PROFESSIONAL DEVELOPMENT SERIES

PERFORMANCE
Managing for Excellence

GEORGE MANNING
Professor of Psychology
Northern Kentucky University

KENT CURTIS
Professor of Industrial Technology and Education
Northern Kentucky University

U257
PUBLISHED BY
SOUTH-WESTERN PUBLISHING CO.
CINCINNATI, OH   DALLAS, TX

Copyright © 1988
by South-Western Publishing Co.
Cincinnati, Ohio

All Rights Reserved

The text of this publication, or any part thereof, may not be reproduced or transmitted in any form or by any means, electronic or mechanical, including photocopying, recording, storage in an information retrieval system, or otherwise, without the prior written permission of the publisher.

ISBN: 0-538-21257-8
Library of Congress Catalog Card Number: 86-62749

3 4 5 6 7 8 E 2 1

Printed in the United States of America

About The Authors

Dr. George Manning *Dr. Kent Curtis*

George Manning is a professor of psychology and business at Northern Kentucky University. He is a consultant to business, industry, and government; his clients include AT&T, Sun Oil, IBM, Marriott Corporation, United Auto Workers, the Internal Revenue Service, and the National Institutes of Health. He lectures on economic and social issues including quality of work life, work force values, and business ethics. He serves as advisor to such diverse industries and professions as energy, transportation, justice, health, finance, labor, commerce, and the military.

He received graduation honors from George Williams College, the University of Cincinnati, and the University of Vienna. He was selected Professor of the Year at Northern Kentucky University, where his teaching areas include management and organization, organizational psychology, and personal adjustment. He maintains an active program of research and study in organizational psychology. His current studies and interests include the changing meaning of work, leadership development, and coping skills for personal and social change.

Kent Curtis has served as an administrator and faculty member at Northern Kentucky University since its inception in 1970. He is a professor in the departments of industrial technology and education. His teaching areas include supervisory development, human relations in business and industry, techniques of research design, counseling, and group dynamics.

He received a baccalaureate degree in biology from Centre College, a master's in counseling from Xavier University, and a doctorate in adult technical education from the University of Cincinnati. He has designed numerous employee and management training and development programs, which are presented to Fortune 500 companies, small businesses, and federal, state, and local government agencies.

Kent also presents open seminars and on-site programs in the areas of time and stress management, communication skills, and team building. His current studies and interests include developing effective "executive pairs" (secretary/manager teams); the manager as an effective teacher; and improving the quality of work life in organizations using employee involvement groups.

PREFACE

Each book in *The Human Side of Work* is special in its own way. *Performance* is the most management-oriented book of the series. It focuses on managing self and managing others. It is full of useful concepts and tools for professional and management development. Optimum individual and work group performance is the goal.

The purpose of the book is to teach principles and practices of excellent job performance. Specific topics include goal setting, performance review, styles of work, career development, performance problems, time management, and programs to improve work group productivity. Exercises and activities are included to personalize the material. The book is an ideal work text for the individual and the manager.

HOW TO USE THIS BOOK

This is a desk book for ready reference, a handbook for teaching others, and a workbook for personal development in the area of job performance. The material is arranged in a logical sequence for learning.

The best approach is to *interact* with the material. Read the narrative, take the tests and exercises, examine the interpretations, and review the principles and techniques — then ask: "How does this apply to me? How can I use this concept or information to improve?" Then take action. Also, use the related readings, cases, and applications to improve your knowledge and skills.

To increase interest and improve overall learning, try the following:

1. Use the learning objectives, discussion questions, and study quizzes included in each part of the book. This will focus your reading, improve comprehension, and increase retention of the material.

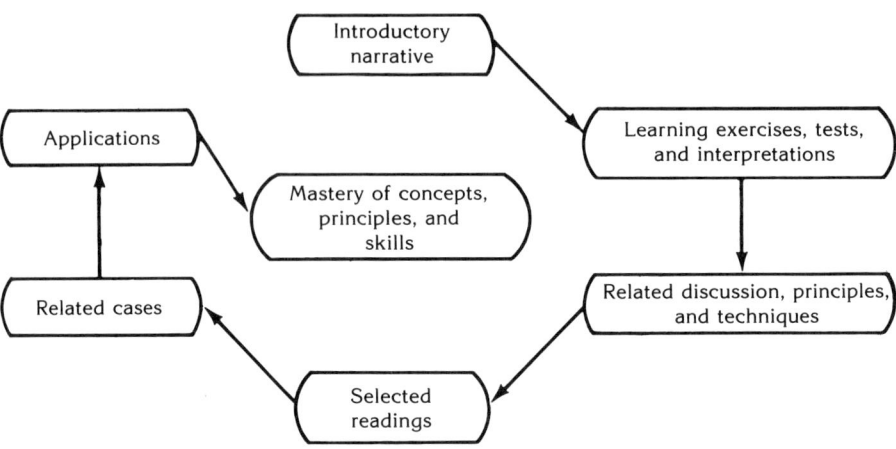

2. Share your tests and exercises with family, friends, and co-workers—those who are interested in your work and career. In this way, you can make tangible use of what you learn and may even help others.
3. Interact with the book. Underline key points; write questions and comments in the margins.

Good luck in your learning!

HOW TO TEACH FROM THIS BOOK

Personalize *Performance*—for yourself and for the student. Use the information, exercises, questions, activities, and tests to complement your own teaching style; use any or all of the materials provided to suit the needs and goals of the group.

Steps

First, scan the material for topics and exercises. Second, outline a curriculum and lesson plan based on time frames and learning goals. Third, arrange learning aids, media, and other resources for smooth instruction. For assistance in this area, refer to the suggested readings, cases, applications, and films that accompany each part of the text. Also, see Appendix A for suggestions on teaching, testing, and grading as well as for information about other books in *The Human Side of Work* series.

Instruction

Multimedia, multimethod instruction usually works best. For each learning session, an ideal combination would be a lecture to set the stage, learning exercises to personalize the subject, discussion to interpret results, and related activities such as cases and readings to increase knowledge and skills. A film, followed by group discussion and panel debate, is an effective way to increase learning. See Appendix C for an annotated list of excellent films.

Final Note

Because this book is easy to read and covers the factual information needed by the learner, class periods should be used primarily for group involvement. Learning activities and group discussion will personalize the subject and result in maximum enjoyment and learning.

Topics and activities include the following:

- What is your *style of work?* Is it like that of Einstein, Darwin, Socrates, or Henry Ford? See pages 34-41.

- How do you stand in matching *personal interests* with *job demands?* See pages 56-64.

- What is your level of job performance? See pages 66-93.

- In relation to time management skills, do you use or abuse the time you have? See pages 104-118.

- Use *behavior modification* to improve work group performance. See pages 118-125.

Performance: Managing for Excellence is popular because it focuses on job performance and career development, two topics of personal importance. However, students won't learn the material unless they get actively involved with it. As the instructor, the more practical and personalized you can make it for them, the better. In this spirit, we conclude with a favorite proverb:

> I listen and I hear;
> I see and I remember;
> I do and I understand.
>
> *Confucius* (551-479 B.C.)

Good luck in your teaching!

Request: We want your suggestions. If you have questions or see a way to improve this book, please write. Thank you.

George Manning
Kent Curtis
Northern Kentucky University
Highland Heights, Ky. 41076

ACKNOWLEDGMENTS

The Human Side of Work is written by many people. It is the result of countless hours and endless effort from colleagues, students, and others who have helped in some important way. From initial draft to final form, many hands bring these books to life. To each we are grateful.

For this book, recognition is given to the following scientists and authors whose ideas and findings provide theoretical framework and important factual data:

Peter Drucker	Phillip Marvin	Irwin Rubin
Andrew DuBrin	James McIntyre	B. F. Skinner
David Kolb	George Odiorne	Francis Stearn
Alan Lakein	Joseph Ohren	Lawrence Steinmetz
Norman Maier	Laurence J. Peter	Robert Townsend
Steven Martin		

Appreciation goes to the following colleagues and supporters for substantive help in research, manuscript review, preparation, and advice:

Jim Alford	Carol Lainhart	Mitch Shapiro
Gene Archbold	William Lindsay	Bill Stewart
Joan Baioni	Rosanna Rizzo Little	Billie Stockton
Anita Bullock	Steve McMillen	Cliff Stone
John Burtchaell	Barry Montgomery	Ralph Tesseneer
Ken Carter	Charles Reynolds	Ann Walker
Dave Davis	Marjorie Scheller	Susan Wehrmeyer
Charlotte Galloway	Shirley Schneider	John Williams
Della Gill	Vince Schulte	Jacqueline Wyatt

We want to thank J. Ellen Gerken for many of the figures, illustrations, and photographs.

George Manning
Kent Curtis

CONTENTS

PART ONE	**PERFORMANCE CONCEPTS**	**5**
	Introduction	6
	Taking Aim and Taking Stock	7
	Exercise: Personal Performance Record	16
	Exercise: How Does Your Supervisor Rate?	18
	Eye of the Beholder	22
	Approach Makes a Difference	25
	Style Plays a Part	31
	Exercise: Styles of Work: Einstein, Darwin, Socrates, or Ford—Which Are You?	31
	Recommended Resources	42
	Reference Notes	42
	Study Quiz	45
	Discussion Questions and Activities	49
PART TWO	**PERSONAL PERFORMANCE**	**51**
	Matching the Right Person with the Right Job	52
	Exercise: Things, People, Ideas—Personal Interest Inventory	55
	What Is Your Level of Job Performance?	66
	Exercise: The Performance Pyramid	67
	Improving Job Performance	72
	Exercise: How Well Do You Know Your People?	75
	Exercise: Putting Your Best Foot Forward	83
	You Can Improve If You Want To	92
	Recommended Resources	93
	Reference Notes	94
	Study Quiz	97
	Discussion Questions and Activities	101
PART THREE	**PRODUCTIVITY IMPROVEMENT**	**103**
	Effective Time Management	104
	Exercise: Time Management Audit—Are You Wasting Your Time?	108

	Programs to Improve Productivity	118
	Conclusion	122
	Recommended Resources	126
	Reference Notes	127
	Study Quiz	129
	Discussion Questions and Activities	131

READINGS 133

What Your Boss Wants to Know	134
Career Problems of Young Managers	143
Walter Cronkite at CBS	168
The Peter Principle	181
That Urge to Achieve	190
What Makes a Top Executive?	199
How to Manage Your Time: Everybody's No. 1 Problem	206
Planning on the Left Side and Managing on the Right	215
The Fertile Tension between Discipline and Impulse	230
Following the Leader: How to Link Management Style to Subordinate Personalities	237

CASES 251

Grandview Morning Press	252
The Dashman Company	254
The Paragon Printing and Lithography Company	257
A Talk with Kirkeby's Son	260
The Vice-President	263
The Reluctant Backhoe Operator	266
The Sales Meeting	268
The Puzzle Block Work Teams	271
Creativity Requires the Right Atmosphere	276
Emery Air Freight	280

APPLICATIONS 283

Employee Performance Review—Rating Scale	285
Employee Performance Review—Paired Comparisons	293
Personality Traits and Job Demands Analysis	297
How Will You Spend Your Life?	303

APPENDIX A   BACKGROUND INFORMATION, TEACHING SUGGESTIONS, AND TESTING AND GRADING 307

Audience	308
Content and Style	308
Testing and Review Process	309
Teaching Formats	311

APPENDIX B	ADDITIONAL REFERENCES	317
APPENDIX C	SUGGESTED FILMS	321
APPENDIX D	MANAGEMENT PERFORMANCE OBJECTIVES	327
APPENDIX E	STUDY QUIZ ANSWERS	333
APPENDIX F	THE RELATIONSHIP OF THE QUIZ QUESTIONS AND THE DISCUSSION AND ACTIVITIES TO THE PART OBJECTIVES	335

Performance

per・form・ance (pĕr-fôr'mans), noun, 1. the act of performing. 2. the execution or accomplishment of work, acts, feats, etc. 3. operation or functioning, usually with regard to effectiveness, as of an airplane. 4. something done or performed; deed or feat. 5. a formal exhibition of skill or talent, such as a theatrical play.

> *A mother was having a hard time getting her son to go to school one morning.*
>
> *"Nobody likes me at school," said the son. "The teachers don't and the kids don't. The superintendent wants to transfer me, the bus drivers hate me, the school board wants me to drop out, and the custodians have it in for me."*
>
> *"You've got to go," insisted the mother. "You're healthy. You have a lot to learn. You've got something to offer others. You're a leader. Besides, you're forty-nine years old, you're the principal, and you've got to go to school."*

Source: Unknown.

PART ONE

Performance Concepts

Learning Objectives

After completing Part One, you will better understand:

1. the importance of ability, experience, and motivation in determining performance levels;
2. how performance objectives (goals) and performance reviews (feedback) help improve job performance;
3. eight principles for setting performance objectives;
4. nine principles for conducting performance reviews;
5. three problems of perception in evaluating performance;
6. the need for using insight instead of trial and error or conditioning to maximize job performance;
7. the characteristics of four styles of work—Einstein, Darwin, Socrates, and Henry Ford;
8. your own style of work and your potential strengths and weaknesses.

INTRODUCTION

Statements such as "Heather is a born artist" imply that performance is a gift of birth. You have also heard that experience teaches, meaning that performance can be learned with practice. Finally, the phrase "Where there is a will, there is a way" supports the power of motivation. The truth involves all three assertions: performance is the result of natural ability, acquired skill, and the desire to achieve. The biographies of great performers bear this out. Consider Michael De Bakey, pioneer heart surgeon; Pelé, world-famous soccer player; and Martin Luther King, Nobel laureate and champion of civil rights. The performance of each was the result of ability, experience, and motivation. In any field of work and at all levels of responsibility, when these elements are present, the quality of performance will show it.

A Perfectly Beautiful Laundress

When I was very young—five years old, as I remember it—I heard my mother say that she had engaged a perfectly beautiful laundress, and being by endowment curious of feminine charm, I hid behind the kitchen sink to have my first look at beauty—my first look and my first disenchantment. The face of my mother's laundress was less beautiful than the soap that she exercised on my jumpers and my stockings, and her figure was, like that of her tub, round, stable, and very wide.

My mother had spoken in a metaphor, inaccessible to my understanding. She had used the word beauty to signify not an attribute of the laundress, but a quality of workmanship for which the laundress, irrespective of her appearance, had become an embodiment.

That which was called beautiful was neither the laundress nor the objects or her laundering, but the performance to which these were machine and medium, a performance made express and visible in the comforting, crisp cleanliness of linens, pajamas, towels, and pillowcases.

The work done was well done; the task and the process were perfectly mastered; the end was well attained, completely and without excess; and my mother, perceiving this unity of intention, method, and product, cast over all of these the aureole of beauty.[1]

The purpose of this book is to teach the concepts and principles of excellent job performance. The goal is to help you to reach the state at which it might be said, "There is a perfectly beautiful performer." Topics covered include goal setting, performance review, problems of perception, the importance of insight, styles of work, matching the right person with the right job, personal performance improvement, employee work habits, effective time management, and programs to improve productivity. Ideas presented in each of these areas have direct and significant influence on job performance (quality of work) and employee satisfaction (quality of work life) and should be of interest to both employee and manager.

TAKING AIM AND TAKING STOCK

Effective job performance requires setting objectives and measuring results. Taking aim and taking stock are important, both for the individual worker and for the work group. The following shows the importance of the individual worker having clear goals and obtaining accurate feedback on performance:

> A group of professional golfers participated in an interesting experiment. Each was given a basket of balls and was asked to drive them as far and as straight as possible, with the fairway lights off. The golfers hooked and sliced their drives, and balls were popping up and dribbling off the tee . . . not at all the performance you would expect from professionals. After they had finished, each was given another basket of balls and asked to drive these as far and as straight as possible—this time, with the lights on. The golfers hit ball after ball, straight as an arrow, 275 to 300 yards down the fairway.
>
> What was the difference between the two experiments? The answer is clear goals and accurate feedback on performance. There were no lights in the first experiment; thus, the golfers could not see the target, nor could they learn the results of their efforts. In the second experiment, lights

ILLUS. 1.1

Quality of work and quality of work life are of concern to both employee and manager.

© SUSAN LAPIDES 1986

Part One • Performance Concepts   7

provided a clear goal and accurate information, so that eyes, hands, and muscles could make adjustments to achieve the desired objective.[2]

The following shows the importance of setting performance objectives and measuring results for the work group:

> The famous industrialist Charles Schwab was visiting a steel mill that was producing far below its potential. The superintendent of the plant couldn't understand why — he had coaxed the employees, threatened them, sworn and cursed, but nothing seemed to work. Schwab asked the superintendent for a piece of chalk, and turning to the nearest worker, he asked, "How many heats did your shift make today?" "Six," was the answer. Without saying a word, Schwab drew a large "6" on the floor and walked away. When the night shift came in, they asked what the "6" meant. A day-shift worker said, "We made six heats today, and Schwab wrote it on the floor." The next morning, when Schwab walked through the mill, he saw "7" on the floor — the night shift had made seven heats. That evening, he returned to the plant and saw that the "7" had been erased, and in its place was an enormous "10." Within a short period of time, one of the lowest producing plants was turning out more work than any other mill in the company. The employees had set performance goals, and they enjoyed recording the results.[3]

Setting performance objectives (goals) and conducting performance reviews (feedback) helps to maximize job performance. Setting objectives meets the worker's need to know what is expected, and providing information on progress meets the need to know where one stands. If you have ever not known what your job was or how well you were doing, you know firsthand the importance of clear objectives and constructive feedback for both personal satisfaction and effective job performance.

ILLUS. 1.2

Properly motivated employees will set high performance goals.

Performance: Managing for Excellence

Performance Objectives—Eight Principles

Employees should have a clear understanding of the performance ideal. Imagine an ambitious person throwing darts at a blank wall, but never accomplishing anything until a bull's eye is drawn, creating a goal. Management consultant Peter Drucker explains the importance of establishing performance objectives:

> Each person, from the highest level to the lowest level, should have clear objectives that reflect and support the objectives of higher level management. As much as possible, lower level employees should participate in the development of higher level objectives as well as their own, thus enabling them to know and understand their own goals as well as their supervisor's expectations.[4]

Setting performance objectives is not a new idea, as shown by the ancient "oath of the physician":

The Hippocratic Oath

I swear by Apollo, the physician, and Asclepius and Health and All-Heal and all the gods and goddesses that, according to my ability and judgment, I will keep this oath and stipulation:

To reckon him who taught me this art equally dear to me as my parents, to share my substance with him and relieve his necessities if required; to regard his offspring as on the same footing with my own brothers, and to teach them this art if they should wish to learn it, without fee or stipulation, and that by precept, lecture and every other mode of instruction, I will impart a knowledge of the art to my own sons and to those of my teachers, and to disciples bound by a stipulation and oath, according to the law of medicine, but to none others.

I will follow that method of treatment which, according to my ability and judgment, I consider for the benefit of my patients, and abstain from whatever is deleterious and mischievous. I will give no deadly medicine to anyone if asked, nor suggest any such counsel; furthermore, I will not give to a woman an instrument to produce abortion.

With purity and with holiness I will pass my life and practice my art. I will not cut a person who is suffering from a stone, but will leave this to be done by practitioners of this work. Into whatever houses I enter I will go into them for the benefit of the sick and will abstain from every voluntary act of mischief and corruption; and further from the seduction of females or males, bond or free.

Whatever, in connection with my professional practice, or not in connection with it, I may see or hear in the lives of men which ought not to be spoken abroad I will not divulge, as reckoning that all such should be kept secret.

While I continue to keep this oath unviolated may it be granted to me to enjoy life and the practice of the art, respected by all men at all times but should I trespass and violate this oath, may the reverse be my lot.[5]

Physicians have used the Hippocratic oath as their performance ideal for over two thousand years.

The following are eight principles for setting performance objectives:[6]

- *Performance objectives should be meaningful.* A manager's objectives should include the health and safety of the work group, excellence in workmanship, a high level of employee morale, and efficient production—all meaningful goals.

- *Performance objectives should be challenging, yet attainable.* An employee whose objectives are either too easy or too difficult will be a morale casualty, and sooner or later, job performance will suffer. Setting unrealistically high goals leads to frustration and failure; pursuing goals that are too low results in wasted opportunity; pursuing the wrong goals results in disillusionment and dissatisfaction.

- *Performance objectives should be measurable.* A manager may have many responsibilities, including operations, fiscal responsibility, and security. Measurable objectives should be set in each of these areas. A sample safety objective is "to achieve a twelve-month record of 'zero' injuries caused by unsafe equipment, facilities, and other conditions under management control." When performance objectives are measurable, the individual knows when, and to what extent, they have been achieved.

- *Performance objectives should be established for a specific time period.* An employee's objectives may be set either by the project or by the calendar, but there should always be a specified time by which objectives are to be accomplished.

- *Performance objectives should be agreed on by those doing the work and those in charge.* An employee's efforts to develop a new product or procedure may be wasted if upper management does not agree about the need for or nature of the project.

- *Performance objectives should be flexible.* An employee should be willing to change the work plan if, in the process, a greater need or opportunity is discovered. Managers should also be open to making changes in a worker's performance objectives. Conditions change, and effective performance requires flexibility.

- *Performance objectives should be written.* If a job is important enough to work on eight hours a day for a long period of time, it is important enough to write objectives for. Memories are fallible, especially if a job has several elements. The palest ink is stronger than the best memory.

- *Performance objectives for work groups should consider the social dynamics of cooperation and competition.* As a rule, work groups perform better if members use teamwork to achieve a common objective. Cooperation within the group should be emphasized and rewarded, and competition between interdependent groups should be discouraged. For example, the administrative staff should not compete with the field staff, and the maintenance department should not compete with the operations department. In contrast, work groups can increase performance by competing against other, independent work groups. A sales team may try to outperform the competition and thus maximize its own performance. Rivalry and contests between autonomous work groups can be an effective motivator.

Performance Review — Nine Principles

After performance objectives have been established, progress should be reviewed to capitalize on strong points and improve weak points. Performance reviews keep communication lines open, help to motivate employees, and give peace of mind to both employer and employee.

Some reviews are easy because feedback is immediate and clear: a baseball player knows he is doing a good job when he hits a home run; the laughter of an audience provides immediate and positive feedback to the comedian. In some types of jobs, however, performance reviews are difficult: the individual may be far removed from the product, as is the case for an executive; factors other than the individual's performance may affect the product, as for a supervisor; or the product may be difficult to measure, as for a social worker or priest. Whether measurement is easy or not, feedback on performance is important for all employees in all occupations. Without this information, employees may waste time and energy worrying about how they are doing and may repeat mistakes.

The following are nine principles for conducting performance reviews:

- *Performance reviews should include three steps: preparation, implementation, and follow-up.* Both the supervisor and the subordinate should be trained in carrying out each of these steps. Figure 1.1 contains a performance review checklist for supervisors and subordinates.

- *Performance reviews should solve job problems and develop employee competence.* Figure 1.2 on page 14 lists characteristics of three types of performance review: the tell-and-sell method, the tell-and-listen method, and the problem-solving method. If the supervisor uses the problem-solving method and plays the role of coach, subordinates usually experience less fear and productivity improves. The following guidelines should be used.

If the employee exceeds standards, the supervisor should (a) congratulate the employee and cite specific examples of good work; (b) review the importance of effective performance for the individual and the organization; (c) discuss the form that recognition will take, remembering that the discussion itself is a form of recognition; (d) ask the employee for ideas that may improve personal performance and the work of the group even more; (e) agree on specific actions each person will take; (f) set a date for a follow-up meeting; and (g) thank the employee for good performance.

FIGURE 1.1

Performance Review Checklist

WHAT TO DO BEFORE THE PERFORMANCE REVIEW

As a subordinate, you should:

- Consider your strong points and formulate a plan to utilize them fully.
- Determine the areas in which you need to improve. Devise a plan to strengthen your performance in these areas.
- Think about what your supervisor can do to help you improve.

As a supervisor, you should:

- Consider your subordinate's strong points and think about how you can reinforce or capitalize on these.
- Think about your subordinate's weak areas and consider actions for improvement.
- Think about what you can do to help your subordinate improve.

WHAT TO DO DURING THE PERFORMANCE REVIEW

As a subordinate, you should:

- Explain your strengths and weaknesses. Be thorough in expressing each one.
- Present ideas to improve future performance; don't dwell on past mistakes, either to save face or to fix blame. Present what you think your supervisor can do to help you improve.
- Listen carefully to your supervisor's reactions; these important indications of attitudes, priorities, and perceptions will be useful in future dealings.
- Obtain final agreement on what each of you will do. Don't settle for "Let's discuss this again at a later date." Try to get as much commitment and agreement as possible.

As a supervisor, you should:

- Tailor the conversation to suit the needs of your subordinate. Stop talking and listen. Have your subordinate begin by explaining each strength and weakness in his or her own words. Provide ample time for the full development of each point; avoid interrupting.
- Ask questions based on your prior preparation as well as on new information developed during the conversation. Encourage your subordinate to do the same.

12 *Performance: Managing for Excellence*

FIGURE 1.1—*continued*

- Ask how you can help your subordinate to do a better job; listen carefully and take notes.
- Establish new performance objectives, standards, and completion dates. Make your expectations clear.
- Remember that a performance review should involve two-way communication. Be prepared to compromise and be flexible. Remember also that you are the supervisor and, as such, are responsible for resolving differences.

WHAT TO DO AFTER THE PERFORMANCE REVIEW

As a subordinate, you should:

- Keep your supervisor informed of progress toward meeting objectives.
- If changes occur that affect your objectives, discuss them as soon as possible with your supervisor.

As a supervisor, you should:

- Develop a system of checks and reminders to be sure that performance objectives are being met.
- Show your subordinate that you want him or her to succeed. Provide positive reinforcement for progress made toward accomplishing objectives.

Source: Steve Martin, "Performance Appraisal—Employee Interview Checklist," Cincinnati, Ohio. Reprinted with permission.

If the employee meets standards, the supervisor should (a) congratulate the employee on performance strengths and cite specific examples of good work; (b) review the importance of good performance for the individual and the work group; (c) ask the employee if anything can be done to increase effectiveness, and listen carefully to ideas; (d) if appropriate, indicate intention to take action; (e) set a date for a follow-up meeting; and (f) thank the employee for good performance.

If the employee does not meet standards, the supervisor should (a) review the areas in which improved performance is necessary; (b) ask the employee to help solve each of the problems; (c) discuss each idea thoroughly; (d) agree on specific actions each person will take; (e) establish a definite date for a follow-up meeting; (f) review any areas of strength; and (g) express confidence in the employee's ability to improve.[7]

- *Performance reviews should be based on mutually agreed-on objectives.* For example, if a repairman and supervisor agree on repair

FIGURE 1.2

Cause-and-Effect Relations in Three Types of Performance Review

	Tell-and-Sell Method (Supervisor Acts as Judge)	**Tell-and-Listen Method** (Supervisor Acts as Advisor)	**Problem-Solving Method** (Supervisor Acts as Coach)
Objective	To evaluate and get employee to change	To communicate evaluation and encourage discussion	To stimulate employee growth and development
Assumptions	Employee wants to correct weaknesses if he/she knows them. Any person can improve if he/she chooses. The superior is qualified to evaluate the subordinate	People will change if defensive feelings are removed	Growth can occur without focusing on faults. Discussion of job problems leads to improved performance
Reactions of employee	Defensive behavior is suppressed. Attempts are made to cover up hostility	Defensive behavior is expressed. Employee feels accepted	Behavior is oriented toward problem solving
Skills required	Persuasiveness; patience	Listening and reflecting feelings; summarizing	Listening and reflecting feelings; using exploratory questions; summarizing
Attitude	People profit from criticism and appreciate help	One can respect the feelings of others if one understands them	Discussion develops new ideas and mutual interests
Motivation	Use of positive or negative extrinsic incentives (motivation is not related to task content)	Reduced resistance to change	Increased freedom; increased responsibility (use of intrinsic motivation in that interest is inherent in the task)
Gains	Success is most probable when the employee respects the supervisor	Employee develops a favorable attitude toward the supervisor, which increases the probability of success	Some improvement is almost assured
Risks	Loss of loyalty; inhibition of independent judgment	Need for change/improvement may not be recognized	Employee may lack ideas. Change may be other than what supervisor had in mind
Values	Perpetuates existing values and practices	Permits supervisor to change views in light of employee responses. Some upward communication	Both employee and supervisor learn, since experience and views are pooled. Change is facilitated

Source: "Three Types of Appraisal Interviews," by Norman R.F. Maier, *Personnel, March–*April 1958, p. 39, copyright © 1958 American Management Association, New York. All rights reserved.

work objectives and do not discuss customer sales, performance evaluation should not be based on sales records.

- *Performance reviews should be tailored to the performance objectives of each job.* Performance requirements for most jobs include the areas of job knowledge, initiative, dependability, work habits, judgment, learning ability, attitude, relationships with people, attendance, appearance and fitness, use of equipment, safety, productivity, and quality. The rating format should be easy to complete and simple to understand. Figure 1.3 shows several sample rating formats.

FIGURE 1.3

Sample Performance Rating Formats

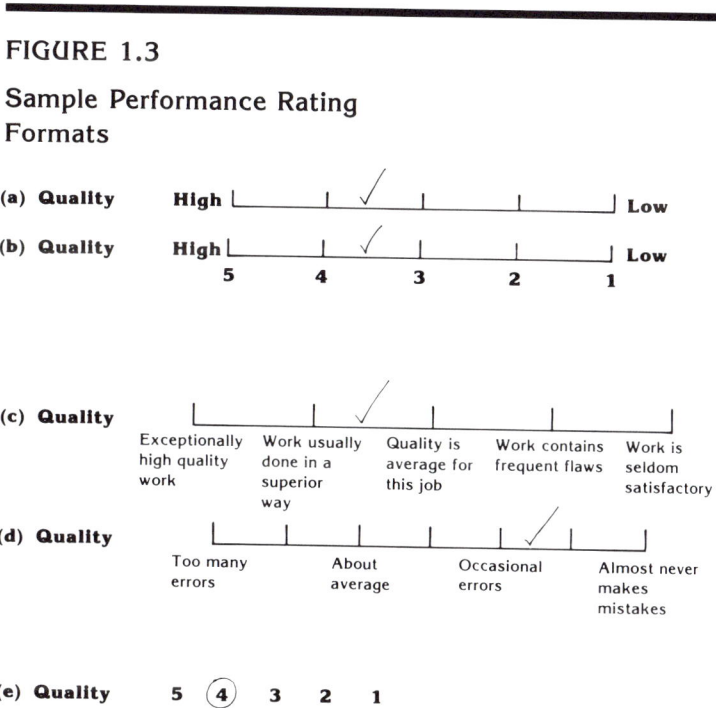

Performance, Part One Exercise • Personal Performance Record 15

FIGURE 1.3—continued

(h) Quality of Work

15	13	⑪	9	7	5	3	1
Rejects and errors consistently rare		Work usually OK; errors seldom made		Work passable; needs to be checked often		Frequent errors and scrap; careless	

(i) Quality of Work — Judge the amount of scrap; consider the general care and accuracy of his work; also consider inspection record.
Poor, 1-6; Average, 7-18; Good, 19-25.   __20__

Source: Based on Norman R. F. Maier, *Psychology in Industrial Organizations*, 4th ed. (Boston: Houghton Mifflin Company, 1973).

- *The subordinate should be involved in evaluating personal performance.* Peter Drucker provides the rationale for employee self-evaluation:

> One has to assume, first, that the individual human being at work knows better than anyone else what makes him or her more productive . . . even in routine work, the only true expert is the person who does the job.[8]

The following questionnaire allows an employee to evaluate personal performance.

PERSONAL PERFORMANCE RECORD

Directions

Read each question and circle the number that best describes your current performance record (0 is lowest; 10 is highest).

Goal Orientation

Am I a self-starter?	0 1 2 3 4 5 6 7 8 9 10
Do I have clear goals?	0 1 2 3 4 5 6 7 8 9 10
Are my goals challenging?	0 1 2 3 4 5 6 7 8 9 10
Do I accomplish my goals?	0 1 2 3 4 5 6 7 8 9 10

Dependability

Is my work done on time?	0 1 2 3 4 5 6 7 8 9 10
Is quantity adequate?	0 1 2 3 4 5 6 7 8 9 10
Is quality adequate?	0 1 2 3 4 5 6 7 8 9 10

Creativity

Am I open to change?	0 1 2 3 4 5 6 7 8 9 10
Do I make improvements in my job?	0 1 2 3 4 5 6 7 8 9 10

Planning

Do I plan ahead?	0 1 2 3 4 5 6 7 8 9 10
Am I prepared for problems and emergencies?	0 1 2 3 4 5 6 7 8 9 10

Communication Skills

Do I listen to others?	0 1 2 3 4 5 6 7 8 9 10
Do I communicate my ideas?	0 1 2 3 4 5 6 7 8 9 10

Job Knowledge

Do I have the necessary facts?	0 1 2 3 4 5 6 7 8 9 10
Are my skills adequate?	0 1 2 3 4 5 6 7 8 9 10
Do I know what I am doing?	0 1 2 3 4 5 6 7 8 9 10

Human Relations

Am I sensitive to others?	0 1 2 3 4 5 6 7 8 9 10
Do I help others?	0 1 2 3 4 5 6 7 8 9 10

Resourcefulness

Do I identify opportunities?	0 1 2 3 4 5 6 7 8 9 10
Do I overcome obstacles?	0 1 2 3 4 5 6 7 8 9 10
Do I cope with change?	0 1 2 3 4 5 6 7 8 9 10

Problem Solving

Do I get the facts?	0 1 2 3 4 5 6 7 8 9 10
Do I consider alternatives?	0 1 2 3 4 5 6 7 8 9 10
Do I ask for advice when appropriate?	0 1 2 3 4 5 6 7 8 9 10
Am I decisive?	0 1 2 3 4 5 6 7 8 9 10
Do I follow up to see if my actions are correct?	0 1 2 3 4 5 6 7 8 9 10

Source: Rosanna Rizzo Little, based on Philip Marvin, Management Goals: Guidelines and Accountability *(Homewood, Ill.: Dow Jones-Irwin, Inc., 1980), 95–113.*

SCORING AND INTERPRETATION

To find your score on the Personal Performance Record, add the circled numbers. Find your score in the following key to determine your current performance level.

Score	Interpretation
0–26	Poor
27–91	Below average
92–168	Average
169–233	Very good
234–260	Excellent

- *Performance reviews should involve two-way communication.* Both subordinate and supervisor should talk and listen; discussion should not be dominated by one individual. Also, positive and negative performance should be discussed. If a secretary is excellent at typing but poor at handling the telephone, typing skills should be recognized and a plan to improve telephone skills should be developed.

Just as subordinates need performance review, so do supervisors. The following questionnaire can be used to evaluate the performance of supervisors and managers.

HOW DOES YOUR SUPERVISOR RATE?

Directions

Rate your supervisor on the following criteria by circling the appropriate response.

Criteria	Responses		
How often is concern shown for subordinates?	Frequently	Sometimes	Seldom
How well does the supervisor know the quality of subordinates' work?	Very well	Fairly well	Not very well
How often is favoritism shown in dealing with subordinates?	Seldom	Sometimes	Frequently
Do subordinates feel free to discuss job-related problems?	Whenever necessary	Sometimes	Seldom
How often are subordinates given incomplete or confusing instructions?	Seldom	Sometimes	Almost always
How often are subordinates told why they are being asked to do a particular job?	Almost always	Sometimes	Seldom

How often are subordinates complimented for good performance?	Almost always	Sometimes	Seldom
How often does the supervisor lose his or her temper when a subordinate makes a mistake?	Almost never	Sometimes	Frequently
How well does the supervisor understand the jobs performed by subordinates?	Very well	Fairly well	Not very well
How often is the advice of subordinates sought in dealing with job-related problems?	Frequently	Sometimes	Seldom
How are suggestions from subordinates received?	Open-mindedly	Skeptically	Negatively
How often are subordinates criticized in the presence of other employees?	Never	Sometimes	Frequently
How often are subordinates told in advance about changes that will affect them?	Almost always	Sometimes	Seldom
How well coordinated is the work of subordinates?	Very well	Fairly well	Not very well
How long are subordinates kept waiting for decisions or information?	A short time	Varies	A long time
How often are promises kept?	Almost always	Sometimes	Seldom
How often are problems seen from the subordinate's point of view?	Frequently	Sometimes	Seldom
How often is blame shifted to subordinates for supervisory errors?	Never	Sometimes	Almost always

Source: Barry Montgomery and Jackie Meeke, Organizational Psychology, Northern Kentucky University, 1982.

SCORING AND INTERPRETATION

To score and interpret the How Does Your Supervisor Rate test, assign a 3 for each item circled in the first column, a 2 for each item circled in the second column, and a 1 for each item circled in the third column. Add these scores and find the total in the following key.

Score	Interpretation
18–23	Poor
24–29	Below average
30–42	Average
43–48	Very good
49–54	Excellent

- *The time, place, and physical setting should be conducive to employee development.* Performance reviews should be conducted in a quiet, comfortable location, with a minimum of interruptions. All calls, except emergencies, should be postponed. If you answer the phone while conducting a review, the employee may think you are not interested.

    A performance review usually takes at least 30 minutes, sometimes much longer. Allow enough time for the employee to become involved in the evaluation. Rushing through in 10 or 15 minutes shows that you do not consider the employee or the review to be very important. The average person spends 2,000 hours every year on the job (40 hours per week for 50 weeks). In light of this, at least one half hour per employee would seem to be time well spent to let workers know where they stand and provide guidance. Most people want to know how they are doing and appreciate the opportunity to discuss job problems in an unhurried way. Finally, avoid scheduling performance reviews for all of your subordinates on the same day. It is demanding work, requiring a lot of effort and concentration.

    When arranging the physical setting, create an atmosphere that encourages two-way conversation. The wrong physical setting can reduce communication. If possible, sit approximately five feet apart, in comfortable chairs of the same height, with no large barriers between you. Sitting on a desk and talking down to your subordinate, or talking to the subordinate from across the room, will inhibit conversation and probably will be resented. Sitting behind a desk clearly and unnecessarily indicates that you are the dominant person; this too may prevent open communication.

- *Supervisors' actions should support their words.* Subordinates notice what supervisors do more than what they say. If a subordinate receives a high evaluation but is not rewarded accordingly, continued high performance will be discouraged; if a subordinate receives a poor evaluation but rewards are unaffected, poor performance is reinforced. Managers encourage the behavior they reward. Consider what would happen if the 100 lowest performing employees in an organization of 1,000 were discharged and their salaries were distributed among the 100 best workers remaining. Soon thereafter, all 900 employees would strive to be more productive. This simple action would encourage positive performance more effectively than all of the words in the dictionary.[9]

- *Performance rating problems should be avoided.* The following are the most common rating problems encountered in conducting performance reviews:[10]

The halo effect. The halo effect occurs when the supervisor allows one characteristic of the employee to influence ratings on other characteristics. A supervisor concerned with neatness may rate an employee poorly on other job factors if the employee is not a neat dresser or does not keep an orderly work area. Another example would be an employee who is always dependable; if the supervisor gives the employee a high rating on loyalty, other areas of performance may be rated high as well, even if these ratings are undeserved.

One way to avoid problems caused by the halo effect is to rate all employees on the same area of performance at the same time.

Leniency. Leniency occurs when supervisors overrate employees. There can be a number of causes for this problem. One is different performance standards among supervisors; one supervisor may have lower performance expectations than another. Another cause could be a supervisor's desire to be popular with employees. Fearing that poorly rated employees will react negatively, the supervisor may give employees high ratings to gain their approval.

The solution to the leniency problem is to train all supervisors in a common interpretation of performance standards. Also, remind supervisors that the purpose of performance reviews is to promote employee development and solve job problems.

Strictness. This is the tendency to underrate employees. Strictness sometimes occurs when the supervisor has had a difficult time as an employee. As a result, the thinking may be, "I had a hard time getting through on this job, and I'm not going to make it easy for them."

The solution to the strictness problem is, again, to train all supervisors in a common interpretation of performance standards and to emphasize the value of positive reinforcement rather than negative conditioning.

Central tendency. This is the tendency to rate all employees as average. The supervisor neither condemns nor praises any employee. A supervisor may do this to avoid being criticized, or the supervisor may feel unable to substantiate ratings.

One solution to the central tendency problem is to train supervisors to use examples of job behavior to back up ratings.

Personal bias. A common rating problem is personal bias toward certain individuals and groups. Legally, an employer may not discriminate in employment practices on the basis of race, creed, color, national origin, or sex. Yet some supervisors do let personal prejudice influence objective appraisal.

The solution to the problem of personal bias is to help supervisors understand their personal biases and to provide training regarding guidelines for nondiscrimination in employment practices and the legal consequences of discrimination.

Recent behavior influence. A supervisor may let recent events carry too much weight in evaluating an employee. A supervisor's perception of current performance, whether good or bad, may weigh more heavily than memories of events that happened six or eight months ago.

One way to reduce recent behavior influence is to document major happenings or critical incidents for later review.

Organizational influences. When supervisors rate employees, they normally take into consideration the purpose of appraisal data: what is the organization going to do with the evaluation? This can influence the supervisor's rating in several ways: (1) a supervisor may overrate employees if pay raises are based on performance reviews. If last year's merit increases were based on the prior year's performance ratings, an unusually large percentage of employees may receive high ratings this year; (2) a supervisor may compete with other supervisors. Not wanting another work group to have better ratings, the supervisor may rate employees excessively high; (3) a supervisor may feel that the appraisal is to be used primarily for employee development and thus may emphasize employees' weaknesses rather than their strengths, probably feeling that employees learn best by concentrating on mistakes.

Organizational influences can be counteracted if management clearly defines and communicates to supervisors the purpose of performance reviews. The best performance reviews solve job problems, develop employee competence, and raise employee morale.

In conclusion, performance reviews improve employee effectiveness by (1) identifying training needs; (2) improving motivation; (3) stimulating self-development; and (4) creating trust and respect between supervisor and subordinate. Effective performance reviews improve the organization by (1) indicating weaknesses in recruitment and selection; (2) identifying the need for changes in policies and procedures; (3) preventing morale problems by acknowledging and rewarding competent service; and (4) providing a means for reclassification or promotion.[11]

EYE OF THE BEHOLDER

As performance objectives are established and performance reviews are conducted, problems of perception can occur. Three common problems are (1) differing perceptions among people—we see things through different eyes; (2) faulty self-perception—our self-image can be distorted; and (3) false perception of circumstances—we fail to see the truth.

ILLUS. 1.3

What you see depends on your perspective.

Differing Perceptions

Sometimes people see things differently. The story of the black and white ball illustrates the problem of differing perceptions.

A man held a ball before a group of children and asked, "What color is this ball?" The children all answered: "White. The ball is white." The old man said, "No, it is not white; it is black." The children were surprised. The wise man had never been wrong before. But they could see that the ball was white, so they said again, "It is white." The old man said: "My children, you believe it is white, but from where I sit, it is black. See?" And he turned the ball so the boys and girls could see the other side. The wise man continued: "So you see, the ball is either black or white, depending on your point of view. And were one to spin it around, it would then be gray. Now children, what color is the ball?"[12]

When setting performance objectives and conducting performance reviews, remember the lesson of the black and white ball—people have a tendency to see things from their own point of view, but a wise person considers all perspectives.

Faulty Self-Perception

The second problem of perception that can arise is faulty self-evaluation. You may misjudge your performance and either overestimate or underestimate yourself. The following story shows how easy it is to misjudge one's own performance:

> Ratatat, a young woodpecker, felt exceedingly vigorous one morning. He looked around the forest and decided to start the day by pecking at a huge oak tree. He had gotten off to a good start when a bolt of lightning split the tree from top to bottom. The little bird hustled out from under the debris, looked up at what was left of the tree, and murmured with a shudder, "My, I did not even know my own strength!"[13]

To see how people, too, can misjudge themselves, consider the following:

> Alice views herself as a gifted actress who will someday make a name in the movies or possibly even on Broadway. She is failing in her drama class, but feels that her native ability makes formal study unimportant. She obtained a small part in the last school play, but had to be replaced because of her poor diction. The drama coach says her chances of ever becoming a successful actress are very small because of her appearance, immaturity, and lack of sensitivity. Alice, however, feels that the coach is unqualified to judge her natural talent.[14]

Performance reviews provide the opportunity to test your self-perception. The opinion of an informed person who wants to help you succeed can be invaluable in solving problems and improving performance.

False Perception of Circumstances

The third problem of perception that can occur is misreading a situation. Employees may believe that a task is impossible, although it is not; supervisors may think subordinates are disloyal, although they are not; a work force may believe it has permanent job security, although it does not. As the following story shows, false perception of a situation can even have life-and-death consequences.

> There was a railway employee in Russia who accidentally locked himself in a refrigerator car. He was unable to escape, and couldn't attract the attention of those outside; so he resigned himself to his fate.

As he felt his body becoming numb, he recorded the story of his approaching death in sentences scribbled on the wall of the car. "I am becoming colder," he wrote. "Still colder, now. Nothing to do but wait. . . . I am slowly freezing to death . . . half asleep now, I can hardly write. . . ." And finally, "These may be my last words." And they were; for when at length the car was opened, they found him dead.

And yet the temperature of the car was only 56°F. The freezing apparatus was, and had been, out of order. There was no physical reason for the employee's death. There was plenty of air; he hadn't suffocated. He was the victim of his own illusion. His conclusions were all wrong. He was so sure he knew.[15]

False perception of circumstances can have negative consequences in the world of work. Performance reviews provide the opportunity for the supervisor and subordinate to work together to see things as they are, to discuss problems, and to agree on solutions.

APPROACH MAKES A DIFFERENCE

Besides setting performance objectives, conducting performance reviews, and seeing things accurately, using the right approach makes a difference in job performance. There are three basic approaches to job performance—conditioning, trial and error, and insight. The least effective is conditioning; the most effective is insight. See Figure 1.4

Conditioning

Studies by the Russian physiologist Ivan Pavlov (1849-1936) demonstrate the effects of conditioning.[16] In a typical experiment, Pavlov presented a dog with a natural stimulus—a piece of meat. The dog reacted

---

FIGURE 1.4

Approaches to Job Performance

APPROACH		DEGREE OF EFFECTIVENESS
REACTIVE CONDITIONING	⟷	LEAST EFFECTIVE
TRIAL AND ERROR	⟷	NEXT MOST EFFECTIVE
INSIGHT	⟷	MOST EFFECTIVE

with a natural response—salivation—and was rewarded by being allowed to eat the meat. The next time the dog was hungry, Pavlov rang a bell (a conditioned stimulus) at the same time that he presented the meat. The dog noted the bell, but salivated at the smell of the meat. The reward was then given. Pavlov found that if this process occurred often enough, the dog would form an association between the sound of the bell and the reward; Pavlov could ring the bell when no meat was present and the dog would salivate. Behavior (performance) was learned by conditioning. Also, as long as reinforcement continued, performance continued. However, if the meat was withheld after ringing the bell, performance (learned by conditioning) would be extinguished. Pavlov's experiment is shown in Figure 1.5

Pavlov's experiments help explain much about human performance; much of our behavior is the product of conditioning. This is good in some cases; good driving skills and hygiene habits may save our lives. However, conditioning can result in ineffective performance as well. Problem

FIGURE 1.5

Four Key Concepts and Their Relationship in Conditioning

RESPONSE

Saliva to food, unconditioned

Saliva to tone, conditioned

STIMULUS

Tone, conditioned

Food, unconditioned

26 *Performance: Managing for Excellence*

behaviors such as overeating, wasting time, and having temper tantrums are often the result of conditioning. When conditioning is the primary approach used in the work setting, mistakes may be made because the employee does not think about the best response to stimuli such as a disagreement with the boss or an unpleasant encounter with a customer. Instead, the employee merely reacts, often making a bad situation worse.

Trial and Error

Trial and error is better than conditioning as an approach to job performance. Consider the following:

> A barracuda (Charlie) was placed in a large tank with a school of mackerels, the natural food for barracudas. A glass partition was used to separate Charlie from the rest of the fish. When he first saw the mackerels, Charlie immediately tried to solve his problem for food—he went after the mackerels. But he swam into the glass partition. Charlie was persistent, so he tried again and again, until he realized . . . there was no way for him to get the mackerels. Self-preservation dictated that he must stop hitting his head against the partition.
>
> At this point, the researchers lifted the partition out of the tank, and what do you think happened? Nothing. Charlie had learned his lesson too well. The mackerels could swim all around him without fear; Charlie never tried to eat them. In fact, Charlie would have died of starvation in a tank full of food, if he had not been moved to another tank.[17]

Figure 1.6 illustrates Charlie the Barracuda's approach to performance.

Charlie's experience helps explain many performance problems; too often the trial-and-error approach is used. How do most people choose the jobs they have? They try this one and say, "That's no good." Then they try that one and say, "That's no good," until, perhaps, they find the one that is just right. Or think of many people's approach to buying cars and choosing a mate. They try this one and say, "That won't do." Then they try that one and think, "That's no good," and so on, until, with luck, they may choose the right one. The inefficiency of the trial-and-error approach can be costly.

The trial-and-error approach can present problems for the employee who wants to do a good job, but continually runs into obstacles. The enthusiastic worker wants to get those mackerels, but runs into one glass partition after another—the boss is unreasonable; the community will not accept new ideas; there is not enough money; the union would never agree; it is against management policy; and so on—until the hypothetical employee thinks: "My commitment is killing me. Every time I try to do something, I run into a glass partition. The answer for me is to quit trying. . . ." And this is exactly what happens. Then, time passes, and conditions change—the boss improves; there is a new spirit in the community; the company's resources grow; the union changes; management is now open to new ideas. But the worker does not know it. The lesson has been learned too well, and the employee is on the shelf. The mackerels can swim all around the employee, and he will not try to get them. There

FIGURE 1.6
Trial-and-Error Performance

Phase I

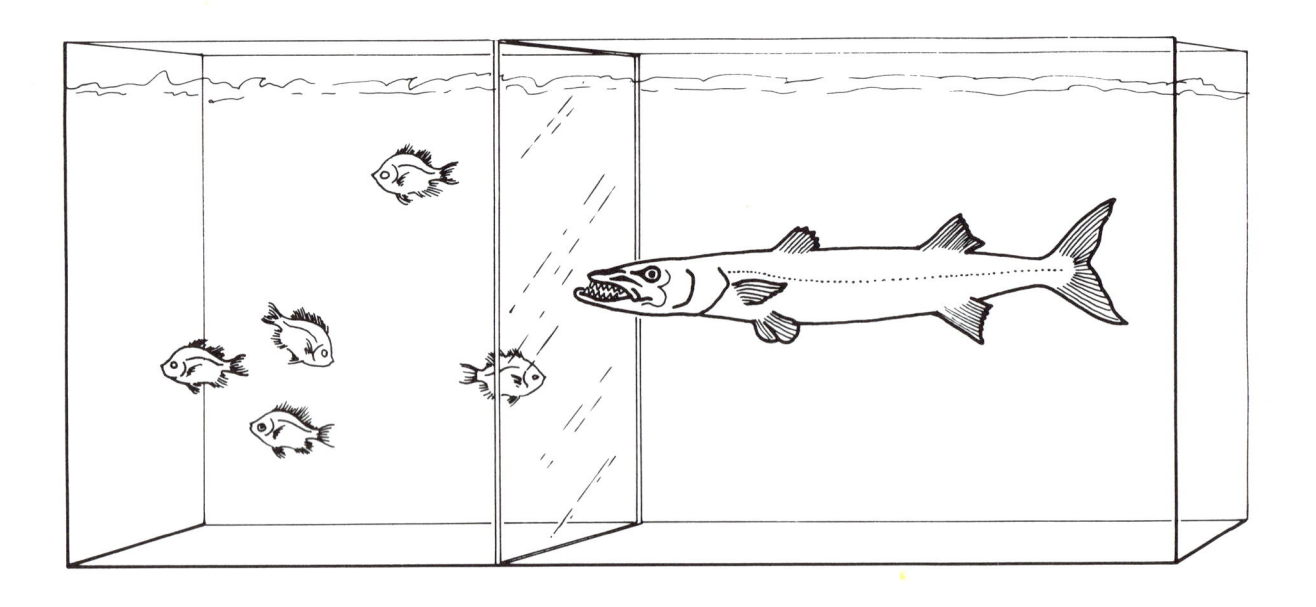

Phase II

28 *Performance: Managing for Excellence*

are many Charlie the Barracudas in the work setting. The problem is in the approach.

Insight

The best approach to job performance is insight. The story of Sultan the Ape makes this point. In 1927, psychologist Wolfgang Köhler discovered Sultan on the Spanish island of Tenerife, and brought him to America. The research Köhler conducted has helped us to better understand human performance problems:

> Köhler placed Sultan in a cage containing nothing except two bamboo sticks. Outside the cage, Köhler hung a string of bananas, the natural food for an ape. The bananas were hung at such a distance that Sultan could not reach them with his arms or legs or by using just one of the sticks. The researcher observed Sultan, and this is what he saw: Sultan sat with a thoughtful look on his face. Then he picked up both bamboo sticks, inserted one into the other, walked over to the edge of the cage, reached out, and pulled in the bananas. There was no reactive conditioning, and there was no trial-and-error behavior. Sultan had solved the problem by using his mind; he had solved the problem through insight.[18]

Figure 1.7 illustrates the insightful approach of Sultan the Ape.

FIGURE 1.7

Performance Using Insight

Many problems go unsolved because of failure to follow the example of Sultan the Ape. As creatures of conditioning and trial-and-error learning, people often fail to tap their full performance potential. The solution is to use insight. Consider the following:

The Candy Store Girls

Four salesgirls in a candy store were paid on commission. One girl always had a long line of customers, while the others had few. The busy girl was asked, "What is the secret of your success?" Her answer was insightful. She had noticed that the other girls always scooped up more than a pound of candy and then took the extra candy away. Her approach was to scoop up less than a pound and add to it.[19]

The Shipping Tycoon

The famous shipping tycoon Emmet J. McCormack told the story of how, as a young boy in the late nineteenth century, he sat, feeling dejected. He had just been turned down by four different employers because none had enough work to justify a full-time office boy. Then he used insight. He went back to each employer and offered his services one-fourth time for a dollar a week. They all hired him, and Emmet J. McCormack became the first syndicated office boy.[20]

The Maintenance Crew

A supervisor of a maintenance crew had two employees who had fought and did not want to make up. The supervisor solved the problem by having each of the workers wash the same window — one on the inside, one on the outside. With nothing to do but look at each other, it didn't take long for both to laugh, and harmony was restored. The supervisor used insight.[21]

The Low Bridge Problem

A large truck had become solidly wedged under a low bridge. Experts on the construction of bridges were consulted about ways to dislodge it, and they offered various suggestions. Because these people were involved daily with bridges, they approached the problem in a conventional way: raise the bridge to release the truck. But a young newsboy, who had not yet been trapped into habitual patterns of thought, had a much better idea. He suggested that the truck be lowered, which was easily accomplished by letting air out of the tires. The newsboy used insight to solve the problem.[22]

In evaluating your own approach to work, are you the product of conditioning, do you use trial and error, or do you use insight in your approach to job performance?

STYLE PLAYS A PART

Regardless of approach — conditioning, trial and error, or insight — each person has a natural or preferred style of work, and each style has potential strengths and weaknesses that can affect job performance. By completing the following questionnaire, you will better understand your own style of work. You will discover whether you are an Albert Einstein, a Charles Darwin, a Socrates, or a Henry Ford, and you will learn the strengths and weaknesses of each. Note that this questionnaire evaluates style of work, not ability.

STYLES OF WORK: EINSTEIN, DARWIN, SOCRATES, OR FORD — WHICH ARE YOU?[23]

Directions

There are ten sets of phrases below. Rank each set by assigning a 4 to the phrase that is most like your style of work, a 3 to the one next most like your style, a 2 to the one next most like your style, and a 1 to the phrase that is least like your style of work. Be sure to assign a different number to each phrase — do not make ties.

Example

__2__ Emotional   __1__ Thorough   __3__ Rational   __4__ Active

E	R	T	A
__1__ Following instincts	__2__ Weighing evidence	__3__ Developing plans	__4__ Accomplishing goals
__2__ Relying on feelings	__1__ Examining facts	__4__ Defining problems	__3__ Trying things out
__4__ Being perceptive	__2__ Measuring effects	__3__ Thinking things through	__1__ Taking action
__1__ Emotional involvement	__4__ Impartial investigation	__3__ Rational analysis	__2__ Practical use
__4__ Having awareness	__1__ Questioning details	__2__ Using logic	__3__ Performing deeds
__1__ Letting intuition guide	__2__ Patiently observing	__3__ Summarizing points	__4__ Applying solutions

_3_ Present oriented   _2_ Reflecting on experiences   _4_ Future oriented   _1_ Concerned with consequences

_4_ Being open to experience   _1_ Recording information   _3_ Organizing ideas   _2_ Applying knowledge

_4_ Being conscious of events   _1_ Studying data   _2_ Forming theories   _3_ Taking risks

_4_ Personal experience   _2_ Unbiased inquiry   _1_ Abstract thinking   _3_ Producing results

SCORING

When you have completed the Styles of Work questionnaire, find the total score for each column and insert in the appropriate spaces:

_28_ Total for E column   _ _ Total for R column   _28_ Total for T column   _26_ Total for A column

Graph your totals for E, R, T, and A on the appropriate axes in Figure 1.8, and connect these scores with straight lines to make a picture of your style of work. The longest line of your four-sided figure indicates your preferred work style.

INTERPRETATION

All jobs involve having experience (E), reflecting on results (R), building theories (T), and taking action (A). These constitute four steps of the work cycle (see Figure 1.9).

The following is a description of this cycle. Included are the strengths and potential weaknesses of each style — Darwin, Einstein, Socrates, and Henry Ford.

Having experiences is followed by reflecting on results (Step 2). If the longest line of your four-sided figure is between E and R (see Figure 1.10), your preferred style of work is like that of Charles Darwin (1809–1882), author of *On The Origin of the Species by Means of Natural Selection* and *The Descent of Man and Selection in Relation to Sex*. About himself, Darwin wrote, "My mind seems to have become a kind of machine for grinding general laws out of large collections of facts."

As a Darwin, your strengths are in observing, recording facts, and identifying alternatives. By style, you are a basic researcher. Darwins are needed in every field — social science, natural science, the arts, business, and the professions — for their thorough data collection and objective analysis. Carried to an extreme, however, the Darwin style of work can

FIGURE 1.8

A Picture of Your Style of Work

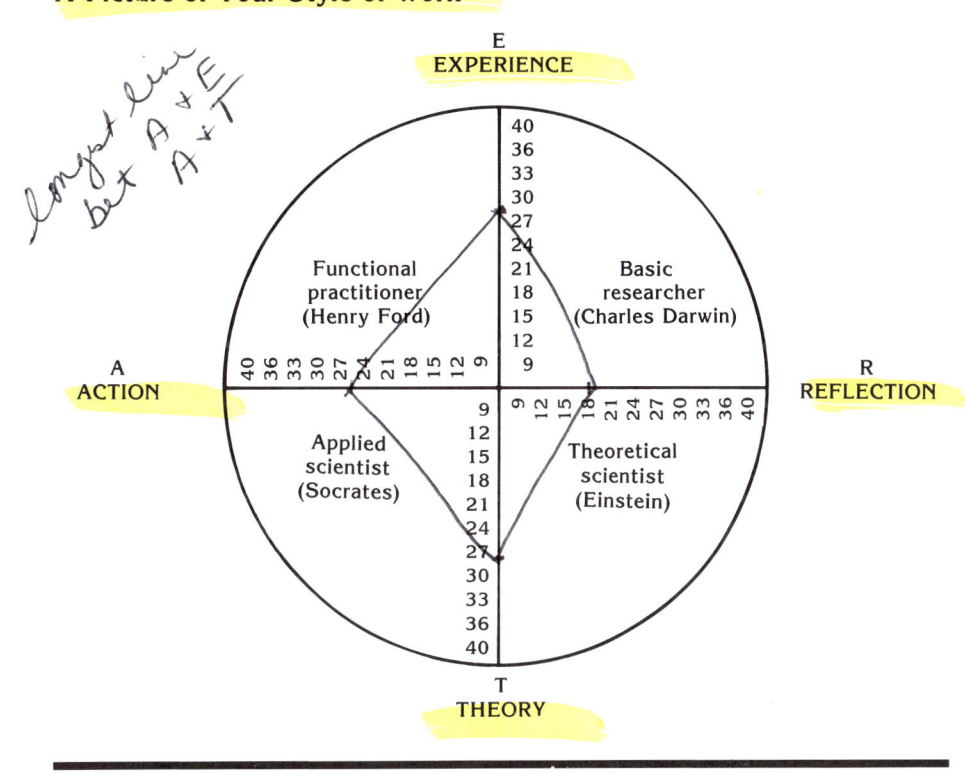

[Handwritten annotation: "longest line bet A & E, bet A & T"]

A circular diagram with two axes:
- Vertical axis: E (EXPERIENCE) at top, T (THEORY) at bottom, with scale marks 9, 12, 15, 18, 21, 24, 27, 30, 33, 36, 40 extending from center in both directions
- Horizontal axis: A (ACTION) at left, R (REFLECTION) at right, with the same scale marks extending from center in both directions

Four quadrants labeled:
- Upper left: Functional practitioner (Henry Ford)
- Upper right: Basic researcher (Charles Darwin)
- Lower left: Applied scientist (Socrates)
- Lower right: Theoretical scientist (Einstein)

A diamond shape is plotted connecting four points on the axes.

---

lead to paralysis as each new fact becomes even more interesting than the last, resulting in indecision. It is important to look before leaping, but it is possible to look so long that one never leaps. Consider the case of Darwin himself, who had developed his theories of human evolution years before another scientist came to similar conclusions and would have received credit for these theories . . . had not Darwin at last published.

After the data are gathered, theory building takes place (Step 3). At this stage, you develop assumptions and formulate ideas. You move from the world of experience into the world of theory, while remaining in the mode of reflecting rather than acting. If the longest line of your figure is between R and T (see Figure 1.11), your preferred style of work is that of the theoretical scientist—the Einstein style. In his description of the world, Einstein wrote, "Physical concepts are free creations of the human mind, and are not, however it may seem, uniquely determined by the external world."

The Einstein style of work is like that of the philosopher and writer. Carried to an extreme, the results can be castles in the air with little practical value. This is the style of the husband whose wife says, "That's good, George . . . but when are you going to *do* something?"

FIGURE 1.9

The Work Cycle

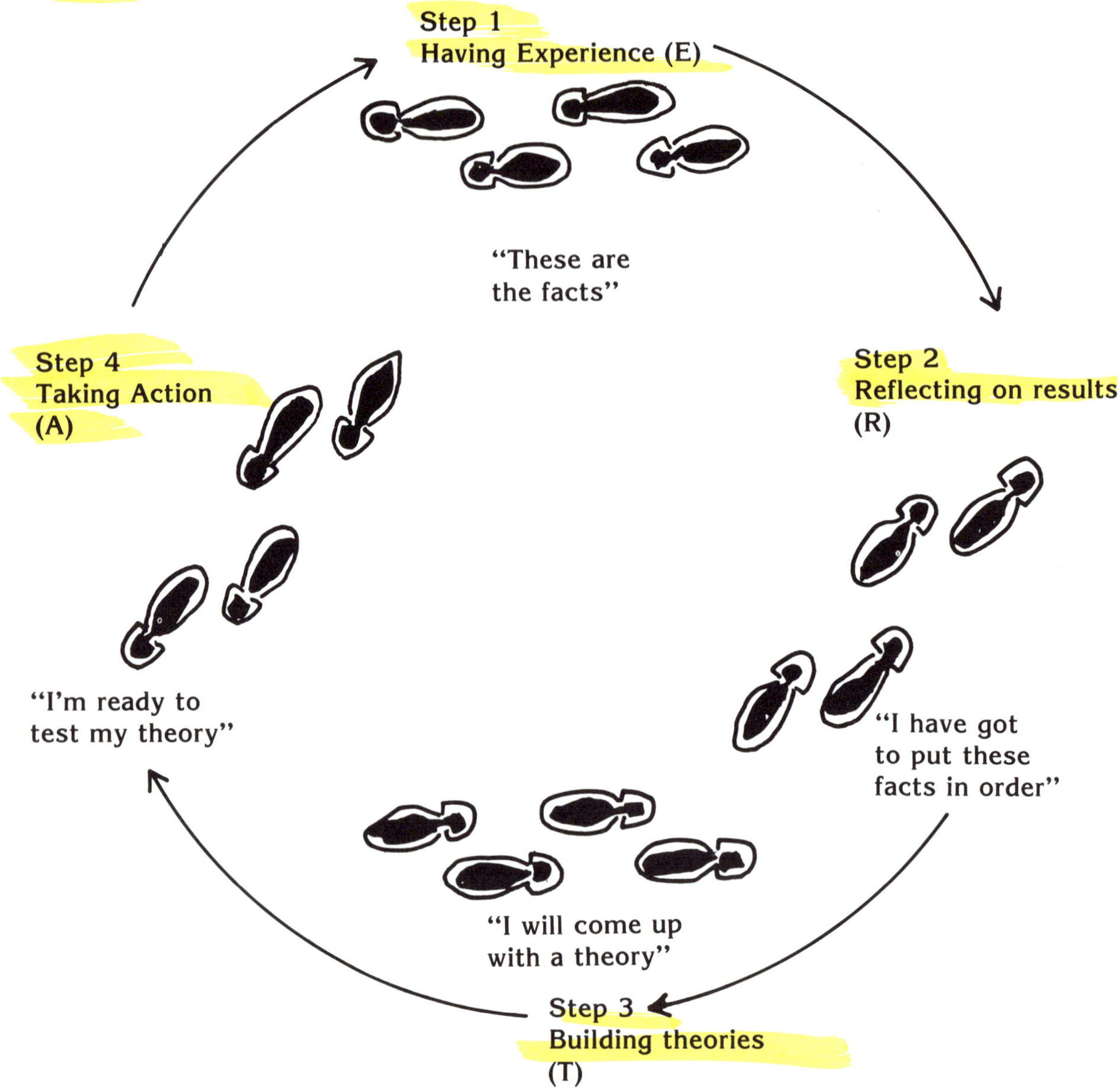

- Step 1: Having Experience (E) — "These are the facts"
- Step 2: Reflecting on results (R) — "I have got to put these facts in order"
- Step 3: Building theories (T) — "I will come up with a theory"
- Step 4: Taking Action (A) — "I'm ready to test my theory"

After theories have been developed, they must be tested (Step 4). If your longest line is between T and A (see Figure 1.12 on page 38), your preferred style of work is that of the applied scientist. Your strength is not in collecting and analyzing but in translating ideas into action. As such, yours is the style of the teacher Socrates (470–399 B.C.):

34 *Performance: Managing for Excellence*

FIGURE 1.10

The Charles Darwin Style of Work

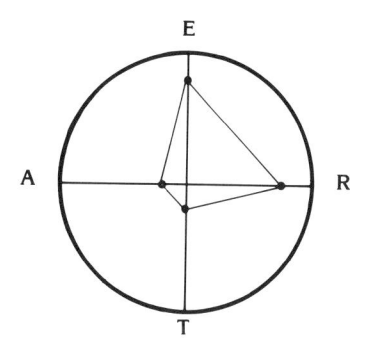

FIGURE 1.11

The Einstein Style of Work

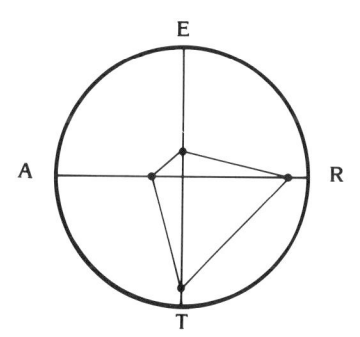

Socrates wrote nothing that was published. Yet we know him as one of the greatest teachers in history, perhaps the greatest of the great men produced by Athens. His name commands admiration, honor, and reverence. Men and women were his objective; to them he had a mission. He wandered through the streets and down to the marketplace, or often he would go to the public gymnasium. Then he started business — the business of teaching. The life of Socrates was a living example of his ideals. His philosophy, as set forth by Plato, marks an epic in human thought. "He brought philosophy down from heaven to earth," wrote Cicero. For Socrates was the founder of moral philosophy. He was scoffed at for taking his examples from common life, but he did so to lead plain men to goodness, truth, and beauty.[24]

Comfortable with ideas, but wanting to apply them, the applied scientist moves from a reflective to an active orientation. This person enjoys

ILLUS. 1.4

Darwin exemplified strengths in observing, recording facts, and identifying alternatives.

coordinating and problem-solving activities. When taken to an extreme, the Socrates style of work may result in impressive, but incomplete performance. This is because these individuals dislike details. The Socrates-type person may give a fine speech but fail to do the thorough research required for excellence.

Taking action automatically results in new experiences (Step 1), so the work cycle never completely ends. In work, and in life, when one problem is solved, another arises. If your longest line is between A and

ILLUS. 1.5

The Einstein style of work is that of a philosopher and theoretical scientist.

THE BETTMANN ARCHIVE, INC.

C (see Figure 1.13), your style of work is like that of Henry Ford (1863–1947), whose strength was in achieving results. Upton Sinclair described Henry Ford, the functional practitioner, as follows:

> Henry Ford was now fifty-five; slender, grey-haired, with sensitive features and a quick, nervous manner. His long, thin hands were never still, but always playing with something. He was a kind man, unassuming, not changed by his great success. Having had less than a grammar-school education, his speech was full of the peculiarities of the plain folk of the Middle West. He had never learned to deal with theories, and when confronted with one, he would scuttle back to the facts like a rabbit to its hole. What he knew he had learned by experience, and if he learned more, it would be in the same manner.[25]

If the functional practitioner knows what needs to be done, the goal will usually be accomplished. This is a person of deeds rather than ideas. But here, as with the other work styles, a strength may become a liability

FIGURE 1.12

The Socrates Style of Work

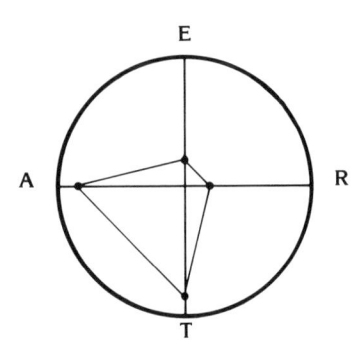

FIGURE 1.13

The Henry Ford Style of Work

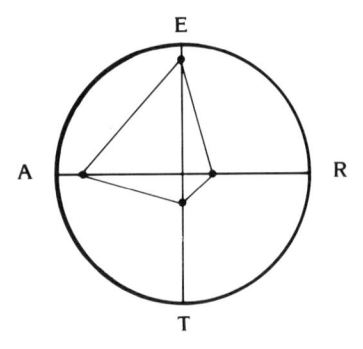

when carried to an extreme. If the functional practitioner does not have sufficient facts, or fails to work from a well-conceived plan, there may be tremendous accomplishment . . . of the wrong thing.

The versatile style of work is represented by Figure 1.14. This individual is equally comfortable with each step of the work cycle—having experiences, reflecting on results, building theories, and taking action. As such, this person does not have structural strengths or weaknesses resulting from work style preference.

There are several important points to remember concerning styles of work:

- All work involves four steps, and each step must be performed well for overall effectiveness. An independent businessperson with a

ILLUS. 1.6

The strengths of Socrates' work style are teaching and problem solving.

THE BETTMANN ARCHIVE, INC.

Socrates style must take extra care to consider details as well as concepts and should remember to get the facts before making decisions, even if this does not come naturally.

- It is possible to have more than one long line in your style-of-work picture. This shows preference for more than one style of work. A person may be equally comfortable as a Henry Ford and a Socrates. Such a person relates to the world in both an experiential and a theoretical sense. In either case, though, this person shows a bias for action.

- When people with different styles of work live or work together, tolerance is required. A Henry Ford boss must be patient with the

ILLUS. 1.7

The characteristics of the Henry Ford work style are goal orientation and accomplishment of results.

THE BETTMANN ARCHIVE, INC.

FIGURE 1.14

A Versatile Style of Work—No Dominant Preference Is Indicated

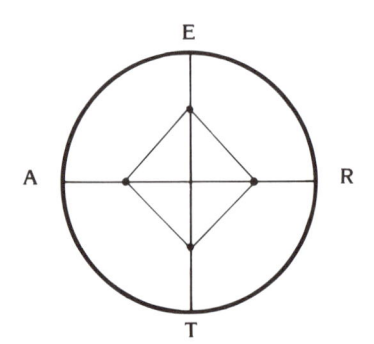

40   *Performance: Managing for Excellence*

seeming lack of effort put forth by an Einstein subordinate, and a Socrates wife must try to understand her Darwin husband's preference for having experiences and reflecting on results over forming ideas and applying knowledge. An understanding and appreciation of the characteristics and needs of each type of worker can go a long way toward improving relations and enhancing productivity.

- Most people have difficulty changing their styles of work. This can be seen in school when a student fails or drops out. It is usually Henry Ford students who fail or drop out, not Einstein types. Often the cause is the nature of the curriculum and the style of instruction, not the ability of the student. The functional practitioner, who wants to apply knowledge and accomplish something tangible, has difficulty relating to data analysis and theoretical discussion.

A work group needs all four types of worker. A balance of basic research, theoretical science, applied science, and functional practice helps to maximize individual as well as work group performance. Consider the following story:

> Fred was a successful research chemist when he suffered a serious heart attack. During his stay in the hospital, his position was filled by a younger employee. Like many large organizations, Fred's company was rich in talent, and others were qualified to do his job.
>
> When Fred recovered and returned to work, he retained his title, his office was the same, and his income was unchanged. However, he had lost a significant part of his job—his duties were now "make work" assignments, while important responsibilities and decision making were handled by others. Whereas Fred had only been physically ill before, he now became depressed, and his overall health began to deteriorate. Fred had been placed on the shelf, and he knew it.
>
> At that time, Fred's company began to develop a new product, and the Styles of Work questionnaire was used to create a balanced team for research and development. On the team was a theoretical scientist, who could write formulas from wall to wall but who few could understand. This was the Einstein. Also on the team was an applied scientist, who could understand the Einstein's ideas and who knew how to bridge the gap between thinking and doing; the team had a Socrates. The team also had a Henry Ford, who was known for his practical nature. He was a goal-oriented person with the ability to produce results. What was missing on the new-product team was a Charles Darwin, a basic scientist, who would be sure that all the facts were gathered and all the data were considered. Fred was chosen to be the team's Darwin.
>
> Within a year, the team developed one of the company's most successful products. A year after that, Fred's wife phoned him at work. By accident, she reached his boss. She said: "Oh, Mr. Johnson, I have been wanting to talk to you for so long. I have wanted to thank you . . . for giving my Fred back to me."[26]

Fred's story shows how the needs of the individual and the needs of an organization are interwoven and how both can be met by creating a balanced work team incorporating all four styles of work.

RECOMMENDED RESOURCES

The following readings, cases, applications, and films are suggested for greater insight into Part One:

Readings — What Your Boss Wants to Know
Career Problems of Young Managers
Walter Cronkite at CBS

Cases — Grandview Morning Press
The Dashman Company
The Paragon Printing and Lithography Company

Applications — Employee Performance Review — Rating Scale
Employee Performance Review — Paired Comparisons

Films — Lifelines: A Career Profile Study
Career Development: A Plan for All Seasons
Job Interview: I Guess I Got the Job
Performance Appraisal: The Human Dynamics

REFERENCE NOTES

1 Joseph Hudnut, *Architecture and the Spirit of Man* (New York: Greenwood Press, 1949), 3.

2 Norman R. F. Maier, *Psychology in Industrial Organizations*, 4th ed. (Boston: Houghton Mifflin Company, 1973), 371.

3 Marvin G. Gregory, ed. *Bits and Pieces* (Fairfield, N. J.: The Economics Press, Inc.).

4 Peter Drucker, *The Practice of Management* (New York: Harper & Row, Publishers, Inc., 1954), 126–29.

5 *World Book Encyclopedia*, s.v. "The Oath of Hippocrates."

6 George S. Odiorne, *Management by Objectives: A System of Managerial Leadership* (New York: Pitman Publishing Corp., 1965), 165–88, and James C. Coleman, *Personality Dynamics and Effective Behavior* (Chicago: Scott, Foresman & Company, 1960), 189–209.

7 Adapted from Robert E. Maloney, *Personnel Report* (Research Institute of America), and Robert E. Maloney, "Taking the Pain Out

of Performance Reviews," *Public Management* 62 (September 1980): 18.

8   Peter Drucker, *Managing in Turbulent Times* (New York: Harper & Row, Publishers, Inc., 1980), 24.

9   Robert Townsend, *Up the Organization* (New York: Alfred A. Knopf, Inc., 1970).

10 Maloney, *Personnel Report*, and Maloney, "Taking the Pain Out of Performance Reviews," 18.

11 Joseph Ohren, *Supervisor's Manual: Performance Evaluation*, (Covington, Ky.: City of Covington, 1982).

12 Source unknown.

13 Will Forpe and John McCollister, *The Sunshine Book: Expressions of Love, Hope, and Inspiration* (Middle Village, N.Y.: Jonathan David Publishers, Inc., 1979), 190.

14 Coleman, *Personality Dynamics and Effective Behavior*, 13.

15 Gordon L. Lippitt, *Quest for Dialogue* (Washington, D.C.: Development Publications, 1966), 21.

16 I. P. Pavlov, *Conditioned Reflexes*, translated by G. V. Anrep (London: Oxford University Press, 1927), and John Dworetzky, *Psychology* (St. Paul, Minn.: West Publishing Co., 1982), 175-76.

17 Stan Kossen, *The Human Side of Organizations*, 2d ed. (New York: Harper & Row, Publishers, Inc., 1978), 387-88.

18 Wolfgang Köhler, *The Mentality of Apes*, translated from the 2d, revised edition by Ella Winter (London/Boston: Routledge & Kegan Paul, Inc., 1927), 4-9, 124-28.

19 Gregory, *Bits and Pieces*.

20 Gregory, *Bits and Pieces*.

21 Gregory, *Bits and Pieces*.

22 Peter Farb, *Humankind* (Boston: Bantam Books, Inc., 1978), 322-23.

23 Billie Stockton, Anita Bullock, and Anne Locke, Northern Kentucky University, 1981, based on "Learning and Problem Solving," in David A. Kolb, Irwin A. Rubin, and James M. McIntyre, *Organizational Psychology: An Experimental Approach*, 3rd ed. (Englewood Cliffs, N.J.: Prentice-Hall, Inc.), 37-53.

24 John Allen, ed., *100 Great Lives* (New York: Journal of Living Publishing Corp., 1944), 20-22, 25.

25 Upton Sinclair, *The Flivver King* (New York: Phaedra, Inc., 1969), 56-57.

26 Team-building story from the authors' files.

STUDY QUIZ

As a test of your understanding and the extent to which you have achieved the objectives in Part One, complete the following questions. See Appendix E for the answer key.

1. High-quality job performance in any field depends on:

    a. practice, tools, and teamwork
    b. ability, experience, and motivation
    c. age, strength, and practice
    d. none of the above

2. Effective performance of any job requires:

    a. leadership and luck
    b. intelligence and dexterity
    c. setting objectives and measuring results
    d. none of the above

3. The Hippocratic oath is an example of:

    a. performance goals
    b. performance feedback

4. Performance objectives should be all of the following except:

    a. meaningful
    b. measurable
    c. challenging
    d. inflexible

5. Competition between interdependent groups should be:

    a. encouraged
    b. discouraged

6. The three steps for performance review are:

    a. practice, evaluate, perform
    b. write, rehearse, deliver
    c. prepare, conduct, follow up

7. The three types of performance review — tell and sell, tell and listen, and problem solving — correspond to the following:

    a. judge, advisor, coach
    b. policeman, referee, teacher
    c. colleague, supervisor, parent

8. Performance rating problems include all of the following except:
   a. halo effect
   b. central tendency
   c. recent behavior influence
   d. job knowledge

9. The lesson of "The Black and White Ball" is:
   a. consider all perspectives when evaluating performance
   b. go by bottom-line results only
   c. find some good point for every bad point
   d. none of the above

10. The moral of "The Powerful Woodpecker" is:
    a. no guts, no glory
    b. the early bird gets the worm
    c. some people overestimate their performance
    d. none of the above

11. The most effective approach to job performance is:
    a. trial and error
    b. conditioning
    c. insight

12. Pavlov's experiments showed the role of _____ in problem solving.
    a. insight
    b. trial and error
    c. conditioning

13. Experiments with Charlie the Barracuda showed the role of _____ in problem solving.
    a. insight
    b. conditioning
    c. trial and error

14. Köhler's experiments with Sultan the Ape demonstrated the importance of _____ as an approach to problem solving.
    a. trial and error
    b. insight
    c. conditioning

15. Four steps in the work cycle are:
    a. having experiences, reflecting on results, building theories, and taking action
    b. Einstein, Darwin, Ford, and Socrates

    c. investigative, inductive, deductive, and intuitive
    d. positive, negative, logical, and emotional

16. Who would be more likely to make an error of commission?
    a. Henry Ford
    b. Albert Einstein

17. Who would be more likely to make an error of omission?
    a. Henry Ford
    b. Albert Einstein

18. Who would be more likely to take action?
    a. Darwin
    b. Socrates

19. Who would be more likely to consider all of the facts before making a decision?
    a. Darwin
    b. Socrates

20. The major point of the Styles of Work exercise is:
    a. there are good and bad work styles
    b. everyone should master every step of the work cycle
    c. likes should seek out likes and avoid those with opposite work styles
    d. all styles are necessary, and people should be tolerant as they live and work with others

DISCUSSION QUESTIONS AND ACTIVITIES

The following questions and activities help personalize the subject. They are appropriate for classroom exercises and homework assignments.

1. Have you ever been wrong in your perceptions at work? Have you ever overestimated or underestimated yourself or evaluated a situation incorrectly? Discuss.

2. Give personal examples of conditioning, trial and error, and insight as approaches to work. Do you have work habits developed by conditioning?

3. Cite a time when you used trial and error to solve a problem.

4. What is the most creative thing you have ever done on the job?

5. What is your preferred style of work—that of Einstein, Darwin, Socrates, or Henry Ford? Does your job or career support your work style? Explain.

    I am versatile – no dominant preference

6. Gather into small groups for the remaining questions and activities. Consider goal setting: what are the pros and cons for setting occupational goals? Give examples to support your view.

Performance, Part One • Discussion Questions

7. Discuss performance appraisal. Cite true-life examples of situations in which performance reviews helped or hurt job performance. What "dos" and "don'ts" do group members recommend for evaluating employees?

8. Discuss the idea of rating supervisors. If you were a manager, would you want to be evaluated by your subordinates? Explain.

9. Identify outstanding performers in various fields. Discuss the importance of ability, experience, and motivation.

PART TWO

Personal Performance

Learning Objectives

After completing Part Two, you will better understand:

1. the importance of matching the right person with the right job;
2. the role of the "vital shift" when job demands change from one focus and process to another—things and doing, people and relating, or ideas and thinking;
3. whether you are most interested in working with things, people, or ideas at this point in your career;
4. the principles and practices by which you can improve job performance in the areas of statesmanship (working through others), entrepreneurship (obtaining results), and innovation (generating new ideas);
5. the principles that constitute good employee work habits;
6. your own level of job performance in the areas of statesmanship, entrepreneurship, and innovation.

MATCHING THE RIGHT PERSON WITH THE RIGHT JOB

An important factor in the performance equation is the match between the interests of the employee and the demands of the job. The following is a discussion of this important concept.

He was called Lucky Lindy, and he was America's favorite hero. In 1927, aviator-adventurer Charles A. Lindbergh flew "The Spirit of St. Louis" from Long Island, New York, to Le Bourget Airport near Paris, France, in 33 1/2 hours, capturing the hearts of people around the world. Lindbergh inspired those who wished to overcome the impossible. He also helped found the fledgling aviation manufacturing and transport industry, as his trip demonstrated the potential for bringing together countries via air travel.[1]

Albert Schweitzer, physician and humanitarian, was loved and respected by people everywhere. His life and work were devoted to the welfare of others. He left his native Germany in 1913 to practice medicine

ILLUS. 2.1

Lucky Lindy, America's favorite hero.

THE BETTMANN ARCHIVE, INC.

ILLUS. 2.2

Albert Schweitzer, the great humanitarian, devoted his life to the welfare of others.

Artist: Arthur William Heintzelman

in deepest Africa, and he remained with his "African children" for fifty years. Schweitzer was a leader and a model for others throughout the world.[2]

Philosopher Bertrand Russell wrote a letter from his deathbed in Wales in 1973. The letter was addressed to the world. Lord Russell was not the first person in history to do this, but he was one of the few from whom the world would await such a letter, and read it when it came. To paraphrase him, "Unless anyone think otherwise, I write to say I enter unto death in the same state I lived my life . . . darkness." Thus the author of *Why I Am Not a Christian*, and the man recognized as one of the foremost thinkers of the twentieth century, bade farewell to the world.[3]

The primary interests of Lindbergh, Schweitzer, and Russell were things, people, and ideas, respectively. Each was personally fulfilled as

ILLUS. 2.3

Bertrand Russell was one of the foremost thinkers of the twentieth century.

THE BETTMANN ARCHIVE, INC.

individual interests meshed with the demands of his work. It is the same for people in all occupations: success and satisfaction come from matching personal interests with job demands. The problem is that some people who enjoy working alone or with their hands are in jobs that require a great amount of interaction with others—dealing with human needs and eccentricities. Also, some people who prefer thought and theories are in positions that require much physical labor and an aptitude for working with materials and machines. Finally, some people are most happy working with and through others, but they have jobs that require solitary effort and abstract thinking.

Because mismatches between the interests of the person and the demands of the job ultimately result in decreased morale and performance, managers should be sensitive to this problem when making work assignments. Whenever possible, the interests of the person should fit the demands of the job. This applies to workers in all fields and at all levels of responsibility. Three examples make the point:

Success as an artist requires the ability to work with things.

> When I was a child, my mother said to me, "If you become a soldier, you will be a general. If you become a monk, you will end up as the Pope." Instead I became a painter, and wound up as Picasso. . . . There are painters who transform the sun into a yellow spot, but there are others who, thanks to their art and intelligence, transform a yellow spot into the sun.
>
> *Pablo Picasso*

The responsibilities of a manager require the ability to coordinate people.

54 *Performance: Managing for Excellence*

> Never tell people how to do things. Tell them what to do and they will surprise you with their ingenuity.
>
> *General George Patton*

> The duties of a judge require the ability to deal with ideas.
>
> Four things belong to a judge: to hear courteously, to answer wisely, to consider soberly, and to decide impartially.
>
> *Socrates*

What are your interests? Are you interested in things, people, or ideas? Complete the following questionnaire to find the answer.

THINGS, PEOPLE, IDEAS — PERSONAL INTEREST INVENTORY

[handwritten: Dictionary of Occupational Titles]

[handwritten: — qualify profile, Career guidance + develop]

Directions

Each of the following questions is worth a total of three points. For each question, assign the most points to the response you prefer and fewer points, in order of preference, to the others. For example, if one response receives three points, the other two must receive zero; if one receives two, then the others must receive one and zero; or each may receive one point.

Examples

Question 1.	0 a.	Question 2.	2 a.	Question 3.	1 a.
	3 b.		0 b.		1 b.
	0 c.		1 c.		1 c.

1. Which activity interests you most?
   - __0__ a. Working with your hands
   - __2__ b. Working with people
   - __1__ c. Reading books

2. Which skills would you invest time in learning?
   - __1__ a. Research and writing
   - __1__ b. Organizing and leading
   - __1__ c. Crafts and art

3. Which job activities would you enjoy most?
   - __1__ a. Counseling and coaching
   - __1__ b. Building and doing
   - __1__ c. Thinking and planning

4. Which trait is most characteristic of you?
   - __1__ a. Helper
   - __1__ b. Doer
   - __1__ c. Scholar

5. Which would you most enjoy doing?
   - __2__ a. Talking with people
   - __0__ b. Writing a book
   - __1__ c. Building a house

6. How do you prefer to use your spare time?
   - __2__ a. Outdoor projects
   - __1__ b. Social activities
   - __0__ c. Thinking

7. Which of these traits is most important to you?
   - __1__ a. Physical coordination
   - __1__ b. Ability to deal with people
   - __1__ c. Mental ability

8. Which jobs most reflect your interests?
   - __2__ a. Teacher, social worker, counselor
   - __1__ b. Engineer, surveyor, craftsman
   - __0__ c. Researcher, historian, author

9. Which ability is your strongest?
   - __2__ a. Communication skills
   - __1__ b. Creative thinking
   - __0__ c. Physical skills

10. Which tasks do you perform best?
    - __1__ a. Operating and maintaining
    - __1__ b. Communicating and motivating
    - __1__ c. Developing and planning

11. Which occupation interests you most?
    - __0__ a. Pilot
    - __1__ b. Judge
    - __2__ c. Politician

12. Which of the following is most interesting to you?
    - __2__ a. Helping others
    - __1__ b. Thinking things through
    - __0__ c. Using your hands

13. Which skills could you learn with the least effort?
    - __2__ a. Leading and negotiating
    - __0__ b. Artwork and handicrafts
    - __1__ c. Language and theoretical reasoning

Performance, Part Two Exercise • Things, People, Ideas

14. What tasks appeal to you most?
    - _0_ a. Developing new theories
    - _2_ b. Helping people with problems
    - _1_ c. Developing a skill

15. What assignment appeals to you most?
    - _0_ a. Working with ideas
    - _2_ b. Working with people
    - _1_ c. Working with things

16. Which is your greatest attribute?
    - _0_ a. Creativity
    - _2_ b. Competence
    - _1_ c. Sensitivity

17. For which occupation do you have natural talent?
    - _3_ a. Counselor
    - _0_ b. Builder
    - _0_ c. Scientist

18. Which subject interests you most?
    - _0_ a. Practical arts
    - _0_ b. Philosophy
    - _3_ c. Human relations

19. To which group would you prefer to belong?
    - _0_ a. Scientific society
    - _3_ b. Outdoor group
    - _0_ c. Social club

20. How do you like to work?
    - _2_ a. In a group, discussing and recommending solutions
    - _1_ b. Alone, using ideas and theories
    - _0_ c. Alone, using tools and materials

Source: Billie Stockton, Anita Bullock, and Anne Locke, Northern Kentucky University, 1981.

SCORING

To obtain your score on the Personal Interest Inventory, complete the following steps.

Step One

Record your scores in the appropriate spaces in Figure 2.1, and total each column. Note that the arrangement of responses is not always alphabetical.

Step Two

Plot your scores and shade the circles in Figure 2.2 representing things and doing, people and relating, and ideas and thinking. This provides a picture of your personal interests.

INTERPRETATION

There are five points to remember about scores on this inventory:

- The numerical scores and circles show the pattern of your interests and indicate the type of work that would be most satisfying to you.

    If A is your largest circle, you are primarily interested in working with your hands and with tools and materials. As such, your interests are much like those of Amelia Earhart, who was happiest when she was flying her plane, pitting her personal skills against the forces of machine and nature. Occupations that call for an orientation toward things include forestry, farming, woodworking, mechanics, and art.

    If B is your largest circle, you are interested primarily in the human side of work. You are most comfortable working with and through others, often for their welfare. Your interests are similar to those of Jane Addams, pioneer social worker, who was happiest when she was working with people. Occupations that require a high degree of interest in people include counseling, supervising, coaching, nursing, and teaching.

    If your largest circle is C, your primary interest is in the world of ideas. Books, ideas, and philosophical discussion stimulate you. Your interest pattern is similar to that of Simone de Beauvoir, one of the most respected women of French literature and an influential leader of the women's rights movement. Positions that call for interest in ideas include professor, scientist, judge, and writer.

- Although interest patterns may change with time, experience, and mood, they are likely to remain the same throughout a person's life. Thus, the early tinkerer is likely to become an inventor; the early teacher will probably remain a teacher; and the early dreamer is likely to become a poet or philosopher.

FIGURE 2.1

Score Matrix

Question	Things		People		Ideas	
1.	a.	0	b.	2	c.	1
2.	c.	1	b.	1	a.	1
3.	b.	1	a.	1	c.	1
4.	b.	1	a.	1	c.	1
5.	c.	2	a.	0	b.	1
6.	a.	2	b.	1	c.	0
7.	a.	1	b.	1	c.	1
8.	b.	2	a.	1	c.	0
9.	c.	2	a.	1	b.	0
10.	a.	1	b.	1	c.	1
11.	a.	0	c.	1	b.	2
12.	c.	2	a.	1	b.	0
13.	b.	2	a.	0	c.	1
14.	c.	0	b.	2	a.	1
15.	c.	0	b.	2	a.	1
16.	b.	0	c.	2	a.	1
17.	b.	3	a.	0	c.	0
18.	a.	0	c.	0	b.	3
19.	b.	0	c.	3	a.	0
20.	c.	2	a.	1	b.	0
		22		22		16
		TOTAL		TOTAL		TOTAL

Part Two • Personal Performance

FIGURE 2.2
Personal Interest Patterns

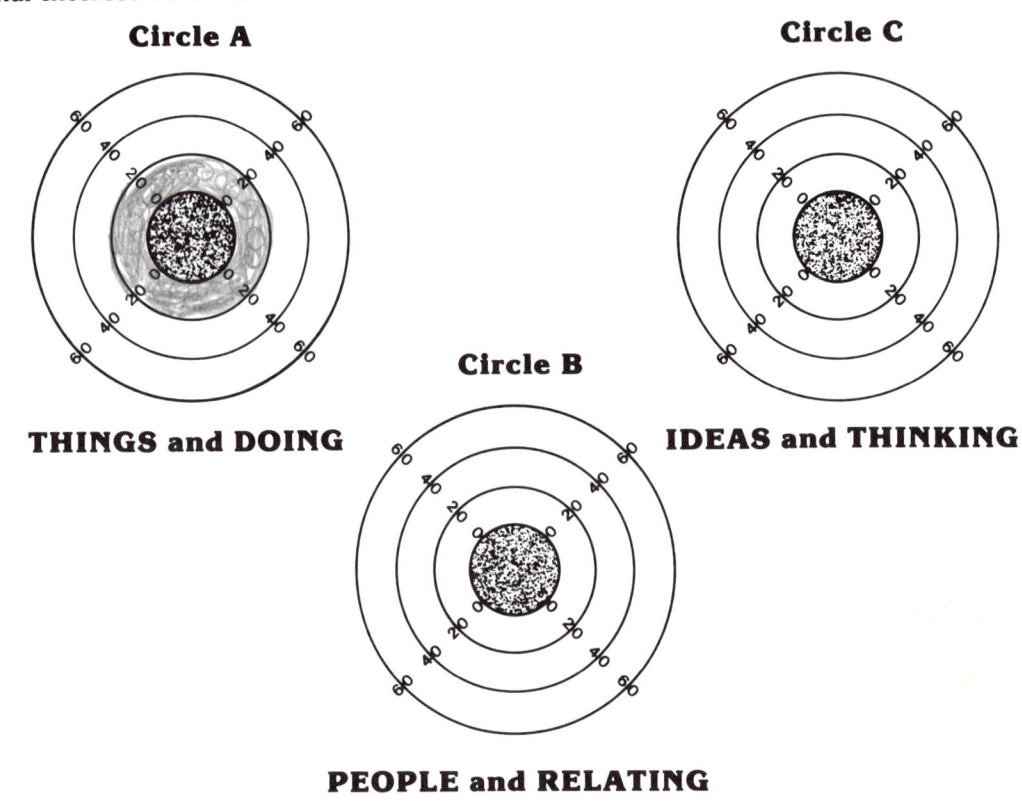

Circle A

THINGS and DOING

Circle B

PEOPLE and RELATING

Circle C

IDEAS and THINKING

- Some people are extremely interested in all three areas—things, people, and ideas. Leonardo da Vinci—artist, administrator, and philosopher—was such a person. There are two cautionary notes to keep in mind if you have high interest in all three areas: beware of running out of energy and becoming fatigued; and beware of the tendency to start projects and fail to see them through to completion.

- The world operates on all three planes—things, people, and ideas. Thus, all three types of people are needed. Having respect for individuals with different interest patterns will help people get along even if they are not exactly alike. Imagine a "doer" wife with a "thinker" husband, or a "relational" wife with a "thinker" or "doer" husband. Ideally, each will tolerate and appreciate the interests of the other.

- The world of work also involves things, people, and ideas. Ideally, the personal interests of members of a work group will match the demands of the work. Imagine the problem if all of the members of a work group were either relational or idea oriented when the job required hands-on skills, or if the work required a good deal of communication and cooperation and all of the members were individual performers, each "into" a distinct skill or specialty. When there is a mismatch between the interests of the group and the demands of the work, compromises must be made. Otherwise, both morale and performance suffer.

Focus of Work, Nature of Work, and Career Stages

Three interrelated concepts—focus of work, nature of work, and career stages—affect job performance. These concepts and the typical progression of careers are shown in Figure 2.3.

FIGURE 2.3

Progression of Careers

FOCUS OF WORK: Things → People → Ideas

NATURE OF WORK: Doing → Coordinating → Thinking

CAREER STAGES: Early Career → Middle Career → Later Career

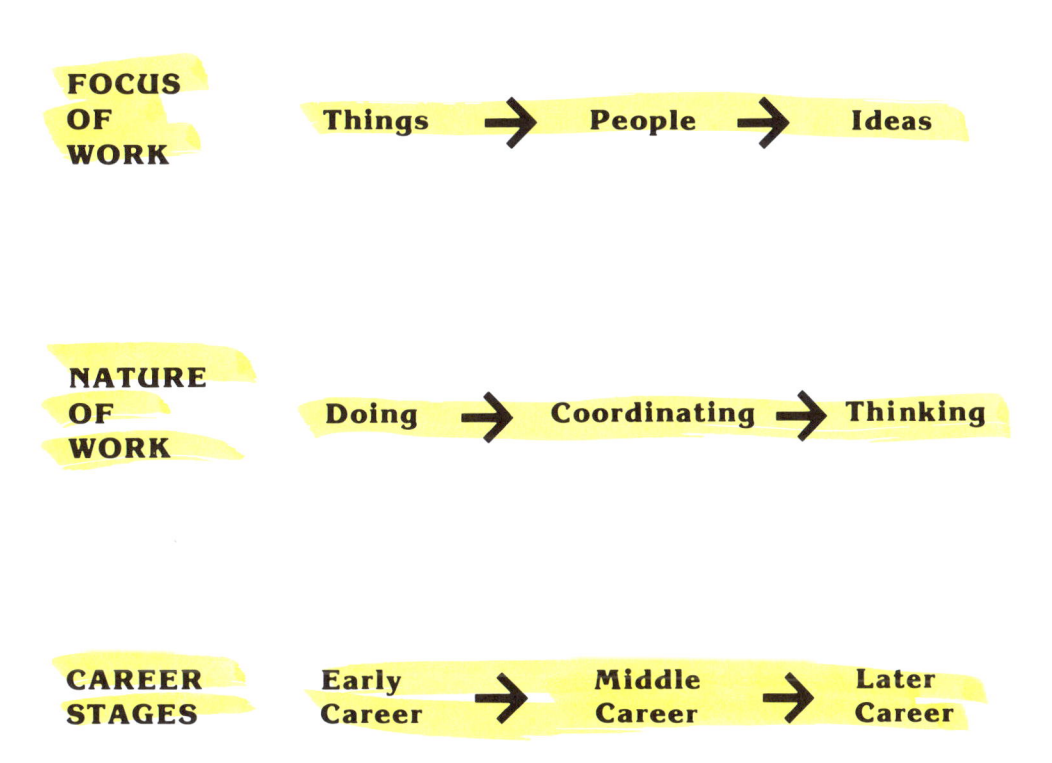

Source: Edgar H. Schein, "The Individual, the Organization, and the Career," Journal of Applied Behavioral Science 7, no. 4 (1971): 401-26; D. T. Hall and M. Morgan, "Career Development and Planning," in W. C. Hamner and F. Schmidt, eds., Contemporary Problems in Personnel, rev. ed. (Chicago: St. Clair Press, 1977); and G. W. Dalton, P. H. Thompson, and R. L. Price, "The Four Stages of Professional Careers," Organizational Dynamics (Summer 1977).

In the early stages of a career, the worker is usually doing something. This may be physical labor, working with tools, machines, and materials, or the job may involve working with people, providing direct service. During this career stage, time is spent learning and applying the skills of the trade or profession. In the beginning, the worker's role may be that of apprentice or trainee. After training, the role may be that of colleague and independent contributor. The type of work performed represents front-line responsibility in the occupation or organization. Police officer, carpenter, salesperson, and technician are job titles typical of this stage.

In mid-career, the worker may spend time coordinating people. An individual may assume leadership and training responsibilities during this period. If so, the nature of the job becomes less that of doing the work and more that of directing the work of others. Work in the middle career stage includes mid-level responsibility in the occupation or organization. Coordinator, foreman, supervisor, and manager are typical occupational titles.

At the highest levels of an occupation or organization, the primary focus of attention is on ideas, such as plans and policies, and thinking is the primary activity. Major duties include determining the long-range direction of the organization, making strategic decisions regarding products and finances, and establishing the ethical tone of the organization. In most cases, the worker is not faced with these responsibilities until the later career stage. Owner, president, chairman, and executive director are common titles of office.

It should be noted that not everyone experiences the career progression outlined here. This may be due to personal choice or to the unique nature of the work. A farmer may choose to maintain a one-person operation for his or her entire working life; similarly, the focus and nature of the artist's work will probably remain the same regardless of career stage.

It is important to match the personal interests of the worker with the demands of the job for all personnel at all levels of an organization. Imagine a president of a department store insisting on displaying merchandise and running the cash register instead of making long-range plans and developing a management team, or a salesperson spending an inordinate amount of energy thinking about price, profit, and public policy rather than focusing on customer service and the care of merchandise. When personal interests and job requirements are mismatched in this way, morale and performance are sure to deteriorate, both for the president and the salesperson.

Management Skills

Figure 2.4 shows the types of skill needed for effective performance at each level of management. The varying amounts of skills needed are represented by the different-sized blocks.

FIGURE 2.4

Types of Skill Needed at Each Management Level

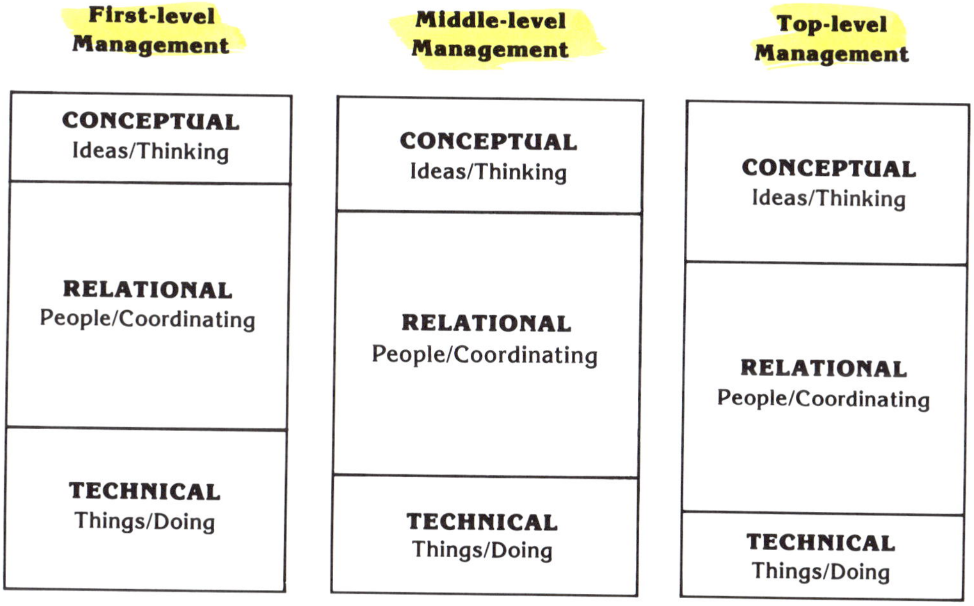

First-level Management
- CONCEPTUAL — Ideas/Thinking
- RELATIONAL — People/Coordinating
- TECHNICAL — Things/Doing

Middle-level Management
- CONCEPTUAL — Ideas/Thinking
- RELATIONAL — People/Coordinating
- TECHNICAL — Things/Doing

Top-level Management
- CONCEPTUAL — Ideas/Thinking
- RELATIONAL — People/Coordinating
- TECHNICAL — Things/Doing

Source: Robert L. Katz, *"Skills of an Effective Administrator,"* Harvard Business Review *(September/October 1974): 90–102.*

A description of each type of skill follows:[4]

Technical Skill. This refers to detailed job knowledge, hands-on expertise, and the specialized use of tools, techniques, and procedures. Both the technical expert and the work group supervisor should have a high degree of technical skill. Examples include a computer specialist designing a program, a lawyer preparing a legal document, and a maintenance supervisor overseeing a repair job.

Relational Skill. This includes the ability to motivate, coordinate, and advise other people, either as individuals or as a work group. Sensitivity in human relations and a willingness to help others are essential elements of relational expertise. Success at all levels of management—first, middle, and top—requires good human-relations skill. Examples include an office supervisor handling an employee performance problem, a sales manager

Part Two • Personal Performance 63

coordinating a sales force, and a plant manager solving a problem between the manufacturing and scheduling departments.

Conceptual Skill. This refers to the ability to think abstractly. Long-range planning, strategic decision making, and weighing of ethical considerations in employee, governmental, customer, and business relations all require conceptual skills. Examples include a personnel vice president evaluating a proposed labor agreement and a company president deciding whether to support a community service project.

Figure 2.5 shows the amount of time each level of management normally should spend on the four processes of management—planning, organizing, directing, and controlling. Note that the conceptual skills needed for planning increase at each higher level of management.

The Vital Shift

The progression through career stages and management levels is not always a smooth one. As seen in Figure 2.6, some of the most difficult

---

FIGURE 2.5

Normal Distribution of a Manager's Time

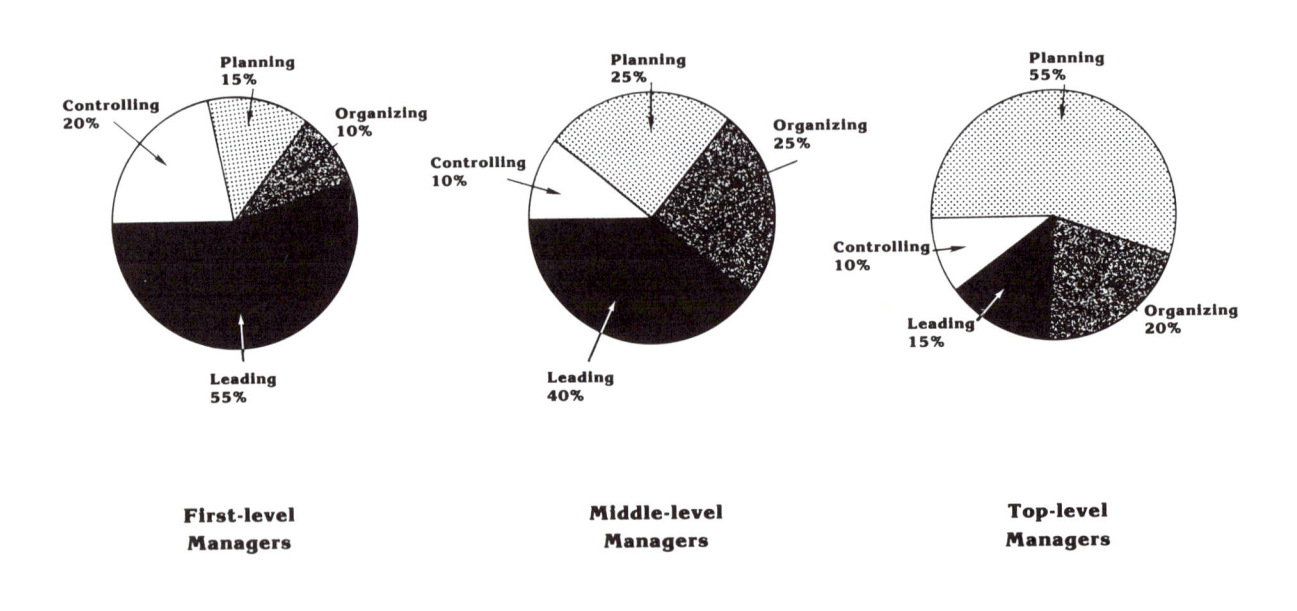

First-level Managers
- Planning 15%
- Organizing 10%
- Leading 55%
- Controlling 20%

Middle-level Managers
- Planning 25%
- Organizing 25%
- Leading 40%
- Controlling 10%

Top-level Managers
- Planning 55%
- Organizing 20%
- Leading 15%
- Controlling 10%

Source: Henry Mintzberg, *The Nature of Managerial Work* (New York: Harper & Row, Publishers, Inc., 1975).

times are the periods of vital shift, when a person leaves one type of work and moves to another.

Moving from a period of doing things, through a period of coordinating people, to a period of thinking about ideas can be difficult because different interests and skills are involved at each stage. When the transition is not made successfully, the result is the overpromotion syndrome popularized by author Laurence J. Peter in *The Peter Principle*. The individual may be dissatisfied because the new work is not interesting or may feel inadequate because needed skills are missing. At the same time, the organization and those it serves are harmed because the individual lacks competence in performing the tasks of the position.[5] Because a round peg does not fit into a square hole (and why should it?), everyone suffers.

The New-Job Tryout

One of the best ways to successfully make a vital shift is to use the new-job tryout. This approach allows an individual to work at a different type of job or level of responsibility for a period of time to see if the work is agreeable and can be performed effectively. If either the person or the

---

FIGURE 2.6

Vital Shifts—Moving from Doer to Coordinator to Thinker

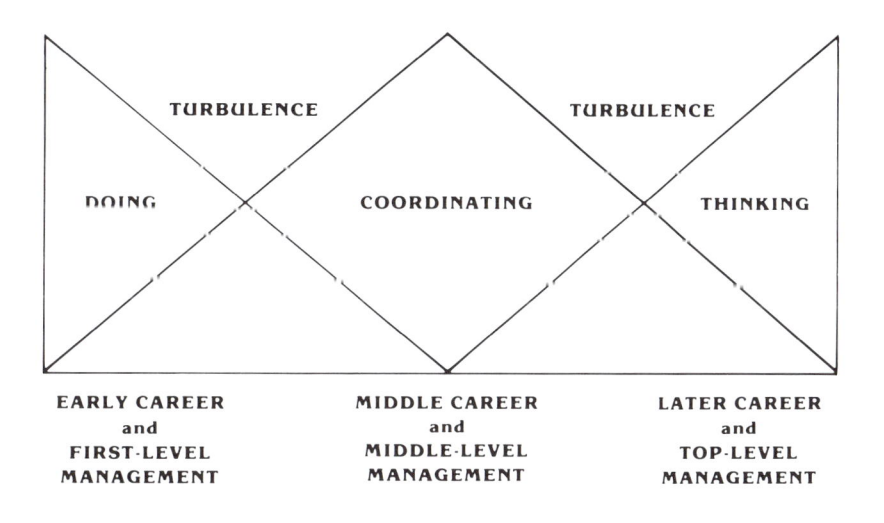

	TURBULENCE		TURBULENCE	
DOING		COORDINATING		THINKING
EARLY CAREER and FIRST-LEVEL MANAGEMENT		MIDDLE CAREER and MIDDLE-LEVEL MANAGEMENT		LATER CAREER and TOP-LEVEL MANAGEMENT

Source: Lawrence L. Steinmetz, The Art and Skill of Delegation *(Reading, Mass.: Addison-Wesley Publishing Co., Inc., 1976), 46-63.*

organization decides the employee should not continue in the new job, the employee's pride is easily preserved because the job was considered to be a two-way tryout. Without such a trial period, fear of embarrassment or an unwillingness to hurt people's feelings may result in a person being retained in an unsuitable position, even when this harms the individual or the organization. The new-job tryout helps to solve this problem. For example, before a permanent job assignment is made, the secretary may try out office management, the tradesman may try out foremanship, or the captain may try out the warden's position.

WHAT IS YOUR LEVEL OF JOB PERFORMANCE?

The following questionnaire allows you to evaluate your performance in your management or professional-level job. Complete the Performance Pyramid alone or with others, such as a co-worker or supervisor. Reviewing and discussing results will help you to remain successful or to make changes where you need to improve. There are seven key points to remember about this performance evaluation:

- Many factors influence job performance, including performance objectives, performance reviews, perception problems, problem-solving approach, work style, and the match between personal interests and job demands.

- Factors measured by the Performance Pyramid are important for success in every field of work, from steel fabrication to computer design, and in every professional-level job, from sales to supervision. Every industry requires the following: *statesmanship* — the ability to work with and through other people; *entrepreneurship* — the ability to achieve results; and *innovation* — the ability to generate new and usable ideas.

- The Performance Pyramid measures job behavior, not personal qualities. To increase objectivity, evaluation is based on actual rather than potential performance.

- Results on the Performance Pyramid are based on a normative group. Scores do not merely show whether your performance is good or bad; they show how your performance compares with that of individuals considered to be top producers and those considered to be poor producers in U.S. business and industry. The measuring stick — the normative group — may be disputed, but at least you know with whom you are being compared.

- Attitudes influence job performance. Scores on the Performance Pyramid may be raised or lowered by changes in your level of morale.

- The behavior of other people and the nature of the job can be assets or obstacles to effective performance.

- How high you score on the Performance Pyramid is less important than what you do about it. It is important to know where you stand in order to capitalize on your strengths and improve your weaknesses.

THE PERFORMANCE PYRAMID

Directions

Read the following sets of statements. In each set, make a check mark next to the statement that is most like your behavior on the job at this point in time. It may be difficult to select one statement over the others, but force a choice.

1. ___ a. You are interested in what will work, not what might work.
   ___ b. You are willing to listen to anyone's ideas.
   _✓_ c. You seek out the ideas and opinions of others.
   ___ d. You are tolerant of those whose ideas differ from yours.

2. ___ a. You rarely get worked up about things.
   ___ b. You measure up to what is expected of you in output.
   _✓_ c. You are one of the top producers of results.
   ___ d. You are busy with so many things that your output does not match that of others.

3. ___ a. When new ideas are introduced, you let others work out the "bugs" before you form an opinion.
   _✓_ b. You continually search for better ways to do things.
   ___ c. Sometimes you think of things that could be improved.
   ___ d. You often make suggestions to improve things.

4. _✓_ a. You go out of your way to help others.
   ___ b. You rarely spend time on other people's problems.
   ___ c. Other people often come to you for help.
   ___ d. You lend a hand if others request your assistance.

5. ___ a. You have selected assignments that have had a good future.
   _✓_ b. Most jobs you have worked on have resulted in significant contributions.
   ___ c. You would be much further ahead if you had not been assigned so many things that turned out to be unimportant.
   ___ d. Some of your time has been wasted on things that you never should have undertaken.

6. ___ a. You have changed the whole approach to your work.
   ✓ b. You have initiated a lot of changes in the work you are doing.
   ___ c. From time to time, you have made a change in the way you do your work.
   ___ d. You go along with established ways of working, without upsetting things.

7. ✓ a. You seek consensus in settling disagreements.
   ___ b. You do not concern yourself with the affairs of others.
   ___ c. You yield a point rather than displease someone.
   ___ d. Once your mind is made up, you prefer not to change it.

8. ___ a. You avoid taking risks under any circumstances.
   ___ b. You avoid taking risks except under rare circumstances.
   ___ c. You gamble on good odds any time.
   ✓ d. You sometimes gamble on being a winner.

9. ___ a. You are well known among your associates for your creativity.
   ✓ b. You often think of new ways of doing things.
   ___ c. You are conservative and rarely experiment with new ideas.
   ___ d. From time to time, you introduce new ideas.

10. ___ a. You often trust the wrong people.
    ___ b. Your judgment of people is usually correct.
    ___ c. You have as little as possible to do with others.
    ✓ d. Your ability to work with people is excellent.

11. ___ a. You prefer doing work yourself rather than planning work for others.
    ___ b. You plan work and hold performance to schedule.
    ✓ c. You make plans, but adjust to day-to-day changes.
    ___ d. You rarely make plans.

12. ✓ a. Your ideas are almost always used.
    ___ b. You frequently say to yourself, "I wish I had thought of that."
    ___ c. Your ideas are sometimes put into practice.
    ___ d. Your ideas are often adopted.

13. ___ a. You rarely have trouble deciding what to do.
    ___ b. You let others make most decisions.

___ c. You wait as long as possible before making decisions.
✓ d. You enjoy making decisions, and you are almost always correct.

14. ___ a. Sometimes you do not accomplish your goals.
___ b. You often do not accomplish your goals.
✓ c. When it comes to getting jobs done, you are one of the best performers.
___ d. If you want something done, you find a way to get it done.

15. ___ a. You recognize that doing things in a new way usually creates confusion.
___ b. You contribute to ideas initiated by others.
___ c. You avoid changing existing methods and procedures.
✓ d. You are constantly looking for ways to improve things.

Source: Philip Marvin, Management Goals: Guidelines and Accountability (Homewood, Ill.: Dow Jones–Irwin, Inc., 1980), 95-113. Used with permission.

SCORING

To evaluate your position on the Performance Pyramid, take the following steps.

Step One

Using the "score matrix" that follows, circle the score you gave yourself for each item under Self-Evaluation. (In question 1, if you checked (c), your score would be 7).

Step Two

If another person evaluated you, circle the score received for each item under Partner's Evaluation. (In question 1, if your partner checked (b), your score would be 5.)

Step Three

Add each column of the score matrix to find your total scores on (A) statesmanship; (B) entrepreneurship; and (C) innovation.

SCORE MATRIX

STATESMANSHIP		ENTREPRENEURSHIP		INNOVATION	
Self-Evaluation	Partner's Evaluation	Self-Evaluation	Partner's Evaluation	Self-Evaluation	Partner's Evaluation
1. a. 1	1	2. a. 1	1	3. a. 1	1
b. 5	5	b. 5	5	b. (7)	7
(c.) 7	7	(c.) 7	7	c. 3	3
d. 3	3	d. 3	3	d. 5	5
4. (a.) 7	7	5. a. 5	5	6. a. 7	7
b. 1	1	(b.) 7	7	b. (5)	5
c. 5	5	c. 1	1	c. 3	3
d. 3	3	d. 3	3	d. 1	1
7. (a.) 7	7	8. a. 1	1	9. a. 7	7
b. 1	1	b. 3	3	(b.) 5	5
c. 3	3	c. 7	7	c. 1	1
d. 5	5	(d.) 5	5	d. 3	3
10. a. 3	3	11. a. 3	3	12. (a.) 7	7
b. 5	5	b. 7	7	b. 1	1
c. 1	1	(c.) 5	5	c. 3	3
(d.) 7	7	d. 1	1	d. 5	5
13. a. 5	5	14. a. 3	3	15. a. 3	3
b. 1	1	b. 1	1	b. 5	5
c. 3	3	(c.) 5	5	c. 1	1
(d.) 7	7	d. 7	7	(d.) 7	7
A 35	A ___	B 29	B ___	C 31	C ___

Step Four

Plot your results on the Performance Pyramid in Figure 2.7, as shown in Figure 2.8. If there is disagreement between your self-evaluation and your partner's evaluation, use either the self-evaluation or an average of the two. In general, you know your own performance best. Discuss points of agreement and disagreement; you may be doing an exceptional job and not communicating this to your partner.

INTERPRETATION

High scores represent your strengths on the job at this point in time; low scores represent the areas in which you should strive to improve. Use the following formula to evaluate your scores:

Scores	Discussion
30–35	Extremely high performers receive these scores. As a result of ability, experience, and motivation, these

70   Performance: Managing for Excellence

FIGURE 2.7

Your Performance Pyramid

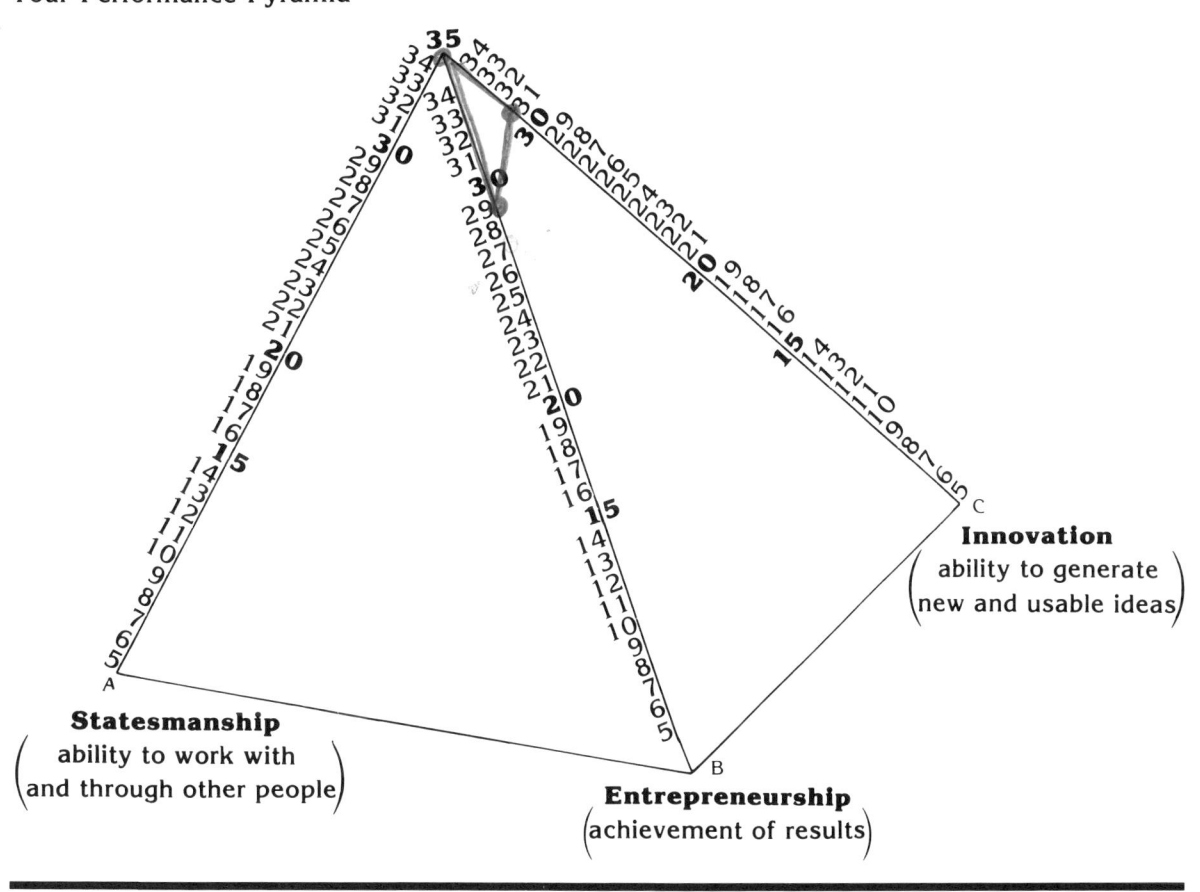

Statesmanship
(ability to work with and through other people)

Entrepreneurship
(achievement of results)

Innovation
(ability to generate new and usable ideas)

	individuals produce top results. If such a person were to leave, it is likely that the organization would suffer significantly.
20–29	Good performers receive these scores. They are pivotal people in their organizations and are solid producers. In college, these scores represent very good work.
15–19	People who receive these scores are "doing their jobs." They are doing what is expected of personnel in their positions—no more and no less. Although these scores are acceptable, they are nothing to write home about.

FIGURE 2.8

Sample Performance Pyramid

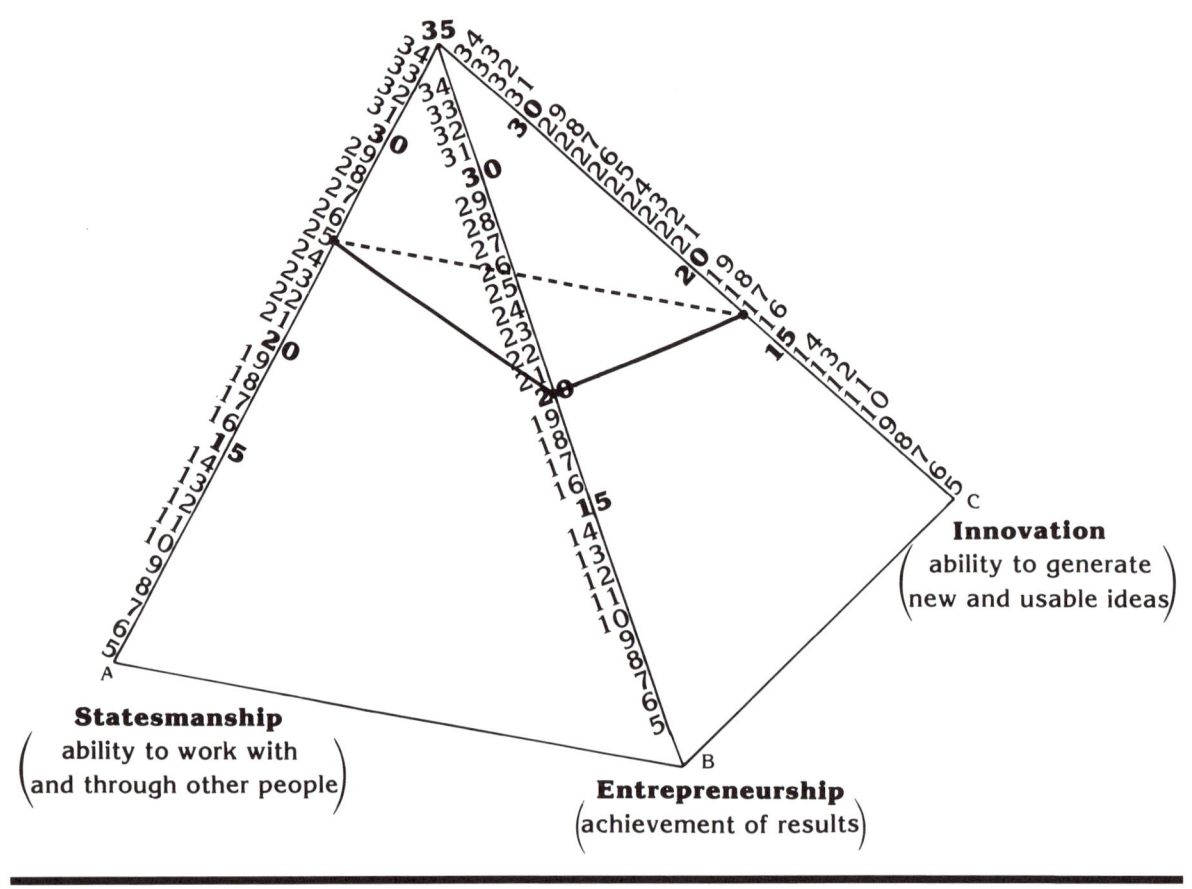

Statesmanship
(ability to work with
and through other people)

Entrepreneurship
(achievement of results)

Innovation
(ability to generate
new and usable ideas)

14 and lower	People whose performance needs improvement receive these scores. Such scores reflect problems in ability, experience, or attitude. Counseling and training should be considered.

IMPROVING JOB PERFORMANCE

Now that you have evaluated your job performance, what can you do to maintain high performance or to improve in the areas of statesmanship, entrepreneurship, and innovation? The answer has four parts:

- First and foremost, you must have the desire to improve; you must not be complacent.
- Second, you must know the essential behaviors that represent statesmanship, entrepreneurship, and innovation.

72 *Performance: Managing for Excellence*

- Third, you must learn principles and practices to perform these behaviors.
- Finally, you must put what you learn into action on the job, where it counts.

The following is a discussion of each area of performance, including behaviors that reflect high performance in that area and principles and techniques that constitute an action plan for improving performance. Implementation of the action plan is not included. Improvement comes from applying what you learn on the job, and that is up to you.

Statesmanship

Statesmanship is the ability to work with and through other people. The statesman is skillful in human relations and is able to multiply personal accomplishment through the efforts of others. The following describes the role of a statesman:

> A statesman is not a dictator, but rather a developer of effective relationships. The statesman is one who guides rather than leads, helping others to make decisions rather than making decisions alone. The statesman believes that if everyone works together, more can be accomplished.[6]

Consider the case of Abraham Lincoln. Throughout his life, Lincoln was always willing to teach others what he had learned himself. From

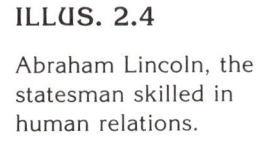

ILLUS. 2.4

Abraham Lincoln, the statesman skilled in human relations.

Part Two • Personal Performance

childhood onward, he was the statesman—storyteller, speech maker, and always the ringleader. One boyhood comrade relates:

> When he [Lincoln] appeared, the boys would gather and cluster around him to hear him talk.... He argued much from analogy and explained things hard for us to understand by stories, maxims, tales, and figures. He would almost always paint his lesson or idea by some story that was plain and near to us, that we might instantly see the force and bearing of what he said.[7]

Examine the following behavior lists. Behaviors in the first list represent a high level of statesmanship; those in the second represent a low level of statesmanship.

High Statesmanship

- You seek out the ideas and opinions of others.
- You go out of your way to help others.
- You seek consensus in settling disagreements.
- Your ability to work with people is excellent.
- You enjoy making decisions, and you are almost always correct.

Low Statesmanship

- You are interested in what will work, not what might work.
- You rarely spend time on other people's problems.
- You do not concern yourself with the affairs of others.
- You have as little as possible to do with others.
- You let others make most decisions.

If you are a supervisor or manager and would like to increase your statesmanship, the following principles and practices constitute an action plan: develop good human relation skills, and use four steps to solve problems.

Develop Good Human Relation Skills. A supervisor should understand human behavior and should know how to bring out the best in employee performance. The following ten principles for developing good human relations will help you to accomplish these goals:

1. *Get to know each subordinate as a person.* Like a craftsman who must know materials and tools, a supervisor must understand each employee's interests, aptitudes, and needs. How well do you know your people? For the answer, complete the following questionnaire.

HOW WELL DO YOU KNOW YOUR PEOPLE?

Directions

In Part I, indicate whether you know each fact about all of your subordinates. In Part II, think about your work group and write the name of the subordinate who answers each description.

Part I: Individual Characteristics

Do you know the following information about each of your subordinates?

	Yes	No
Full name	_____	_____
Age	_____	_____
Marital status	_____	_____
Spouse's name	_____	_____
Number of children	_____	_____
Approximate ages of children	_____	_____
Years of service	_____	_____
Career goals	_____	_____
Personal goals	_____	_____
Special interests	_____	_____
Educational level	_____	_____

Part II: Work Group Characteristics

Write the name of the subordinate who answers each description.

1. Who is the oldest employee by age? _____
2. Who is the oldest employee by years of service? _____
3. Who can handle the largest number of different jobs? _____
4. Who is the fastest worker? _____
5. Who does the best quality of work? _____
6. Who has the fewest accidents? _____
7. Who is your most skilled employee? _____
8. Who is the best suited to help train new employees? _____

9. Who should be in charge when you are not available? _____
10. Who is your most dependable employee? _____
11. Who is the best natured? _____
12. Who is the most cooperative? _____
13. Who is the most intelligent? _____
14. Who is the best all-around employee? _____
15. Who needs your help the most? _____

Source: Rosanna Rizzo Little; based on Philip Marvin, *Management Goals: Guidelines and Accountability (Homewood, Ill.: Dow Jones-Irwin, Inc., 1980).*

SCORING AND INTERPRETATION

To rate yourself on the How Well Do You Know Your People test, give yourself one point for each yes answer in Part I and one point for each answer you completed in Part II. Add up your total score and circle it on the scale below. The lower your total score, the less you know your people; the higher your score, the more qualified you are as a statesman.

Statesmanship Skills

Low 1 2 3 4 5 6 7 8 9 10 11 12 13 14 15 16 17 18 19 20 21 22 23 24 25 26 High

2. **Let subordinates, associates, and supervisors know where they stand.** You should communicate your expectations, then keep people informed on how they are doing. If criticism is necessary, do it in private; if praise is in order, give it in public.

3. **Give credit where due.** Have you yourself ever done a good job that went unnoticed? Look for extra or unusual performance from your subordinates, and give recognition as soon as possible. You should not wait until Christmas to thank an employee for something done well in the summer. If you do, for six months the employee probably will be thinking, "If my boss doesn't care, why should I?" In addition, you will have missed the opportunity to reinforce good performance. Psychologist Gordon Allport writes:

> Not only does human learning proceed best when the incentive of praise and recognition is used, but the individual's capacity for learning actually seems to expand under this condition.[8]

4. *Tell people as soon as possible about changes that will affect them (and tell them why).* Keep people informed, and tell them why change is necessary. Many people dislike change, even if it is inevitable, and they especially dislike sudden changes. Therefore, new ideas and methods are more easily accepted when introduced gradually, over a period of time. Also, be sure to tell those who will be affected by the change why something must be done; this is a sign of respect that meets a basic human need. Remember, most people prefer to be informed of change as soon as possible and to be told why change is necessary.

5. *Make best use of each person's ability.* No two workers are exactly alike, so let each subordinate shine as only that person can. Take the time to look for potential not now being used. Also, never stand in a subordinate's way. To do so creates resentment, reduces morale, and ultimately results in reduced performance.

6. *Lend a helping hand.* This shows that you care about your subordinate's well-being, meeting a basic human need. The following story helps to make the point:

    A painter asked Albert Einstein to sit for a portrait. The famous mathematician replied, "No, no, no. I do not have the time." "But I desperately need the money I'll get for the picture," the painter pleaded. "Well, that's another story," Einstein replied. "Of course I'll sit."[9]

7. *Give people time to talk.* One-to-one discussions and small-group meetings meet employees' needs to express themselves and also meet the organization's needs for information exchange and coordination of work. Employee involvement activities, such as quality circles and quality-of-work-life programs, are especially useful to give people time to talk.

8. *Design jobs and assign duties that are meaningful to subordinates.* The statesman realizes that people work for different reasons—survival, security, fellowship, respect, and self-fulfillment. Whenever possible, match the worker with the job so that the individual can satisfy personal needs by doing a good job.

9. *Let people participate in decisions that affect them, and encourage a friendly group atmosphere.* Whenever possible, tap the constructive power of group involvement to develop plans, products, and procedures and to solve job-related problems.

10. *Make sure your subordinates know the goals of the organization, and be sure each person knows what is expected of him or her.* Not knowing organizational goals and personal responsibilities wastes energy, erodes goodwill, and causes mistakes to be made.

Use Four Steps to Solve Problems. In addition to expertise in human relations, statesmanship requires problem-solving ability. The following is a four-step method for solving any problem—technical or human—at work or at home.

1. *Get the facts.* As Mark Twain said, "Get the facts first; then you can distort them as much as you please." You simply cannot solve a problem without first knowing the facts, so (a) review all records; (b) talk with the people concerned; (c) consider opinions and feelings (people act on their feelings); and (d) look at all sides. Seeing things from more than one point of view can help in the problem-solving process. Abraham Lincoln tried to understand the views of both the North and the South when he said:

   > I have no prejudice against the Southern people. They are just what we would be in their situation. If slavery did not now exist among them, they would not introduce it. If it did now exist among us, we would not instantly give it up. This I believe of the masses of North and South.

2. *Weigh and decide.* After getting all of the facts, you must weigh each fact against the others, fit the pieces together, and consider alternatives. Consider the effects that different courses of action will have on individuals and groups. Sometimes it is a good idea to sleep on a problem so that you do not jump to conclusions or overreact. It is easy to rush the thinking step of the problem-solving process and forget critical details. Benjamin Franklin emphasized the importance of considering details when he wrote, "A little neglect may breed mischief; for want of a nail, the shoe was lost; for want of a shoe, the horse was lost; for want of a horse, the rider was lost; for want of a rider, the war was lost."

3. *Take action.* After you have gathered the facts and determined a course of action, carry out your plan. Harry Truman realized the importance of this step in the problem-solving process. He believed it was the task of statesmen to take action; this was why he said, "The buck stops here" and "If you can't stand the heat, get out of the kitchen."

   There are many people who occupy positions that require statesmanship but who are indecisive and fail to act. Have you ever been affected by someone in authority—supervisor, parent, or public official—who could not, or would not, take action? William James wrote, "There is no more miserable human being than one in whom nothing is habitual but indecision."[10] Statesmen will act decisively and will not pass the buck.

4. *Follow up.* Follow-up is an essential, but often neglected, step in the problem-solving process. Some people say "I'm so busy taking action that I don't have time to follow up." With this attitude, they may be making the same mistakes over and over. At the least, they are not learning from experience.

Statesmen check to see if the actions they take are effective or not. They ask, "Did my action help the quality of work and the quality of work life?" If not, they admit the error immediately and try to find a better solution to the problem. Contrast the statesman's willingness to admit a mistake with the approach taken by many people: "Right or wrong, that is my decision." By taking time to follow up on actions and being willing to admit mistakes, the statesman achieves three important goals: (a) the respect of all who are watching; (b) another chance to solve the problem; and (c) the opportunity to set an example of honesty and thoroughness in problem solving.

In summary, statesmanship requires good human relation skills and problem-solving ability.

Entrepreneurship

Entrepreneurship is the ability to achieve results, regardless of obstacles. It takes entrepreneurship to build a plant on time, to produce a quality product, to balance books properly, and to close a sale successfully. Although an entrepreneur is action oriented, such an individual knows that it is not just action, but achievement, that counts. Effective performance in any field requires entrepreneurship. Consider the entrepreneur Henry Ford, who founded and built the Ford Motor Company. Ford believed in honesty and hard work and often asked, "Did you ever see dishonest calluses on a man's hands?" Ford's story follows:

Profile of an Entrepreneur

How it began

. . . But in the month of April, there came a burst of strenuous effort; the inventor worked two days and nights without rest or sleep, and at two o'clock in the morning came in to tell his wife that the machine was ready, and he was about to make a test. It was raining, and she came out under an umbrella to see what happened.

There was a crank in front, and you had to turn it over to start the engine. It made a mighty sputtering, then a roaring, and shook the vehicle most alarmingly; but it held together, and Mr. Ford got in and started. He had a kerosene lamp in front, and by this dim light went down the street paved with cobblestones. Mrs. Ford stood in the rain for a long time, wondering if she would ever see her husband again.

The young inventor was gone a long time, and came back pushing the contraption. A nut had come loose, with all the shaking. But he was exultant; in spite of bumpy cobblestones and muddy ruts, he had gone where he wished to go. "You're wet clear through," said his wife, as he let her lead him into the kitchen, take off his wet things, hang them up, and give him hot coffee. He was talking excitedly all the time. "I've got a horseless carriage that runs," said Henry Ford.

ILLUS. 2.5

MAXIMA is the result of the managerial and entrepreneurial abilities of Joshua I. Smith.

The MAXIMA CORPORATION

The early years

. . . He observed when they [the cars] bumped into each other, and devised plans to keep them from doing so. He examined materials, read contracts, discussed selling campaigns, and prepared advertisements shrewdly addressed to the mind of the average American, which he knew perfectly, because he had had one for forty years. It was his doctrine that any man who wanted to succeed in business should never let it out of his mind; and he had practiced this half a lifetime before he began to preach it.

In the first year the sales of the Ford Motor Company brought Ford a million and a half dollars, nearly one-fourth of which was profit. From then on, all his life, Henry Ford had all the money he needed to carry out his ideas. He took care of his money, and used it for that purpose.

The drive to succeed

. . . Henry Ford went on expanding his business. There was nobody to stop him now; he was master of his own house. He and his wife and son were the three directors of the Ford Motor Company; also they were the sole stockholders. There was a housecleaning, and those who did not see eye to eye with the master got out. The war had done something to Henry; it had taught him a new way to deal with his fellow men. No more crusades, no more peaceships, no more idealists getting hold of him and wasting his time. From now on, he was a businessman, and he held a tight rein on everything. This industry was his. He had made it himself; and what he wanted of the men he hired was that they should do exactly what he told them.

Tough times for the men

. . . Under this new deal, the chassis came to him [the worker] with spindlenuts already screwed on; it was Abner's job to put in a cotter-pin and spread it. The next man wielded a scoop, pasting a gob of brown grease into the cavity; by the time he had smoothed it level, the chassis had moved on to another, who screwed on the hubcap. Abner's job rested his tired legs, but his back began to ache abominably, and his arms were ready to give out from being held up in front of him continually. But he hung on like death and taxes, for he was over forty, the dangerous age for workers in any factory. "We expect the men to do what they are told," wrote Henry.

Mission accomplished

. . . Henry had a seemingly inexhaustible market for his cars. He was employing more than two hundred thousand men, paying wages of a quarter of a billion dollars a year. He had developed fifty-three different industries, beginning alphabetically with aeroplanes and ending with wood-distillation. He bought a broken-down railroad, and made it pay; he bought coal-mines, and trebled their production. He perfected new processes — the very smoke that had once poured from his chimneys was now made into automobile parts.[11]

Compare the two behavior lists that follow. The first list represents a high level of entrepreneurship; the second represents a low level of entrepreneurship.

High Entrepreneurship

- You are one of the top producers of results.
- Most jobs you have worked on have resulted in significant contributions.
- You gamble on good odds anytime.
- You plan work and hold performance to schedule.
- If you want something done, you find a way to get it done.

Low Entrepreneurship

- You rarely get worked up about things.
- You would be much further ahead if you had not been assigned so many things that turned out to be unimportant.
- You avoid taking risks under any circumstances.

- You rarely make plans.
- You often do not accomplish your goals.

Entrepreneurship in any field requires good work habits and the willingness to take risks, and both of these qualities depend primarily on the individual worker. The following action plan will help you to maximize entrepreneurship: exercise good work habits, and be willing to take risks.

Exercise Good Work Habits. The achievement of results requires a positive attitude and the ability to stick to a job until it is done, even with little help from others. A Polish proverb says, "If there is not enough wind, row." The following poem shows the kind of attitude that is necessary to accomplish difficult tasks:

> Some said it couldn't be done.
> But he, with a chuckle, replied
> That maybe it couldn't, but he would be one
> Who wouldn't say so until he tried.
>
> So he buckled right in with a bit of a grin,
> If he worried, he hid it.
> He started to sing, as he tackled the thing
> That couldn't be done—and he did it.[12]

Edgar Guest

The chronology of Abraham Lincoln's career shows the results of a positive attitude and determined effort:

- in 1831, he failed in business;
- in 1832, he was defeated for the legislature;
- in 1833, he again failed in business;
- in 1836, he had a nervous breakdown;
- in 1843, he was defeated for Congress;
- in 1855, he was defeated for the Senate;
- in 1856, he lost the race for the vice presidency;
- in 1858, he was defeated for the Senate;
- in 1860, he was elected president of the United States.[13]

A good worker goes the extra mile. If you have good work habits, your employer will want to keep you, and you will be rewarded both financially and personally as word gets out that you are a valuable employee. The following questionnaire evaluates work habits for all jobs at all levels of responsibility.

PUTTING YOUR BEST FOOT FORWARD

Directions

The following are fifteen qualities employers like to see in their personnel. These work habits are important in all fields of work and at all levels of responsibility. They are important for new employees and for experienced professionals. Evaluate your current job performance by circling the appropriate number (1 is low; 10 is high).

Job Knowledge

Make it your business to know what to do, when to do it, and why you are doing it.

1   2   3   4   5   6   7   8   9   10

Dependability

If your work requires being on time, be on time. You should be ten minutes early for the work day if at all possible. Tardiness lowers your image (this includes lunch and work breaks). Also, if you say you will do something, do it. Be known as a person who can be counted on.

1   2   3   4   5   6   7   8   9   10

Cooperation

Take interest in other people, and strive to be helpful. Everyone appreciates someone who is willing to lend a hand. Show others you are interested in doing a good job for them. Learn to understand and get along with all types of people.

1   2   3   4   5   6   7   8   9   10

Concentration

Always pay attention to what is going on; that is how you learn. You should try to learn something new every day. People are more interested in those who show initiative and concentration. Don't sleepwalk through your day; this is how accidents occur and opportunities are missed.

1   2   3   4   5   6   7   8   9   10

Industry

If you are not eager to do your job, either you are in the wrong line of work or you have allowed yourself to get lazy. If it is the first, find another job; if it is the second, overcome your laziness. It will pay off. Be a self-starter; don't wait for others to generate a spark in you. It is your life, and you control what you do now and with your future.

1   2   3   4   5   6   7   8   9   10

Communication

No one likes excuses after the fact, even if they are legitimate. If you can't accomplish a task as assigned, inform those who should know as soon as possible. The more you communicate, the better your relationships will be.

1 2 3 4 5 6 7 8 9 10

Flexibility

Don't be overly rigid. Most jobs require flexibility to get the best results. Be open to changing your approach, your schedule, and even your goals if it will help increase job performance.

1 2 3 4 5 6 7 8 9 10

Dedication

You have to be dedicated to your job if you are to succeed. Don't automatically take the attitude that you are being exploited by others. A job is usually a two-way street. You are helping your employer, but you are also acquiring knowledge and experience that will benefit you; also, you are being paid. Most business owners and managers work nearly ten hours a day trying to keep their operations going, and this creates jobs. Employee dedication is needed as well, and it is usually greatly appreciated.

1 2 3 4 5 6 7 8 9 10

Avoidance of Conflict

Avoid arguments on the job. If you do become part of a conflict, try to solve the problem in private, as soon as possible, and without hurting anyone. Remember, seeing things from the other person's point of view helps to solve unnecessary conflict.

1 2 3 4 5 6 7 8 9 10

Patience

At times, you may feel dissatisfied with your job. If so, wait a fair amount of time before deciding whether to change jobs. In the meantime, talking to the people with whom you work may help you to feel a part of the group and may help you to enjoy what you are doing.

1 2 3 4 5 6 7 8 9 10

Neat Personal Appearance

Impressions are important, so dress appropriately for work. Always be careful about personal hygiene, and keep your clothes presentable.

1 2 3 4 5 6 7 8 9 10

Conscientious Use of Break Time

Avoid taking more break time than you truly need (including paid personal time). Would you like paying an employee to kill time? Put yourself in your employer's position, and then look at yourself. Are you giving a full day's work for a full day's pay?

1   2   3   4   5   6   7   8   9   10

Wise Use of Spare Time

During the normal workday, there may be times when you are temporarily out of work. Keep your eyes open for something to do during these periods. It costs money and time for one person to keep another person busy. Learn to look for things to do, and if you cannot find something, ask. Never just sit or stand around.

1   2   3   4   5   6   7   8   9   10

Excellence

Study or practice your work so that you are truly good at it. This will boost your ego and make you more valuable to your employer, which will usually be reflected in your wages. Do not become complacent with current success. Remember, a professional in any field knows what it takes to perform well, but always strives to improve.

1   2   3   4   5   6   7   8   9   10

Trustworthiness

Be honest in all of your dealings. Word travels quickly, and a poor reputation can be acquired faster than a good one.

1   2   3   4   5   6   7   8   9   10

Source: Steve McMillen, Northern Kentucky University, 1984. Based on training materials from the National Association of Homebuilders, Manpower Department, 1025 Connecticut Ave., N.W., Washington, D.C. 10036.

SCORING AND INTERPRETATION

To score and interpret the Putting Your Best Foot Forward test, add up your total and read the evaluation and discussion that follow.

Score	Evaluation	Discussion
135–150	Outstanding	Extremely high performers receive these scores. These

		individuals produce top results, and their work habits are excellent.
105–134	Very good	Good performers receive these scores. They are solid producers in their organizations. In college, these scores would represent a high level of work.
75–104	Ordinary	People who receive these scores are "doing their jobs" — no more and no less. Although acceptable, these scores are only ordinary.
15–74	Below Standard	These scores reflect problems with ability, experience, or attitude. Counseling and training should be sought.

Be Willing to Take Risks. Besides good work habits, entrepreneurship requires the ability to overcome fear. Fear can have terrible consequences, as the following story shows:

> In an ancient fable, an oriental monarch met Pestilence going to Baghdad. "What are you going to do there?" asked the King. "I'm going to kill 5,000 people," said Pestilence. On the way back, the monarch met Pestilence again. "You liar," thundered the monarch, "You killed 25,000." "Oh, no," said Pestilence. "I only killed 5,000 people. It was Fear that killed the rest."[14]

Fear of failure can have negative consequences in the work setting. Fear can paralyze a person to the extent that opportunities are missed and achievement is reduced. As the following poem illustrates, entrepreneurship requires courage:

> He had his doubts when he began;
> The task had stopped another man;
> And he had heard it whispered low,
> How rough the road was he must go;
> But now on him the charge was laid,
> And of himself he was afraid.
>
> He wished he knew how it would end;
> He longed to see around the bend;
> He had his doubts that he had strength,
> Enough to go so far a length;
> And all the time the notion grew,
> That this was more than he could do.
>
> Of course, he failed. Whoever lives with doubt,
> Soon finds his courage giving out;
> They only win who face a task,

And say the chance is all I ask;
They only rise who dare the grade,
And of themselves are not afraid.

There are no ogres up the slope;
It is only with human beings that man must cope;
Whoever fears the blow before it's struck,
Loses the fight for lack of pluck;
And only he the goal achieves,
Who truly in himself believes.[15]

Edgar Guest

In summary, hard work (good work habits) and self-confidence (willingness to take risks) are essential for entrepreneurship.

Innovation

Innovation is the ability to generate new and usable ideas. Not satisfied with the status quo, the innovator explores, questions, and studies new ways of doing things. Innovation accounts for advances in all fields of work, from agriculture to architecture. Important products we take for granted today are the result of yesterday's innovations—Thomas Edison's electric light, the Wright brothers' airplane, and Alexander Graham Bell's telephone are but a few examples.

Within the past hundred years, the growth of knowledge has accelerated at an ever-increasing rate, and development in some fields has been astounding. Consider that the speed of travel has increased by ten squared (10^2), the speed of processing information by ten to the sixth power

ILLUS. 2.6

Thomas Edison, the young inventor.

(10^6), the speed of communication by ten to the seventh power (10^7), and the ability to control disease by ten squared (10^2). Within the last half century, we have developed jet travel, computers, space satellites, immunology, and many other innovations that have the potential for helping the human race. Currently, creative people are making discoveries in such fields as laser technology, microprocessing, fiber optics, and genetic chemistry.[16]

The creative process is not unique to human beings; it can be seen in other animals as well:

> Primatologists put out various foods, such as wheat and potatoes, that were not part of the macaque's natural diet, to attract the animals to feeding grounds near the open seashore where they could more easily be observed. Within four hours after a dominant male in one group had sampled the wheat that had been left and then begun eating it, the entire group followed his lead. . . . Because a mound of wheat had simply been piled on the beach, the monkeys found it difficult to separate grains of wheat from grains of sand. Year after year, the monkeys painstakingly picked out the grains of wheat with their fingertips—until a young female arrived at the novel solution of scooping a handful of the mixture and running on her hind legs to the sea. When she opened her hands in the water, the heavier sands sank immediately while the wheat grains floated on the surface, where they could easily be scooped up. This method of sifting wheat eventually became a tradition within the group, much as it must have in human groups that early developed the cultural innovation of winnowing wheat to separate the chaff from the grain. Wheat-sifting by macaques represents true protoculture: a modification in behavior different from that of other groups belonging to the same species and faced with the same potentials and limitations in the environment— one that is transmitted throughout the group and from generation to generation.[17]

Compare the following lists of behaviors. The first list represents a high level of creativity; the second represents a low level of creativity.

High Innovation

- You continually search for better ways to do things.
- You have changed the whole approach to your work.
- You are well known among your associates for your creativity.
- Your ideas are almost always used.
- You are constantly looking for ways to improve things.

Low Innovation

- When new ideas are introduced, you let others work out the "bugs" before you form an opinion.
- You go along with established ways of working, without upsetting things.
- You are conservative and rarely experiment with new ideas.

- You frequently say to yourself, "I wish I had thought of that."
- You avoid changing existing methods and procedures.

How do you develop creativity? How can a person increase innovative ability? The following action plan will help you to develop new and useful ideas: have an open mind, avoid innovation blocks, have a questioning attitude, and use a new-ideas system.

Have an Open Mind. An essential quality of the innovator is openness to change and to new experience. The innovator does not consider creation to be a place, but rather a direction, and does not consider himself to be a completed book, but rather a book in the process of being written. The following story shows the importance of openness to change:

> Two caterpillars were crawling across the grass when a butterfly flew overhead. They looked up. One nudged the other and said, "You couldn't get me up in one of those things for a million dollars."[18]

Charles F. Kettering, the famous inventor, emphasized the importance of keeping an open mind when he wrote:

> I don't want men of experience working for me. The experienced man is always telling me why something can't be done. The fellow who has not had any experience doesn't know a thing can't be done—and goes ahead and does it. . . . There exist limitless opportunities in any industry. Where there is an open mind, there will always be a frontier.[19]

The innovative person remembers the bumblebee—nothing that flies is less qualified to do so. The bumblebee's wings are small and its body is large; yet, despite the laws of aerodynamics, the bumblebee flies. We often hear about an idea that doesn't sound as if it would work. However, *non tentare, non pugnare*—if you haven't tried it, don't knock it. Innovation requires an open mind.[20]

Avoid Innovation Blocks. Do any of the following prevent you from being as creative as you could be?

- *Excessive need for order.* Institutions—church, school, industry, and government—provide a sense of order. But it is possible to be too orderly. When everything happens according to plan, innovation is ordered out of existence. As the Hungarians say, to make an omelet you have to break a few eggs. For creativity, order should be viewed as a tool, not a goal.

- *Reluctance to play.* Creativity requires playfulness, daydreaming, and questioning "what if?" and "why?" Innovative people play with things, people, and ideas. Those who are afraid to play because they think they will look silly or because they feel guilty about having fun rarely come up with creative ideas.

- *Myopic vision.* Some people pride themselves on seeing things "as they are." But if you see things only as they are, you miss seeing what they could be; this is the essence of innovation. A shoe can be a hammer, a pillow, or something from which to drink water.

- *Fear of risk.* Society punishes failure, so we become afraid to "stick our necks out." Yet the wisdom of the ages says, "Nothing ventured, nothing gained."
- *Reluctance to exert influence.* If children are taught to be "seen and not heard," they may not want to attract attention or appear to be "different" when they become adults. Most people have the feeling that the majority has to be right. But often, the majority keeps on doing things one way when there is a new and better way available.
- *Closed-mindedness.* What if Christopher Columbus had been as certain as most people in his day that the world was flat? Research has shown that the more that people feel they really know something, the less open they are to new information and ideas in that area. This is called the "specialist disease."[21]

Have a Questioning Attitude. People are creatures of habit. Some habits are good because they help us survive. Good driving habits and hygiene habits are examples. Other habits, such as drinking too much or procrastinating, are harmful and prevent success. People may have poor habits and not know it, unless they ask themselves two questions: "Am I doing the right thing?" and "Is there a better way to do it?" Many people sleepwalk through their days, never stopping to ask themselves these two questions. For these individuals, creativity is never realized because it is never considered. The following poem shows the importance of having a questioning attitude:

*The Calf Path — The Beaten
Path of Beaten Men*

One day through an old-time wood,
A calf walked home, as good calves should;
But made a trail,
A crooked trail, as all calves do.
Since then three hundred years have fled,
And I infer the calf is dead.
But still, he left behind his trail,
And thereby hangs my mortal tale.

The trail was taken up the next day,
By a lone dog that passed that way.
And then a wise sheep,
Pursued the trail, over the steep,
And drew the flocks behind him too,
As all good sheep do.
And from that day, over hill and glade,
Through those old woods, a path was made.

This forest path became a lane,
That bent, and turned, and turned again.

This crooked lane became a road,
Where many a poor horse with his load,
Toiled on beneath the burning sun.
And thus a century and a half,
They followed the footsteps of that calf.

The years passed on in swiftness fleet,
And the road became a village street.
And this became a city's thoroughfare.
And soon the central street was a metropolis.
And men, two centuries and a half,
Followed the footsteps of that calf.

A moral lesson this tale might teach,
Were I ordained, and called to preach.
For men are prone to go it blind,
Along the calf paths of the mind;
And work away from sun to sun,
To do just what other men have done.
They follow in the beaten track,
And out, and in, and forth, and back;
And still their devious course pursue,
To keep the paths that others do.

They keep these paths as sacred grooves,
Along which all their lives they move.
But how the wise old wood gods laugh,
Who saw the first old-time calf.
Ah, many things this tale might teach,
But I am not ordained to preach.[22]

Samuel Foss

Use a New-Ideas System. Being open to change, avoiding innovation blocks, and having a questioning attitude are three ingredients of creativity; but a fourth element is necessary — we need a system to generate new and usable ideas. One such system comes from the English writer Rudyard Kipling. Kipling, who was known for his creativity, was asked how he could come up with so many good ideas; what was the secret of his success? His famous answer was:

I keep six honest serving-men;
They taught me all I knew;
Their names are What and Where and When,
And How and Why and Who.
I send them over land and sea;
I send them east and west;
But after they have worked for me,
I give them all a rest.

I let them rest from nine till five,
For I am busy then,
As well as breakfast, lunch, and tea,
For they are hungry men:
But different folk have different views:

> I know a person small—
> She keeps ten million serving-men,
> Who get no rest at all.
> She sends 'em abroad on her own affairs,
> From the second she opens her eyes—
> One million Hows, two million Wheres,
> And seven million Whys.[23]
>
> *Rudyard Kipling*

By asking six simple questions—who, what, why, when, where, and how—and by constructively answering them, you can usually find new and workable solutions to any problem.

In summary, innovation requires openness to change, avoidance of innovation blocks, a questioning attitude, and an effective system to generate new ideas.

YOU CAN IMPROVE IF YOU WANT TO

It is possible to improve job performance, and the rewards are great. Consider the following story:

> When Gene Malusko first went to work for his company, he was hired as a laborer. Before long, it was apparent that Gene would become either a union steward or a supervisor because he had the ability to work with and through other people—Gene could talk people into things; he was a statesman. Gene chose supervision because he had a family to raise and needed the money. For the next year, Gene was a successful foreman—he had good relations with his subordinates, and he had a good production record.
>
> Then Gene became interested in advancing to general foreman. As he considered those who had been promoted in the past, he realized that they had each excelled at obtaining results. The quality and efficiency of their production had stood out over that of the other supervisors. This convinced him to set forth on a self-improvement program to improve entrepreneurship, the delivery of results.
>
> Thereafter, when Gene arrived at work, he began working immediately, and he worked diligently until he went home. He developed a reputation for making his production quota each day, and he could be counted on to help out in emergencies. Gene was also willing to stick his neck out and take risks when the situation warranted it. He overcame self-doubt with the attitude, "Nothing ventured, nothing gained." With confidence in himself and good work habits, Gene developed a superb record of achievement. Gene exhibited entrepreneurship, and within two years, he was promoted to general foreman.
>
> Gene performed very well as a general foreman on the strength of his ability to work with people (statesmanship) and his ability to obtain results (entrepreneurship), and after a mere three years in this capacity, he was selected as the youngest superintendent in the history of the company.
>
> Two years later, Gene was talking with a friend about future plans when he stated that his goal was to be a general manager. He wondered aloud, "What do those guys have that I don't?" The answer was creativity. A good general manager must work with and through others, which Gene

did; must achieve results regardless of the obstacles, which Gene did; and must come up with new and usable ideas, which Gene almost never did.

Gene's friend told him about the ideas of Charles Kettering and the importance of keeping an open mind; he pointed out the six common blocks to innovation; he gave him "The Calf Path—The Beaten Path of Beaten Men," emphasizing the need to question things; and finally, he told him about Rudyard Kipling's six honest serving-men, a system of constructive self-questioning.

Until this time, Gene had not thought much about why things were as they were; he had rarely questioned whether there was a better way to do something; and he had never been given a system for generating new ideas. For Gene, a new dimension of management performance was unveiled, and he set about to improve his creativity.

Each day, Gene would go into his work area and ask himself six questions—who, what, why, when, where, and how—to analyze the production bottlenecks and employee problems he encountered. He would ask: Who should do this work, the machine operator or the inspector? What should be done, milling or planing? Why should this be done, production or politics? Where should the work be done, in the office or the field? When should the work be done, on the first shift or the second? And how should the work be done, by man or by machine? And, like Kipling, Gene always found a better way.

Gene worked at constructive questioning until it became a habit, and he gained a reputation as a creative person. He added innovation to the qualities of statesmanship and entrepreneurship that he had already mastered, and two years later, Gene Malusko was promoted to general manager.[24]

Gene's story is one of professionalism. He learned what it would take to perform his job well; he performed good work; yet he constantly tried to improve. He was not complacent. As a result of development as a statesman, an entrepreneur, and an innovator, Gene Malusko improved his job performance and achieved personal satisfaction as well.

RECOMMENDED RESOURCES

The following readings, cases, application, and films are suggested for greater insight into Part Two:

Readings	— The Peter Principle That Urge to Achieve What Makes a Top Executive?
Cases	— A Talk with Kirkeby's Son The Vice-President The Reluctant Backhoe Operator
Application	— Personality Traits and Job Demands Analysis
Films	— What Can I Contribute? Need to Achieve

The Self-Motivated Achiever
Women in Management: Threat or Opportunity?

REFERENCE NOTES

1. Charles A. Lindbergh, *Autobiography of Values* (New York: Harcourt Brace Jovanovich Inc., 1976).

2. George Marshall and David Poling, *Schweitzer* (Garden City, N. J.: Doubleday & Company, Inc., 1971).

3. Ronald W. Clark, *The Life of Bertrand Russell* (New York: Alfred A. Knopf, Inc., 1975).

4. Robert L. Katz, "Skills of an Effective Administrator," *Harvard Business Review* (September/October 1974): 90-102.

5. Laurence J. Peter and Raymond Hull, *The Peter Principle* (New York: William Morrow & Co., Inc., 1969).

6. Phillip Marvin, *Management Goals: Guidelines and Accountability* (Homewood, Ill.: Dow Jones-Irwin, Inc., 1980), 166-67.

7. Will Forpe and John C. McCollister, *The Sunshine Book: Expressions of Love, Hope and Inspiration* (Middle Village, N. Y.: Jonathan David Publishers, Inc., 1979.

8. Gordon W. Allport, "The Ego in Contemporary Psychology," *Psychological Review* 50 (1943): 466.

9. Forpe and McCollister, *The Sunshine Book*, 112.

10. William James, as quoted in J. M. Cohen and M. J. Cohen, *The Penguin Dictionary of Quotations* (New York: The Viking Press, 1977), 204.

11. Upton Sinclair, *The Flivver King* (New York: Phaedra, Inc., 1969), 6, 7, 19, 65, 69, 70, 78.

12. Edgar Guest, as quoted in Forpe and McCollister, *The Sunshine Book*, 5.

13. Forpe and McCollister, *The Sunshine Book*, 89.

14. Forpe and McCollister, *The Sunshine Book*, 99.

15. "The Doubter," Edgar Guest, from the course training materials of William J. Stewart, University of Cincinnati, 1970.

16. Warren Bennis, *The Unconscious Conspiracy* (New York: AMACOM Book Division, 1976), 127-28.

17. Peter Farb, *Humankind* (New York: Bantam Books, Inc., 1980), 31.

18. Source unknown.

19. *The Reader's Digest Great Encyclopedic Dictionary* (Pleasantville, N. Y.: Reader's Digest Association, 1966), 2039.

20 Robert P. Levoy, "Getting Your Money's Worth from Courses," Professional Practice Consultants.

21 Source unknown.

22 Samuel Foss, "The Calf Path," as found in Peter J. Frost, Vance F. Mitchell, and Walter R. Nord, *Organizational Reality: Reports from the Firing Line*, 3d ed. (Glenview, Ill.: Scott, Foresman & Company, 1986), 486–87.

23 John Beecroft, *Kipling: A Selection of His Stories and Poems* (Garden City, N.Y.: Doubleday & Company, Inc., 1956), 383–84.

24 Case from the authors' files.

STUDY QUIZ

As a test of your understanding and the extent to which you have achieved the objectives in Part Two, complete the following questions. See Appendix E for the answer key.

1. The three types of interests—in things, in people, and in ideas—correspond to the following individuals, respectively:

    a. Schweitzer, Russell, and Lindbergh
    b. Russell, Lindbergh, and Schweitzer
    c. Lindbergh, Schweitzer, and Russell

2. There are two problems facing people who have a high degree of interest in all three areas—things, people, and ideas:

    a. fatigue; tendency to not complete tasks
    b. public resentment; personal rejection
    c. lack of ability; lack of time

3. The typical progression of careers is as follows:

    a. coordinating, thinking, doing
    b. doing, thinking, coordinating
    c. doing, coordinating, thinking

4. The "vital shift" refers to:

    a. the change in emphasis when a person leaves one type of work and moves to another
    b. a change in employee attitude
    c. a change in the human resources/physical facilities mix
    d. a new form of automatic transmission

5. The Peter Principle refers to:

    a. a religious practice in the Catholic Church
    b. the tendency of organizations to promote individuals to their level of incompetence
    c. the tendency of individuals to take on more work than they can perform
    d. the principle of vertical versus horizontal organizational structure

6. The three key performance elements in managerial and professional jobs are:

    a. statesmanship, entrepreneurship, and innovation
    b. intelligence, social status, and work records
    c. leadership, teamwork, and experience
    d. none of the above

7. People with low statesmanship:
   - (a.) let others make most decisions
   - b. seek out the ideas and opinions of others

8. People with high statesmanship:
   - a. rarely spend time on other people's problems
   - (b.) go out of their way to help others

9. A statesman gets to know each subordinate personally.
   - (a.) True
   - b. False

10. A statesman lets people know what is expected of them and provides feedback about how they are doing.
    - (a.) True
    - b. False

11. A statesman is quick to give credit for a job well done.
    - (a.) True
    - b. False

12. A statesman discourages one-to-one discussions and small-group meetings.
    - a. True
    - (b.) False

13. A statesman holds information closely and postpones telling people about changes that will affect them.
    - a. True
    - (b.) False

14. The four steps statesmen take to solve problems are as follows:
    - (a.) get the facts, weigh and decide, take action, follow up
    - b. study, rehearse, state, record
    - c. involve others, take charge, decide action, implement decision
    - d. none of the above

15. A statesman who makes a mistake will:
    - (a.) admit the mistake
    - b. stonewall the decision
    - c. ignore the effects of the error
    - d. blame others
    - e. none of the above

16. Entrepreneurship means:
    a. financial individualism
    b. the ability to achieve results
    c. corporate activity
    d. none of the above

17. The two key ingredients of entrepreneurship are:
    a. good work habits and a willingness to take risks
    b. an extroverted personality and social connections
    c. intelligence and financial resources
    d. none of the above

18. People with a high level of entrepreneurship:
    a. gamble on good odds
    b. rarely make plans

19. People with a low level of entrepreneurship:
    a. rarely get worked up about things
    b. plan work and hold performance to schedule

20. All of the following are effective work habits except:
    a. dependability
    b. cooperation
    c. concentration
    d. flexibility
    e. patience
    f. unquestioning obedience

21. Entrepreneurship requires the ability to overcome _____.
    a. love
    b. fear
    c. nature
    d. none of the above

22. Innovation is the ability to generate:
    a. new and usable ideas
    b. a high production volume
    c. chaos in social order
    d. none of the above

23. A person wth a high level of innovation:
    a. constantly looks for ways to improve things
    b. rarely experiments with new ideas

24. A person with a low level of innovation:
    a. changes whole approaches to work
    b. goes along with established ways

25. A person can increase personal innovation by having a questioning attitude and using a new-ideas system.
    a. True
    b. False

26. Common blocks to innovation include excessive need for order and reluctance to play.
    a. True
    b. False

27. Rudyard Kipling's famous questions to increase creativity were: who, what, why, when, where, and how.
    a. True
    b. False

28. Examples of statesmanship, entrepreneurship, and innovation, respectively, are:
    a. Lincoln, Ford, and Edison
    b. Magellan, Newton, and Napoleon
    c. Michelangelo, Churchill, and Roosevelt

DISCUSSION QUESTIONS AND ACTIVITIES

The following questions and activities help personalize the subject. They are appropriate for classroom exercises and homework assignments.

1. Do your personal interests match the demands of your job?

2. Have you experienced or witnessed the Peter Principle at work?

3. What are your strengths and weaknesses on the Performance Pyramid? What key steps can you take to maintain or improve your job performance?

4. What are your occupational and career goals — in one year; in five years; for the rest of your life? Using one to five pages, discuss.

5. Gather into small groups for the remaining questions and activities. Consider the importance of statesmanship, entrepreneurship, and innovation in a company or organization. For each area, cite a true-life person or incident and the effects the person or incident had.

6. What can an organization do to maximize statesmanship, entrepreneurship, and innovation among its employees? What policies and practices would you recommend?

7. Discuss the pros and cons of the new-job tryout. Give actual examples.

8. Discuss the work habits employers want in all employees. Describe your own strengths and weaknesses.

PART THREE

Productivity Improvement

Learning Objectives

After completing Part Three, you will better understand:

1. your time management skills. You will know if you are using your time effectively;
2. a three-step method for improving the performance of any work group or organization.

EFFECTIVE TIME MANAGEMENT

The French writer-philosopher Voltaire asked an interesting question in his book *Zadig or the Book of Fate*. "What, of all things in the world, is the longest and the shortest, the swiftest and the slowest, the most divisible and the most extended, the most neglected and the most regretted, without which nothing can be done, which devours all that is little and enlivens all that is great?"

To this, Zadig answered, "Time." Then he said: "Nothing is larger, since it is the length of eternity; nothing is shorter, since there is never enough of it to satisfy our wants. Nothing is faster for the person who is happy; nothing is slower for one who is sad. In smallness, time is infinitely divisible; in greatness, time has no limit. People neglect time, but they regret the loss of it. There is no action that can be done without time. Time stores in darkness whatever is unworthy, and makes immortal all that is truly great."[1]

One of the most important factors in job performance is effective use of your time. You know you have a time management problem when:

- you are always late for meetings and appointments;
- you are typically behind in your work, school, or personal responsibilities;
- you often feel hurried, harried, and hassled;
- you don't have enough time for basics—sleeping, eating, family affairs;
- you often feel fatigued—worn out physically and mentally;
- you often forget appointments, meetings, and other responsibilities;
- you are constantly working;
- you can't meet deadlines—even if you are constantly working;
- your activities are fragmented, disjointed, and incomplete.

Time is both personal and finite. It is personal in that the best statement of who you are is the way you spend your time. Your use of time reflects your needs, goals, and accomplishments as does no other single thing. Time is finite in that each person has only 24 hours a day. Figure 3.1 shows how most people spend their time each day.

FIGURE 3.1

How You Spend Your Time

Based on surveys and observations of thousands of people, the average person's day looks something like this:

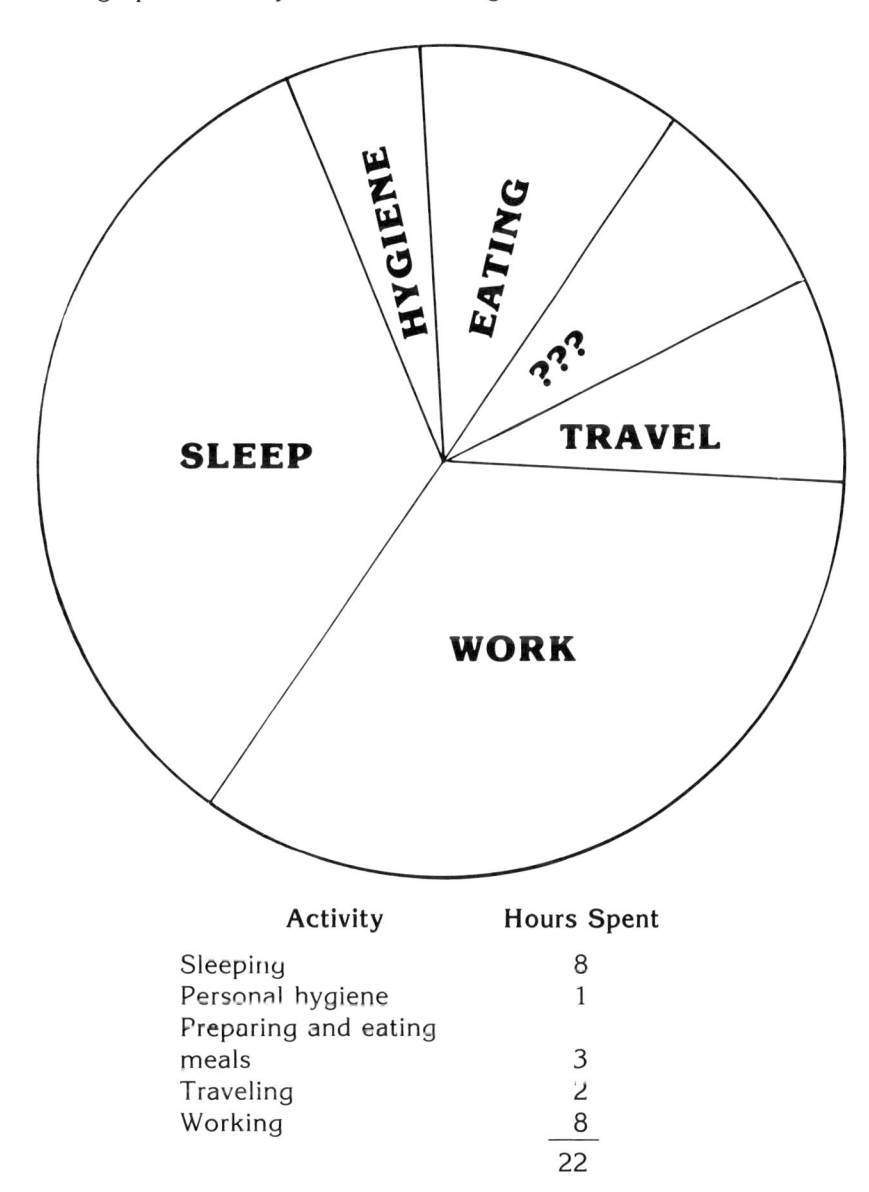

Activity	Hours Spent
Sleeping	8
Personal hygiene	1
Preparing and eating meals	3
Traveling	2
Working	8
	22

On the average, this leaves about two hours each day to do all of the other things that make life worth living. However, most people, by their own accounts, waste at least two hours a day.

Source: "How We Spend Our Time," adapted from Time Management Center, P.O. Box 5, Grandville, Mich. 49418. Reprinted with permission.

Getting full benefit from the 24 hours you have each day depends primarily on your attitude toward time and on your time management skills.

The Importance of Attitude

The following shows an attitude toward time and life that will help you to get the most out of both:

Just for Today . . .

Just for today, I will try to live through this day only and not tackle all of my life's problems at once. I hope I can do something for someone and keep the memory of it for a lifetime.

Just for today, I will try to be happy. This assumes to be true what Abraham Lincoln once said: "Most folks are as happy as they make their minds up to be."

Just for today, I will adjust myself to what is and try not to adjust everything to my own desires. I will take my "chances" as they come and fit myself to them.

Just for today, I will exercise myself in two ways: I will do somebody a good turn and not get found out. I will do at least two things I don't want to do just because they are good for me.

Just for today, I will be agreeable. I will look as fit as I can, talk softly, listen intently, act courteously, criticize not one bit, try not to find fault, and try to regulate no one except myself.

Just for today, I will have a program. I may not follow it exactly, but I will have it. I will try hard to save myself from two pests — hurry and indecision.

Just for today, I will have a quiet moment or two all by myself and relax. During this brief period, somehow, I will try to better myself and try to get a better perspective of my life.

Just for today, I will be unafraid to enjoy what is beautiful and what is common and to believe that as I give to the world and the people in it, so will the world benefit.[2]

William J. Stewart

Time Management Skills

The following story shows the importance of time management skills. Does the situation sound familiar?

Bill slid behind the wheel of his car. It was late, and he was very tired. As he thought back over his day, he said to himself, "Man, this job is killing me!" He remembered arriving at work early and seeing the stacks of paperwork and return-call messages demanding his attention. At least three of these were "hot items," requiring immediate action. In his briefcase were four letters he had written the night before to give to his secretary and bits of a major report due by week's end. In addition, there was the note in his pocket from his wife: "Call the repairman." Bill remembered the desperation he had felt as he gathered his strength to dive into the problems of the day. He felt like a rat, trapped in a familiar maze and running a habitual treadmill. Finally, where was that coffee? He sure wished he had a cup of coffee. Problems and people were to pour forth in a relentless stream for ten consecutive hours.

Now, as he sat in his car, Bill thought: "The day has not gone well . . . nor has the week. Come to think of it, the whole year has been one crisis after another for the entire operation." Several of his key people seemed to feel "under siege" as well. Others didn't seem to feel anything at all. It was as if they were physically at work, but mentally absent—undedicated and not very productive. Lately, it was as if everyone fell into one of two camps—the unhelpful and the shell-shocked. Neither camp had many smiles or many relaxed moments to savor accomplishments. In fact, big-picture-wise, he himself had trouble identifying the accomplishments of his operation. Bill thought: "Why is this? Why do we lurch from personnel problems to financial crises to production emergencies, one after another? Why do we always seem to be fighting fires?"[3]

Bill's problem is called the "firehouse syndrome." The symptoms are a high level of frustration, overworked employees, burned-out managers, and decreased productivity. The results are high stress levels, low morale, and organizational breakdown. Often, the solution to the firehouse syndrome is better use of one's time. Bill could probably help his subordinates, his organization, and himself by improving his time management skills. If you are a manager, complete the following questionnaire to see if you are managing time effectively.

ILLUS. 3.1

The "firehouse syndrome" results in overworked employees, burned-out managers, and decreased productivity.

Photo courtesy BASF Corporation Information Systems

TIME MANAGEMENT AUDIT — ARE YOU WASTING YOUR TIME?

Directions

Circle Yes or No for each of the following questions.

1. Does everyone in your organization, including yourself, have a common understanding of the goals of the organization?

    Yes   No

2. Does everyone in your organization, including yourself, have a clear understanding of job duties in order of priority?

    Yes   No

3. Is there a calendar and bulletin board available to all employees, showing important schedules and events?

    Yes   No

4. Is the telephone communication system for your organization the most efficient possible?

    Yes   No

5. Is the mail system for your organization the most efficient possible?

    Yes   No

6. Is the physical layout of departments, offices, and equipment the most efficient possible?

    Yes   No

7. Do you have regularly scheduled meetings that facilitate communication upward, downward, and sideways and that facilitate the coordination of work?

    Yes   No

8. Have you asked your subordinates, "What do I do that wastes your time or reduces your effectiveness?"

    Yes   No

9. Do you and your subordinates maintain daily appointment books or "to-do" lists and check off tasks as they are completed?

    Yes   No

10. Do you prioritize your own work, always working on the most important items first?

        Yes   No

11. Do you have accurate and easy-to-read clocks convenient to work stations?

        Yes   No

12. Can employees quickly and easily obtain any information needed in conducting day-to-day business?

        Yes   No

13. Is the flow of work such that things rarely get overlooked and work rarely gets done twice (such as mail being misplaced or two people writing the same report)?

        Yes   No

14. Is there effective communication and cooperation between line and staff employees?

        Yes   No

15. Are you a decisive person?

        Yes   No

16. Do you always use the most effective communication medium when relating to others—telephone, television, letter, report, conference, group discussion, or one-on-one meeting?

        Yes   No

17. Whenever possible, do you schedule meetings to last no more than 1 1/2 hours?

        Yes   No

18. Does the formal structure of your organization facilitate the quick and accurate flow of information?

        Yes   No

19. Do you and your subordinates achieve results rather than simply stay busy?

        Yes   No

20. Does the equipment in your organization—cars, typewriters, tools—function properly?

                Yes   No

21. Do you do all you can to be sure there are money, materials, methods, and manpower available to do the job, with no time wasted?

                Yes   No

22. Do you write clearly and legibly so that others know what you mean and waste no time deciphering your scribbles?

                Yes   No

23. Do you and your subordinates schedule sufficient time to perform each vital function—planning, implementing, and evaluating work?

                Yes   No

24. For all business meetings—group or one-on-one—do you prepare a list of topics you want to address, and then address them?

                Yes   No

25. Are you effective at saying no when necessary?

                Yes   No

26. Do you use travel and waiting time productively?

                Yes   No

27. Is your own desk and work area well organized and free of clutter?

                Yes   No

28. Are unnecessary interruptions effectively controlled?

                Yes   No

29. Do you utilize secretarial and clerical staff as well as you could?

                Yes   No

30. Do you periodically ask "What is the best use of my time right now?"—and then act on the answer?

                Yes   No

SCORING AND INTERPRETATION

To find your score on the Time Management Audit, add up the number of yes answers you circled and enter the total on the appropriate line on the hourglass in Figure 3.2. Fill in the space below this line to obtain a graphic illustration of your time management effectiveness.

If you did not get a perfect score (30), go back to the items marked no and take steps to correct your time management deficiency. This may require the help of others who may be part of the problem or who may be affected by your poor time management practices. You will know you have mastered your use of time when, besides having achieved a perfect score on this test, you can sit quietly for at least two or three hours during your work week to think about your organization, your work group, and yourself. Every manager needs such time for thinking. You won't have this time if you have wasted it.

Rules for Effective Time Management

People make many mistakes that result in wasted time, unfinished tasks, a sea of paperwork, and missed opportunities. The following are rules for preventing or solving the most common time management problems.[4]

- *Know what is expected of you.* Good time management begins with knowing what you are supposed to accomplish and in what order of priority. Reviewing your responsibilities and objectives with your supervisor is of fundamental importance. This review should result in mutual understanding of what you will be accountable for and what your supervisor will do to help you succeed.

  A manager in a computer software firm was criticized by the owner for being ineffective. Asked why, the owner replied, "You have failed to keep the systems analyst off my back." The manager was surprised, and responded, "This must have been a hidden purpose of my job. You never told me that before." From that point on, the manager increased his effectiveness by dealing with the complaints and concerns of the systems analyst.[5]

- *Set priorities.* Concentrate your time, energy, and talents on the tasks most important to you and your organization. Busy people need a system for prioritizing activities. One of the best methods is the "to-do" list. Make a list of activities for each day and assign a one, two, or three rating to each item on the list. Number one items are top priority; they have the highest value because they *must* be done. Number two items have a medium value and *should* be done. Number three items have the lowest value; they are worthwhile tasks (otherwise they should not be on the list), but they are not critical. People who make best use of their time work on number one items first, then number twos, and relegate number threes to a place that is out of sight but accessible if needed or after ones and twos have

FIGURE 3.2

How Effective Are You?

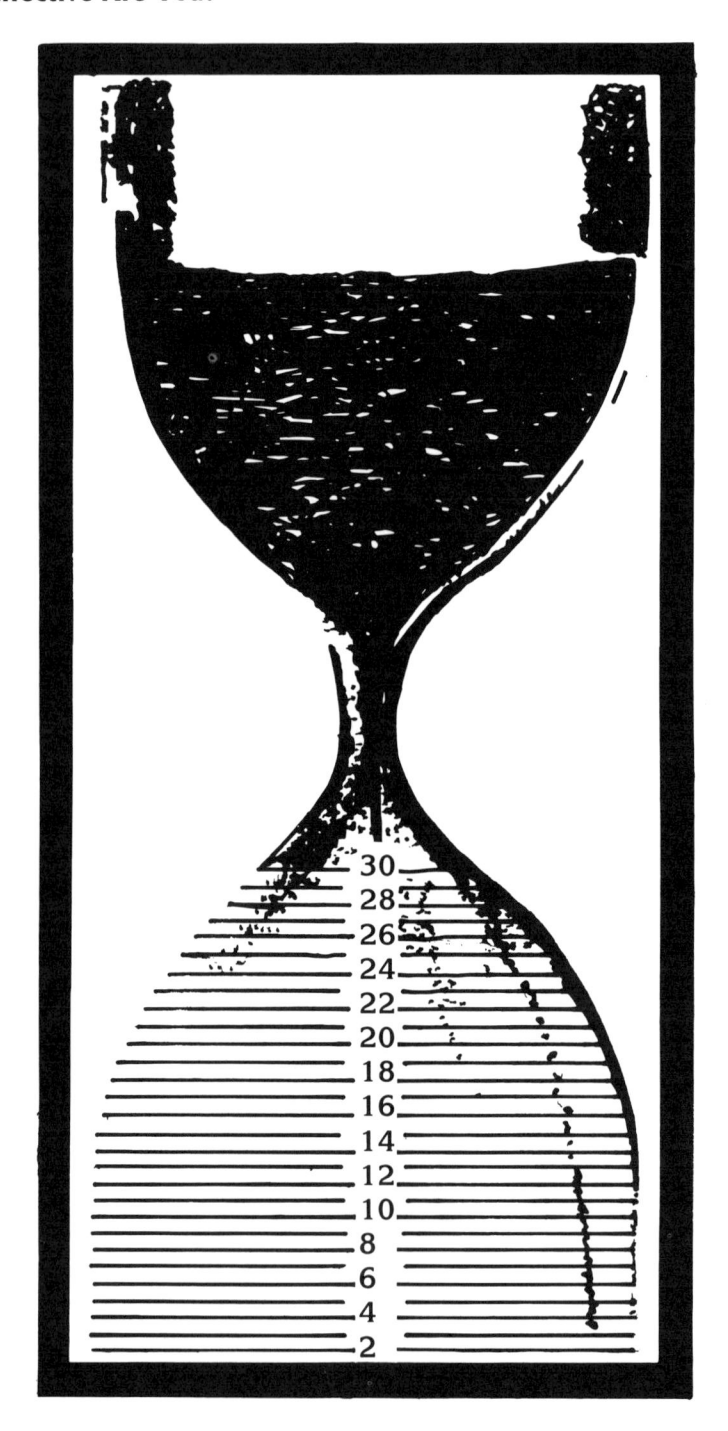

Performance: Managing for Excellence

been completed. The following story illustrates how effective this method can be:

> A well-known story about the efficiency of a to-do list concerns Charles Schwab when he was president of Bethlehem Steel. He called in Ivy Lee, a consultant, and said, "Show me a way to get more things done with my time, and I'll pay you any fee within reason."
>
> "Fine," Lee replied. "I'll give you something in twenty minutes that will step up your output at least fifty percent."
>
> With that, Lee handed Schwab a blank piece of paper, and said: "Write down the six most important tasks that you have to do tomorrow, and number them in order of their importance. Then put this paper in your pocket, and the first thing tomorrow morning look at item one and start working on it until you finish it. Then do item two, and so on. Do this until quitting time, and don't be concerned if you have finished only one or two items. You'll be working on the most important ones first anyway. If you can't finish them all by this method, you couldn't have by any other method, either; and without some system, you'd probably not even have decided which was the most important."
>
> Then Lee said: "Try this system every working day. After you've convinced yourself of the value of the system, have your employees try it. Try it as long as you wish, and then send me a check for what you think it's worth."
>
> Several weeks later, Schwab sent Lee a check for $25,000 with a note proclaiming the advice to be the most profitable he had ever followed. This concept helped Charles Schwab earn $100 million and turn Bethlehem Steel into the biggest independent steel producer in the world.
>
> You may think Charles Schwab was foolish to pay $25,000 for such a simple idea. However, Schwab thought of that consulting fee as one of his best investments. "Sure, it was a simple idea," Schwab said. "But what ideas are not basically simple? For the first time, my entire team and I are getting first things done first."[6]

- *Start each day by making a to-do list.* Make this practice as habitual as brushing your teeth. Write down all of the things you want to accomplish that day, and rank these in order of importance. The small amount of time you invest in doing this will repay you many times over. Two points to remember: make sure your to-do list is on one sheet of paper rather than several sheets. Also, make the list on a pad or piece of paper small enough to carry in your pocket or purse; it should go where you go. If you are ever tempted to keep your to-do list in your head, remember what Ziggy said: "I made a mental note to remember something very important I had to do today . . . but I lost the note."

- *Eliminate time wasters.* Good time management requires combining similar tasks and eliminating unnecessary ones. You should eliminate meetings that serve no useful purpose, eliminate unnecessary paperwork, and strive for efficiency in travel. Why take several trips to town when all errands could be combined? Why take a trip by plane if a telephone call will accomplish the same purpose?

- *Make good use of waiting time.* In our complex and interdependent society, we often run into delays—at the repair shop, in the bank, or at the airport. Be prepared to use this time productively. Reading, writing, thinking, talking, resting, and exercising are all preferable to wasting time.

- *Log your day.* Keep track of what you do each day for a period of one month. It is good to know how you are spending your time, and the analysis may reveal surprises.

    One bank asked its branch managers to record the time they spent under three headings—time with customers, time with administrative duties, and time with staff. Analysis showed that too much time was spent on internal administration and too little time was spent on marketing and staff development.[7]

- *Learn how, when, and why to say no.* One of the best time management techniques is the effective use of the words yes and no. If saying yes helps accomplish important goals, by all means do so. But if saying yes prevents you from accomplishing more important things, learn how to say no in a tactful way. If your supervisor interrupts your work with an additional assignment, discuss how the new task will affect existing ones. Obtain a clear understanding of the priorities of all your assignments.

- *Stock up and clean house.* Having the correct tools and materials, and knowing where they are, saves time and energy. Proper supplies and an orderly work area are basic to good time management. A few hours of housecleaning and stocking up several times a year will usually improve efficiency.

- *Provide enough time.* The saying "Haste makes waste" is true. If you do not give yourself sufficient time to accomplish a task, mistakes and decreased performance are inevitable. As a rule of thumb, complex meetings involving employee counseling, project planning, and staff development require at least one hour from the moment they begin. A one-hour minimum is usually necessary to establish a productive atmosphere, share basic information, deal with important issues, draw conclusions, make decisions, agree on future steps, and end the work session on a positive note.

- *Work when you are fresh.* If you have an especially critical day ahead, rest up the night before. Otherwise, fatigue may affect judgment and results.

- *Focus your efforts.* A fundamental rule of effective time management is to concentrate on the task at hand. Frustration and mistakes result from trying to do too many things at once. Often it is not the quantity of time spent on a project that counts, but the quality of time.

- *Attack uninteresting tasks when your energy level is high.* People have the tendency to do what they enjoy, postponing uninteresting or unpleasant jobs until their enthusiasm and energy are so low that these jobs become even less enjoyable, and therefore harder to accomplish. By working on low-interest tasks when your energy is high—whatever time of day that is—you will get more done in the long run. When you complete the uninteresting tasks and turn to interestng assignments, you will feel stimulated and energized.

- *Don't build a castle when a log cabin will do.* The extra refinement may not be worth the expense when a log cabin will accomplish the same purpose. This principle applies in time management as well; in some instances, the best possible performance may be far better, and far more expensive, than is necessary. For example, a manager usually should not spend time performing tasks subordinates could do. Even if the manager can do a better job, the loss in efficiency, employee growth, and overall productivity of the work unit may not be worth the extra refinement.

- *Practice good telephone techniques*. Avoid taking telephone calls while you are in important meetings and problem-solving sessions. If you are working with others, these interruptions will reduce both efficiency and goodwill. Save your calls, and set aside a certain period of time to respond to them. Returning calls one half hour before or after lunch, one half hour before the end of the workday, and the first half hour of the following workday is effective for many people.

    Initiating telephone calls when others are most available and receptive is another good practice. For example, you should avoid calling a company president on the morning of the monthly board meeting. In general, it is best to initiate telephone calls early in the morning, late in the morning, early in the afternoon, and late in the afternoon of the business day. Remember, the telephone can be both a time helper and time waster. One study found that 25 percent of the time spent on the telephone was used in waiting.

- *Use efficient mail and paperwork practices*. Set aside a specific time of the day or week to read mail and do paperwork. If you try to read incoming mail and paperwork as it arrives, the quality of your work probably will deteriorate because your efforts will lack a clear focus. A good technique is to reserve the last hour or so of the workday for correspondence and paperwork.

    Effective time management requires handling each piece of paper as few times as possible. Each item should be dispatched in one of the following ways: (a) read the item for information and discard it; (b) make a personal response, such as making a telephone call or dictating a memo, and then file the item; (c) route the item to others for follow-through; (d) store the item for future personal attention.

- *Keep a schedule.* Establish a work schedule that is efficient and satisfying, and try to follow it as much as possible. The idea of having a plan for the day is an old one, as shown in Figure 3.3.

FIGURE 3.3

Ben Franklin's Daily Regimen

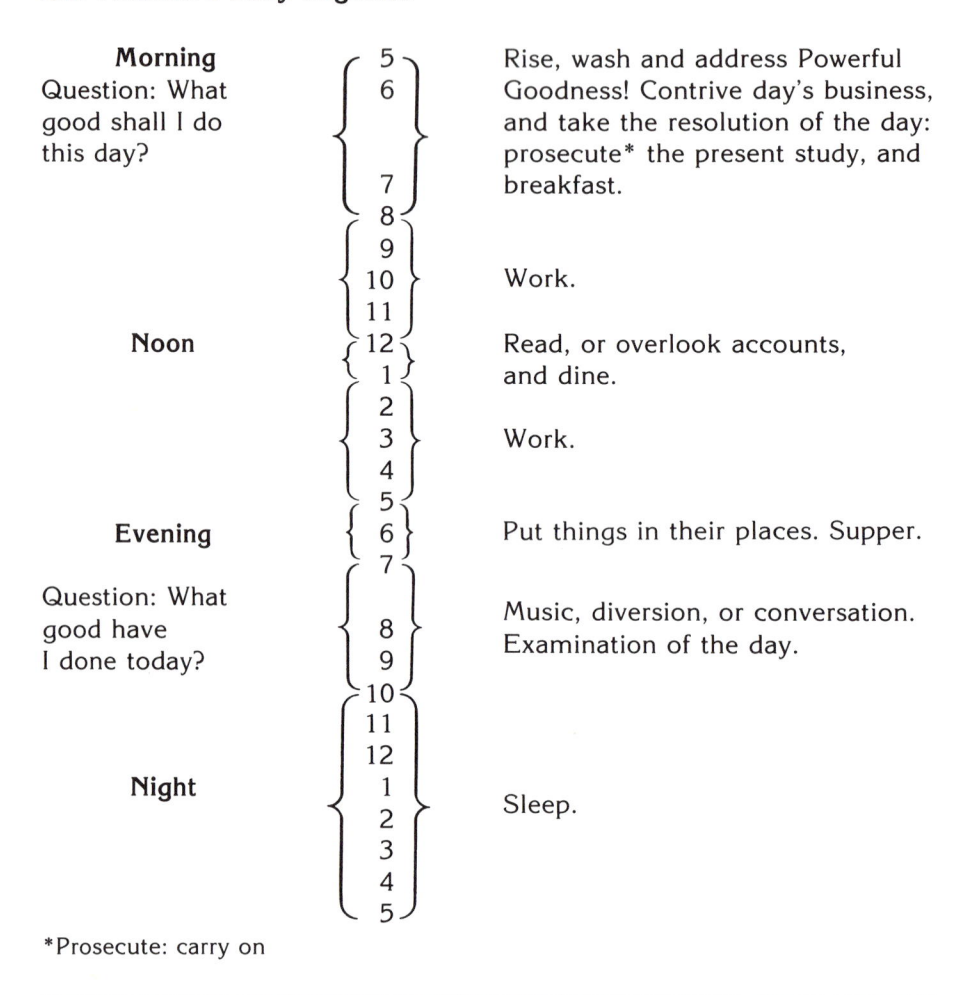

Morning Question: What good shall I do this day?	5 6 7	Rise, wash and address Powerful Goodness! Contrive day's business, and take the resolution of the day: prosecute* the present study, and breakfast.
	8 9 10 11	Work.
Noon	12 1	Read, or overlook accounts, and dine.
	2 3 4	Work.
Evening	5 6 7	Put things in their places. Supper.
Question: What good have I done today?	8 9	Music, diversion, or conversation. Examination of the day.
Night	10 11 12 1 2 3 4 5	Sleep.

*Prosecute: carry on

Figure 3.4 shows a more modern weekly schedule for effective time management.

- *Keep a delegation file.* Time and energy are wasted when managers fail to follow up on tasks they delegate. Relying on memory is not good enough. A good technique is to use a file or calendar to record assignments and review progress.
- *Use meetings effectively.* A meeting is a two-edged sword. It can be useful and productive, or it can waste valuable time. Keep in mind that all who attend meetings are individuals who may have something valuable to contribute and who are contributing their own valuable time. The following are important points to consider when planning and conducting a meeting:

FIGURE 3.4
Weekly Schedule for Effective Time Management

TIME	MONDAY	TUESDAY	WEDNESDAY	THURSDAY	FRIDAY	SATURDAY	SUNDAY
8:00 a.m. – 9:00 a.m.	Secretary	Phone	Dictation	Correspondence			
9:00 a.m.	Central office and staff meetings	Appointments; conferences; creative and productive work	Employee evaluation, training, and counseling activities	Appointments; conferences; creative and productive work	Review and planning		
11:30 a.m.							
11:30 a.m. – 12:00 noon	Secretary	Phone	Dictation	Correspondence			
12:00 noon – 1:00 p.m.	LUNCH						
1:00 p.m.	Field visits	Preparation for board meeting	Appointments; conferences; creative and productive work	Field visits	Review and planning		
4:00 p.m.							
4:00 p.m. – 5:00 p.m.	Secretary	Phone	Dictation	Correspondence			
6:00 p.m.		Board meeting	Business related meetings and activities				
10:00 p.m.							

Approximately 48 hours per week are devoted to work-related activities.

a. Assure yourself that a meeting is necessary. Know the purpose of the meeting and what you expect to accomplish.
b. Schedule the meeting far enough in advance to allow participants time to prepare.
c. Inform each participant of the nature of the meeting and the specific role you wish the person to play—providing information, recording minutes, generating ideas, making decisions.
d. Control the size of the meeting by inviting only those individuals who can benefit or contribute.
e. Prepare an agenda, limiting the topics of discussion to a number that can be reasonably handled in one session. Usually, meetings should convene and end within a period of 1 1/2 hours.
f. Advise people in advance if you expect them to make a presentation.
g. Begin and end on time.
h. During the meeting, be specific and clear and use data to support your statements.
i. Try to understand why people act in different ways, and use this knowledge to avoid personal rivalries. When necessary, reject ideas—not people.
j. Know when to delegate. You can remove some of the burden from your shoulders and keep everyone involved as well.
k. Before adjourning, review the purpose of the meeting, the accomplishments, and what participants are to do next.
l. After the meeting, see that minutes are prepared and that everyone gets a copy.[8]

PROGRAMS TO IMPROVE PRODUCTIVITY

Productivity is an important management concern. Both individual and work group performance are important. Three steps should be followed to maximize employee productivity:

- set high performance objectives;
- provide accurate feedback on results;
- use meaningful rewards to reinforce performance.

These simple steps are the keys to top performance in every line of work and at every level of responsibility.

The following are sample behavior modification programs that have been successfully used to improve the performance of front-line employees in the transit industry and of management personnel in the retail industry.[9] The principles and techniques used in these programs apply to all individuals, work groups, and organizations, both private and public.

Employee Development

The purpose of a mass transit organization is to provide safe, dependable, efficient, and courteous transportation to the public. The performance of the operator is critical in meeting this mission because this is the person who deals directly with the passenger. In order to improve driver performance, one transportation organization sponsored a six-hour passenger relations program. Participants learned human relation principles and were asked, "What are the day-to-day actions a driver should perform to provide the best possible service to the public?" Figure 3.5 lists the performance objectives developed by the 250 participants.

For a period of three months after attending the training session, each operator completed a self-evaluation, based on the list of performance objectives, at the end of each work shift. Drivers checked off the behaviors they had performed and left blank those they had not. This paper-and-pencil checklist provided personal feedback on performance. At the end of every month for three months, each driver also met privately with the supervisor, who had been a fellow participant in the passenger relations program. The supervisor held these meetings to review performance checklists, discuss job problems, and express appreciation for employee participation in the program. These meetings emphasized the positive and ignored the negative. If a driver had a good performance record, this was praised; if a driver had a poor record, he or she was thanked for keeping the checklist and encouraged to continue trying to implement the agreed-on performance objectives; if a driver failed to keep records, this fact was ignored, and a discussion was held reviewing and reaffirming the importance of the performance objectives.

ILLUS. 3.2

The goal of mass transit is to provide safe, dependable, efficient, and courteous service.

Queen City Metro/Cincinnati, OH

FIGURE 3.5

Operator Performance Objectives

A coach operator should:

1. Start and stop smoothly.
2. Avoid smoking when carrying passengers.
3. Clean up trash around driver's quarters when leaving the bus.
4. Address adults by name if known and by "Sir" or "Ma'am" if name is not known. Never call a youngster by a nickname—Junior, Sonny, Peanut, Sister, etc.—unless requested.
5. Have exact working tools—transfers, punch, change, ticket refunds, etc.—when starting the job.
6. Greet all passengers in a friendly manner.
7. Try to solve problems that arise in carrying out the job. Do not complain to passengers about other employees.
8. Wave recognition to police officers, fire fighters, school guards, truck drivers, and other uniformed public workers.
9. Always use hand and arm signals in traffic; say "thank you" in this manner whenever possible.
10. Wait for slow arrivers, making sure that all who want rides get them.
11. Never run ahead of schedule.
12. Pull to the curb if possible; avoid puddles.
13. Give clear, friendly, and sensible answers to the public.

Source: Transit Authority of Northern Kentucky (TANK), 1973.

The following were the results of the employee development program:

- Safety records showed substantial improvement, and there were also significant financial savings.
- Passenger complaints decreased, and the organization's public image improved.
- Employees set a national record for increased ridership.
- Employee morale and pride increased.
- Relations between managers and employees improved.

Management Development

The tasks of management are to plan, organize, direct, and control the work of the organization. In order to better accomplish these tasks, one retail company instituted a management development program for the 60 members of its management team. The goal of this program was to improve performance in the areas of management values, leadership principles, stress management, delegation skills, effective listening, time management skills, and public speaking. The management team was divided into four groups, each of which included representatives from every level and division of the company. The purpose was to build relationships between group members, solve common performance problems, and build team spirit (esprit de corps).

Each week for seven weeks, in a three-hour workshop, the management team studied one of the areas targeted for improvement. At the end of each workshop, team members agreed on performance objectives. Then, at the end of the following week, each participant completed a checklist on personal performance. If the performance objective was accomplished, it was checked; if not, it was left blank. The checklists appear in Appendix D.

At the end of each week, a coordinator for each group collected the performance checklists and gave the group a percentage completion score. This score was based on the total of actual checks of all the group members, divided by the total checks possible, multiplied by 100. (For example, a total of 80 checks, divided by 160 possible checks, multiplied by 100, would result in a 50% performance record for the group.) When the groups reported their weekly results, high performance records were praised. If low performance was reported, appreciation for participation was expressed and the importance of the performance objectives was reviewed.

The same three-step process was followed for each area targeted for improvement: (1) a workshop was conducted to study the subject and agree on performance objectives; (2) individual and group records were kept on performance during the following week; and (3) reinforcement for good work was provided in the form of recognition.

The following were the results of the management development program:

- Management improved in each performance area. Figure 3.6 shows the performance improvement record for each group.
- Employee turnover and grievances declined; many subordinates complimented their managers for improved management practices.
- The financial performance of the company improved dramatically.
- Management morale and pride increased.
- Communication and cooperation on the management team improved.

Other Examples

Figure 3.7 lists other organizations that have used a similar three-step method to improve employee productivity and the results they experienced.

FIGURE 3.6

Performance Improvement Record

Area Targeted for Improvement	Percentage of Follow-Through Group 1	Group 2	Group 3	Group 4	Performance Averages for All Groups
Management values	88%	86%	98%	90%	91%
Leadership principles	94%	92%	96%	91%	93%
Stress management	93%	94%	94%	91%	93%
Delegation skills	89%	87%	92%	87%	89%
Effective listening	92%	92%	94%	92%	93%
Time-management skills	90%	90%	91%	90%	90%
Public speaking	88%	89%	91%	90%	90%
Group averages for all performance areas	91%	90%	94%	90%	

The overall percentage of follow-through by the entire management team for all areas of improvement was 91%.

CONCLUSION

What can you do to improve job performance and manage for excellence? What skills can you acquire, and what personal motivation can you add, to enhance the natural ability you already possess? How can you achieve the quality of work characterized by the perfectly beautiful laundress?

If you are not content to remain at your present level of performance, you should begin today to exhibit the behaviors and apply the principles and practices of statesmanship, entrepreneurship, and innovation. In addition, you should capitalize on your style of work (Einstein, Darwin, Socrates, or Henry Ford); you should use the insight of Sultan the Ape in your approach to job performance; and you should be sure that your personal interests (things, people, or ideas) match the demands of your job.

You should practice the work habits that all employers want in their employees, set performance objectives that are meaningful and obtainable, and get accurate feedback on your efforts through performance review. You should also use your time effectively. If you are not doing this now, take steps to improve your time management practices. Finally, if the productivity of your work group is not as high as it should be, set challenging performance objectives, provide constructive feedback on results, and use meaningful rewards to reinforce employee effort.

You hold the key to job performance and managing for excellence. Using the key is up to you. In this spirit, remember the power of ten two-letter words: If it is to be, it is up to me. The rewards in quality of work and quality of work life are worth the effort.

FIGURE 3.7
Results of Positive Reinforcement and Similar Behavior Modification Programs in Organizations

Organization and Person Surveyed	Length of Program	Number of Employees Covered/Total Employees	Type of Employees	Specific Goals	Frequency of Feedback	Reinforcers Used	Results
Emery Air Freight John C. Emery Jr., President Paul F. Hammond, Manager, Systems Performance	1969–1975	500/2,800	Entire work force	a. Increase productivity b. Improve quality of service	Immediate to monthly, depending on task	Previously only praise and recognition; others now being introduced	Cost savings can be directly attributed to the program
Michigan Bell—Operator Services E. D. Grady, General Manager, Operator Services	1972–1975	2,000/5,500	Employees at all levels in operator services	a. Decrease turnover and absenteeism b. Increase productivity c. Improve union-management relations	a. Lower level—weekly and daily b. Higher level—monthly and quarterly	a. Praise and recognition b. Opportunity to see oneself become better	a. Attendance performance has improved by 50% b. Productivity and efficiency have continued to be above standard in areas where positive reinforcement (PR) is used
Michigan Bell—Maintenance Services Donald E. Burwell, Division Superintendent, Maintenance & Services Dr. W. Clay Hammer, Consultant	1974–1976	220/5,500	Maintenance workers, mechanics, and first- and second-level supervisors	Improve a. Productivity b. Quality c. Safety d. Customer-employee relations	Daily, weekly, and quarterly	a. Self-feedback b. Supervisory feedback	a. Cost efficiency increased b. Safety improved c. Service improved d. No change in absenteeism e. Satisfaction with supervisor and co-workers improved f. Satisfaction with pay decreased
Connecticut General Life Insurance Co. Donald D. Illig, Director of Personnel Administration	1971–1975	3,000/13,500	Clerical employees and first-line supervisors	a. Decrease absenteeism b. Decrease lateness	Immediate	a. Self-feedback b. System feedback c. Earned time off	a. Chronic absenteeism and lateness have been drastically reduced b. Some divisions refuse to use PR because it is "outdated"

Part Three • Productivity Improvement 123

FIGURE 3.7—*continued*

Organization and Person Surveyed	Length of Program	Number of Employees Covered/Total Employees	Type of Employees	Specific Goals	Frequency of Feedback	Reinforcers Used	Results
General Electric Melvin Sorcher, Ph.D., formerly Director of Personnel Research, now director of Management Development, Richardson-Merrell, Inc.	1973–1976	1,000	Employees at all levels	a. Meet EEO objectives b. Decrease absenteeism and turnover c. Improve training d. Increase productivity	Immediate—uses modeling and role playing as training tools to teach interpersonal exchanges and behavior requirements	Social reinforcers (praise, rewards, and constructive feedback)	a. Cost savings can be directly attributed to the program b. Productivity has increased c. Worked extremely well in training minority groups and raising their self-esteem d. Direct labor cost decreased
Standard Oil of Ohio T. E. Standings, Ph.D., Manager of Psychological Services	1974	28	Supervisors	Increase supervisor competence	Weekly over 5 weeks, (25-hour) training period	Feedback	a. Improved supervisory ability to give feedback judiciously b. Discontinued because of lack of overall success
Weyerhaeuser Company Gary P. Latham, Ph.D., Manager of Human Resources	1974–1976	500/40,000	Clerical, production (tree planters), and middle-level management and scientists	To teach managers to a. Minimize criticism and maximize praise b. Make rewards contingent on specified performance levels c. Use optimal schedule to increase productivity	Immediate—daily and quarterly	a. Pay b. Praise and recognition	a. Using money, obtained a 33% increase in productivity with one group of workers, an 18% increase with a second group, and an 8% decrease in a third b. Currently experimenting with goal setting and praise and/or money at various levels in organization c. With a lottery-type bonus, the cultural and religious values of workers must be taken into account

City of Detroit Garbage Collectors	1973–1975	1,122/1,930	Garbage collectors	a. Reduction in paid man-hour per ton b. Reduction in overtime c. 90% of routes completed by standard d. Effectiveness (quality)	Daily and quarterly, based on formula negotiated by city and sanitation union	Bonus (profit sharing) and praise	a. Citizen complaints declined significantly b. City saved $1,654,000 first year after bonus paid c. Worker bonus—$307,000 first year or $350 annually per man d. Union somewhat dissatisfied with productivity measure and is pushing for more bonus to employees e. 1975 results not yet available
B. F. Goodrich Co. Donald J. Barnicki, Production Manager	1972–1976	100/420	Manufacturing employees at all levels	a. Better meeting of schedules b. Increase productivity	Weekly	Praise and recognition; freedom to choose one's own activity	Production has increased over 300%
ACDC Electronics Division of Emerson Electronics Edward J. Feeney, Consultant	1974–1976	350/350	All levels	a. 96% attendance b. 90% engineering specifications met c. Daily production objectives met 95% of the time d. Cost reduced by 10%	Daily and weekly feedback from foreman to company president	Positive feedback	a. Profit up 25% over forecast b. $550,000 cost reduction on $10M sales c. Return of 1,900% on investment including consultant fees d. Turnaround time on repairs went from 30 to 10 days e. Attendance is now 98.2% (from 93.5%)

Source: Reprinted, by permission of the publisher, from "Behavior Modification and the Bottom Line," pp. 12–24, by W. C. Hamner and E. P. Hamner; Organizational Dynamics, Spring 1976. Copyright © 1976 American Management Association, New York. All rights reserved.

ILLUS. 3.3

Job performance and managing for excellence depends on you.

RECOMMENDED RESOURCES

The following readings, cases, application, and films are suggested for greater insight into Part Three:

Readings	— How to Manage Your Time: Everybody's No. 1 Problem
	Planning on the Left Side and Managing on the Right
	The Fertile Tension between Discipline and Impulse
	Following the Leader: How to Link Management Style to Subordinate Personalities
Cases	— The Sales Meeting
	The Puzzle Block Work Teams
	Creativity Requires the Right Atmosphere
	Emery Air Freight
Application	— How Will You Spend Your Life?
Films	— Creative Problem Solving
	A Psychology of Creativity
	Problem-Solving Strategies
	Managing Time
	The Time of Your Life
	Managing in a Crisis
	Business, Behaviorism, and the Bottom Line

REFERENCE NOTES

1. Voltaire, *Zadig or the Book of Fate* (New York: Garland Publishers, Inc., 1974).

2. William J. Stewart, University of Cincinnati, 1970.

3. Stan Kossen, *The Human Side of Organizations*, 2d ed. (New York: Harper & Row, Publishers, Inc., 1978), 203–5.

4. Lawrence Steinmetz, *The Art and Skill of Delegation* (Reading, Mass.: Addison-Wesley Publishing Co., Inc., 1976); Alan Lakein, "Time Management Ideas," from the film *The Time of Your Life* (Cally Curtis Films, 3384 Peachtree Rd. N.E., Atlanta, Ga. 30326); Alan Lakein, *How to Get Control of Your Time and Your Life* (New York: Peter H. Wyden, Inc., 1973); and Andrew J. DuBrin, *Contemporary Applied Management* (Plano, Tex.: Business Publications, Inc., 1982), 66–72.

5. DuBrin, *Contemporary Applied Management*, 67.

6. Michael Le Beouf, *Working Smart: How to Accomplish More in Half the Time* (New York: McGraw-Hill, Inc., 1979), 52–54.

7. DuBrin, *Contemporary Applied Management*, 68.

8. Keith Davis, *Human Behavior at Work: Organizational Behavior*, 6th ed. (New York: McGraw-Hill, Inc., 1981), 184–90.

9. Cases from the authors' files.

STUDY QUIZ

As a test of your understanding and the extent to which you have achieved the objectives in Part Three, complete the following questions. See Appendix E for the answer key.

1. The best statement of who you are is made by:
   a. the clothes you wear
   b. the way you spend your time
   c. your physical features

2. The average person has at least ____ hours of free time every day (time not spent on sleeping, personal hygiene, eating, travel, and working).
   a. 10
   b. 8
   c. 6
   d. 4
   e. 2

3. Getting full benefit from the 24 hours you have each day depends primarily on your _____ and _____ .
   a. family; friends and colleagues
   b. money; occupation or job
   c. attitude; time management skills

4. Time wasters include poor communication systems, inadequate tools, and poor work procedures.
   a. True
   b. False

5. The first rule for effective time management is to:
   a. know your goals
   b. buy a watch
   c. read a book
   d. study other people

6. A critical time management skill is to:
   a. set priorities
   b. write reports
   c. read journals
   d. give speeches

7. All of the following are good time management practices except:
   a. using waiting time wisely
   b. stocking up and cleaning house
   c. learning when to say no
   d. focusing your efforts
   e. using good telephone techniques
   f. using meetings effectively
   g. making a to-do list
   h. doing all tasks personally

8. Behavior modification is a technique to:
   a. overcome prejudice
   b. control minds
   c. improve performance

9. The three steps of behavior modification are: set performance objectives, provide feedback on results, and reinforce good performance.
   a. True
   b. False

10. Behavior modification can be used to improve employee performance in such areas as production, sales, and service.
    a. True
    b. False

11. Behavior modification can be used to improve management performance in such areas as stress management, delegation skills, effective listening, and time management.
    a. True
    b. False

DISCUSSION QUESTIONS AND ACTIVITIES

The following questions and activities help personalize the subject. They are appropriate for classroom exercises and homework assignments.

1. Overall, how would you rate your time management effectiveness? What steps can you take to maintain or improve your performance?

2. What are the critical elements of your job? What are the most important tasks for you to accomplish?

3. What distractions and time wasters do you face?

4. Gather into small groups for the remaining questions and activities. Develop a behavior modification program to improve performance in an existing work group: (a) identify a work group with critical performance behaviors (examples—teachers, machine operators, police officers, food service employees, salespeople, nurses, etc.); (b) meet with members of the work group and help them to agree on critical performance behaviors; (c) prepare a one-page checklist of critical performance behaviors (typically, ten to fifteen points); (d) enlist the cooperation of members in monitoring their own performance and using the checklist to document behaviors they exhibit (typically, daily); (e) review progress with the work group members (typically, weekly); (f) reward their participation and progress (provide recognition and reinforcement); (g) report your results to the discussion group.

5. Discuss the pros and cons of behavior modification (setting objectives, providing feedback, and rewarding results) as a tool to increase productivity. Give examples of situations in which behavior modification would work and situations in which it would not work.

READINGS

What Your Boss Wants to Know   134

Career Problems of Young Managers   143

Walter Cronkite at CBS   168

The Peter Principle   181

That Urge to Achieve   190

What Makes a Top Executive?   199

How to Manage Your Time: Everybody's No. 1 Problem   206

Planning on the Left Side and Managing on the Right   215

The Fertile Tension between Discipline and Impulse   230

Following the Leader: How to Link Management Style to Subordinate Personalities   237

Editor's Note: Some of the facts in the readings chosen for this book may appear to be out of date; however, the articles have been selected because of the overall importance of the subject matter.

What Your Boss Wants to Know

Most articles and books on any aspect of employer-employee relations are addressed to supervisors and managers and are focused on how to deal with employees or what to do for employees. This article reverses the usual pattern and gives suggestions on what an employee or a supervisor should do for his boss. Before you mark this article as "must reading" for your subordinates, perhaps you should scan it for some ideas as to how to improve relations between you and your superior.

One of the cardinal rules to follow in getting along with your superior can be summarized as: "Never let your boss be surprised." This means that your boss should hear first from you about any unusual success you have had or any unusual service you have extended to subordinates, associates, or customers. It also means that he should hear about your boners from you rather than by stumbling on them himself or hearing of them through the grapevine. In short, a great deal of your success on your job will depend on keeping your boss informed.

PRELIMINARY ESSENTIALS

In order for you to fulfill the obligations and duties which are inherent in your position and in order to keep your superior informed so that he will not be surprised, you must master three preliminary essentials:

1. Acquire a knowledge of the duties and responsibilities of your position.
2. Understand the needs (the accountability) of your superior.
3. Understand your superior.

Knowledge and Responsibilities

Keeping your boss informed does not mean that you should try to substitute for the daily newspaper or for a trade or professional magazine. You are not expected to keep him informed on world events or general economic conditions. Neither are you expected to be an essential link in

Source: Robert D. Gray, "What Your Boss Wants to Know," *The Oil and Gas Journal* (30 August 1954). Reprinted by permission.

the grapevine and pass on to him rumors or gossip within the organization. It is, however, your responsibility to see that he is not surprised about the duties and responsibilities which have been assigned to you.

The chances are that you have received a job description. Have you read it recently? In one way or another you probably have a fairly clear idea of what is involved in your position. If this is not clear to you, you should seek an early discussion with your superior to clarify your duties and responsibilities. It is impossible to do a job unless one knows what that job is.

Many job descriptions, however, do not clarify the three degrees of delegation of authority and responsibility. A few things may have been delegated to you completely and you may have the entire responsibility for carrying them out. This complete degree of delegation implies that you have the authority and the responsibility to make decisions on certain problems without reporting them to your superior. Many persons assume that everything that is delegated to them is in this category. The truth of the matter is that only the most routine items can be so classified.

Most of the work which has been delegated to you will be in a second category: you have been delegated the authority and responsibility to take action on certain problems, but it is expected that you will report your actions to your superior. It is usually not necessary to report each decision as it is made; the reporting can be accomplished through regular, periodic reports which may be made daily, weekly, monthly, or even annually. On the other hand, any decision in this category which is of an exceptional nature and which may involve your superior should be reported to him directly and immediately on a special report.

Most job descriptions list merely the duties and responsibilities which are completely assigned to you or which are delegated to you with an implication that you should report your decisions from time to time. Actually, however, every job also includes an implied delegation of authority and responsibility to make recommendations on any other subject that affects the operations of your job, of related jobs, your department, and of the company as a whole. Every employee and especially everyone in management, should recognize his obligation to make suggestions on any problem or situation that may come to his attention.

When you list all of the matters that have been definitely delegated to you and when you consider the larger numbers of subjects on which there is an implied responsibility for you to make suggestions, you can realize that there is a great amount of information resulting from the duties and responsibilities of your position that should be passed on to your superior.

Understanding Superior's Needs

One of the most common errors in management is to assume that delegation of authority and responsibility means that the authority and responsibility have been passed from one person to another. You may think that the duties and responsibilities which have been delegated to you are now your problem and are no longer of any concern to your superior. You may likewise feel that the matters which you delegate to your subordinates are now their problem and should not concern you. Such is not the case. It is important that both authority and responsibility be delegated and redelegated until they reach the lowest possible level. These actions are necessary in order that decisions can be made promptly. But no one can "wash his hands" of a problem by delegating it.

The board of directors of your company has certain authority and responsibility which have been delegated to it by the stockholders. All authority, however, has not been delegated to the board of directors. For example, it is usually necessary to have the stockholders of a company approve a pension plan. The board of directors in turn delegates certain authority and responsibility to the officers, and they in turn delegate it to their subordinates. Usually, and unless there is a specific provision to the contrary, one may delegate to a subordinate any authority and responsibility which have been delegated to him.

In spite of the delegation of this authority and responsibility, the board of directors is still responsible to the stockholders for the effective operation of the company; in turn the officers are accountable to the board of directors and certain executives are accountable to the officers. Everyone is still responsible or accountable for what has been delegated to him even though he in turn has delegated it to somebody else.

It is important to understand this in order to realize that your superior needs to know what decisions you have made. It is not just idle curiosity on his part that makes him want reports from you as to what you have been doing. Your superior is, in turn, having to report to his superior about the decisions which he has made, and he must include as his decisions the ones you have made. If you realize that your boss is responsible for your decisions and actions, that he must account to his superior for his own actions and also for your actions and the actions of your subordinates and the actions of others in your department, you can see the necessity of keeping your boss informed.

Understand Your Superior

In addition to understanding the accountability or needs of your superior, it is essential that you understand your superior as an individual. This understanding may affect the form and kind of your reports. For example, if he likes charts you should try to present as much material as possible in that form. On the other hand, if he does not like to read graphs, then the material should be presented to him in some other form. If your boss is color-blind, you should not use colors on charts. If he is hard of hearing, the reports should usually be written. On the other hand, if his eyesight is failing, give him as many oral reports as possible.

If he is scheduled to leave on a business trip or on his vacation, make your reports as far in advance as possible. Only the most urgent matters should be taken up with him when he is ready to leave. Likewise when he returns, and if you know that his desk is piled high with an accumulation of items, give him a chance to get settled before you report minor items. Urgent items, however, should not be delayed in being reported to him. At times it may even be proper to make this report to him by letter or by telephone while he is on his trip, or even while he is on his vacation. You must use judgment, but presumably you have judgment or you would not be holding your present position.

WHAT TO REPORT

The large number of specific duties and responsibilities which have been assigned to you, and the even larger number of general responsibilities which are inherent in your position, can be divided into four main categories. These categories are helpful in planning what to report and when to make the report:

1. Progress on long-term or continuing projects.
2. Completion of assignments.
3. Deviation from approved plans.
4. Anticipated problems.

Progress on Long-Term Projects

Some of your specific duties may include work on projects which can be classified as continuing or long-term. You may even feel that some parts of your work are never completed. If your boss is to know what is going on, he should receive periodically a progress report from you. Many of these progress reports can be reduced to a special form. There may be some items on which, or there may be certain occasions when, he needs a daily report on progress. Other subjects may be properly reported weekly, biweekly, monthly, quarterly, semi-annually, or even annually. It is well to discuss some of these items frankly with your superior in order to find out just how frequently he wants to know how the work is progressing. His request for periodic reports may be influenced by the date of reports that he has to make at departmental conferences or in other forms.

Completion of Assignments

In addition to keeping your superior posted on how work and other assignments are progressing, it is necessary for you to let him know when specific jobs or assignments have been completed. Most executives have learned through bitter experience that it is what attorneys call "an assumption contrary to the facts" to assume that a job has been done because someone was told to do it.

Have you ever griped about your boss not complimenting you on a job well done? This is a frequently expressed complaint among employees and supervisors. In making this complaint it never occurs to the person involved that the failure of a supervisor to compliment his subordinate upon a job well done may be really the subordinate's fault. It is so easy to blame someone else. But how can a supervisor give credit where credit is due when he does not know that any credit is due?

If your superior assigned a task to you and then later complimented you upon its completion, and if you knew that you had not completed the assignment, you might think that your boss had made a mistake or that he was pretty dumb or you might even think that he was being sarcastic. Your boss can't compliment you until he knows that the work has been completed. If you want to receive credit for completing an assignment, it is up to you to let your superior know that the assignment has been completed. If you do not want to be nagged as to whether or not a job has been done, it is up to you to see that your boss knows how you are getting along on the job, and also that he knows when it has been completed.

No one can guarantee that you will receive praise for completing your assignments. Your boss may think that one of the reasons why you are paid is to complete assignments, and he may feel that if you receive your paycheck regularly you are being complimented sufficiently. More and more supervisors are beginning to realize, however, that praise when praise is due is an essential part of good management. While reporting on the completion of assignments may not insure proper recognition, the failure to report such assignments will certainly result in your not receiving any credit for performing the job. Many of your completed assignments can probably be reported in the form of regular periodic reports. Certain special projects assigned you, however, may require the submission of a special report indicating that your assignment has been completed. If you have been engaged in a continuing project on which you have submitted one or more interim or progress reports, the final report should clearly indicate that in your estimation at least the assignment has been completed.

Deviations from Approved Plans

Subjects so far discussed upon which you should report to your superior emphasize the "good" things: progress on continuing or long-term projects and completion of assignments. The third type of subject to be covered in reports may not be so pleasant.

You and your boss may have agreed upon a definite schedule of work or you may have mapped certain plans involving production or maintenance or some other phase of your activity. Or you may merely have been handed a schedule of work. Regardless of how the schedule was developed, you do know that you have certain procedures to be followed or certain deadlines to be met or you know that you are to perform certain jobs in a certain sequence.

Suddenly you are aware of the fact that it is going to be necessary to deviate from these approved plans. It may be because of illness of a key worker, or delay in receiving parts from a supplier, or because of a breakdown of equipment. What are you going to do?

At this point it is important for you to know how much authority and responsibility have been delegated to you. This is clearly not a matter of taking action without a report. The chances are that this is a situation in which you should take action, but make a report. It is possible, however, that this is a situation in which you should make a recommendation to your superior. Whether you are empowered to take action or not, it is imperative that you make an immediate report to your superior.

The necessity for a deviation from the approved plans as far as your operations are concerned may require other changes in other plans affecting other sections or departments. The quicker your boss knows about this change, the easier it will be for him to prevent this problem, regardless of how large or small it may seem to you, from snowballing into a major problem. Your boss, if he is aware of the deviations that have been made and the reasons for them, may be in a position to suggest an alternative course of action, or he may be able to authorize other changes which will help to compensate for this necessary deviation.

There are two types of situations which should be classified as deviations from approved plans: (1) lack of progress and (2) mistakes or boners. Both of these situations may call for prompt and special reports.

Lack of progress should not be relegated to a mere detail on a progress report. Usually certain progress has been planned; therefore, lack of this progress becomes a deviation from approved plans. The quicker this can be detected and reported, the sooner remedial action can be started.

Likewise, mistakes or boners must be considered as deviations which require immediate reporting in order to minimize any serious effects. Your boss can overlook a mistake provided that the same mistake is not made too often and especially if the mistake is reported promptly. If the mistake is ignored or concealed and is then discovered by the boss, he has two legitimate criticisms to make of the employee: (1) original error and (2) the fact that it was overlooked or concealed. This second "mistake" is more serious than the original one. It may not seem easy to admit an error, and it is not easy, but it is a lot less painful than receiving a double reprimand for the boner and for not reporting it.

Anticipated Problems

Many junior executives and even some higher executives may feel that the reports suggested so far will cover all possible situations in any job. The discussion has already covered the making of either regular or special reports on progress, on completion, and on deviations from approved plans. These three types of subjects do cover all of the work that is normally assigned specifically to an individual.

It must be remembered, however, that whether the job description is specific or whether it is indefinite, it does include for every position the responsibility and authority to make recommendations on any subject which may be of assistance to the company.

The successful businessman must always be thinking in the future. He may want to know what has happened in order to have information to assist future development. This information will help him learn from his mistakes and from the mistakes of others. But the key decisions always look toward the future. It is proper to take time out occasionally to celebrate the accomplishments of the past week, month, or year. But the major interest in a company is not how much money was made last year, but how the company can make money in the current year and in the years to come. As a result, the really valuable executive is one who anticipates the problems which are ahead and who is able to make some suggestions toward their solution.

Today's problems must be solved, but they might not have been so serious today if they had been properly anticipated. Looking ahead may prevent problems, or at least minimize them.

HOW TO REPORT

You can keep your boss informed through either oral or written reports. An oral report has apparent advantages in not seeming to require much time for preparation, and, apparently, in not taking much time of your superior. These advantages, however, are more apparent than real. An effective oral report should be carefully prepared. If it is not carefully prepared, it may take a considerable period for discussion in order to bring out all of the facts. The real advantage of an oral report is the chance to discuss the problem and to have two-way communication between you and your superior. The principal disadvantages of oral reports are that there is no record of the report, and it is difficult to transmit the report to others.

While a written report seems to take time to prepare and while a good written report does take time to prepare, it has the advantage of providing a permanent record in the files. In addition, it permits referral of the problem to higher authority. Your boss may not have the authority to approve some or all of the recommendations which you make. If the suggestions are in the form of a conversation between you and your superior, he must either write a report himself, or he must pass on your recommendations in another conversation with his superior. The time taken in preparing a good written report is offset by the time saved when your superior has to write only a covering note saying either specifically or in effect, "I concur with these recommendations." Your written report can be easily referred to higher authority and you can be sure that credit will be given where it is due.

On most major problems it is well to combine oral and written reports. This combination can be made by having a conversation with your superior and then preparing a memorandum summarizing the conversation. Again this memorandum can be referred to higher levels in the company. The other combination is to submit a written report to your superior, and follow it up immediately or within a short time with a conversation. The boss may want time to read and consider your report before discussing it with you.

The preparation of reports can be facilitated and the reports themselves can be clarified if you check to make sure that the report clearly answers the following six questions:

1. What is the subject matter of the report? What is the problem?
2. Why is the report being made? Why is this a problem?
3. How can it be solved, or performed?
4. Who is to do it?
5. When is it to be done?
6. Where is it to be done?

The first two questions concerning *what* and *why* should always be first. The question of *why* explains the *what*. The other questions as to how, who, when, and where can be arranged in various sequences, depending upon the specific subject of the report.

OVERALL ESSENTIALS

If you want to keep your boss informed, you must consider four general essentials:

1. *Get all the necessary facts.* It is difficult, but not impossible, to make a proper decision with only some of the facts. You yourself will be very much embarrassed if you cannot answer the questions that your boss asks in discussing the problem. If you do not know some of the facts, admit it. One of the few things that your boss cannot possibly excuse is a misrepresentation of facts.

2. *Distinguish between facts and conclusions.* Facts are things that can be seen or observed or measured. Conclusions are interpretations of facts. Most people who believe something think that this belief is a fact. Because of this tendency, they frequently get themselves into difficulty.

3. *Submit recommendations.* Whenever you are reporting about a present or potential problem, be sure to have a recommendation as to what should be done. You have almost unlimited authority and responsibility to submit suggestions and recommendations.

4. *Have an alternative plan.* In making your recommendation, either include, or be prepared to submit, an alternative solution. There are very few problems, especially where people are involved, that can be solved in only one way.

QUESTION

Evaluate yourself as a subordinate. Do you know your job? Do you know your boss's needs? Do you keep your boss informed? Do you perform your job well?

_____

_____

_____

Career Problems of Young Managers

Drawing on interviews with more than one hundred managers, discussions with several hundred more, and published literature, this article examines some of the common difficulties experienced by young specialists and managers and offers some advice on career management. Hopefully, no one is so unlucky as to confront them all, but knowledge forewarned is courage armed.

EARLY FRUSTRATION AND DISSATISFACTION

The early years of one's first permanent job can be difficult. The young college graduate's job expectations often exceed reality, eliciting feelings of underutilization that can result in departure.[1] The causes of this condition rest with the young person, organizational policy, and incompetent first supervisors.

Conflicting Expectations

Business school graduates often are trained through cases to think like managers and to solve top-level executive problems. If they enjoyed this perspective in college, they may expect real work to be similar and their actual authority to equal the synthetic authority in class. But this takes years to achieve, so they frequently experience difficulty in adapting to changed time horizons that accompany the transition from school to work. Many students have been accustomed to almost immediate gratification and to short time spans — this semester, next academic year, a few years to graduation. The passage of time and status changes are clearly signaled by changes in routine and frequent vacations.[2]

A permanent job is quite different. The time horizon is much longer, fewer events mark time passing, and it is a full year until a two-week vacation. Not surprisingly, some young employees attempt to perpetuate

Source: Ross A. Webber, copyright © 1976 by the Regents of the University of California. Reprinted from California Management Review 18, no. 4. *By permission of The Regents.*

the school perspective by changing jobs frequently and taking off on unofficial vacations. However understandable the behavior, older managers perceive it as immature.

These older managers may also be at fault because they don't provide young specialists and managers with sufficient challenge. Large organizations tend to treat newly employed college graduates as all the same and to assign them to boring tasks that could be performed by people with less education. Management argues that young people's expectations are unrealistic and they must prove themselves before being assigned more important jobs.[3] But many young people detest being treated as "average" or as a member of a category like everyone else. They want to be considered unique, if not special, because their culture stresses the individual.[4]

Corporate culture, however, emphasizes efficiency in handling large numbers of people identically until individuals have demonstrated their uniqueness. Paradoxically, management's attitudes and policies may promote the very "immature behavior" that is given as the reason for the policies in the first place. Obviously, patience and understanding are needed on both sides.

Before concluding that it is better to work for a small organization, one should realize that situations change. Beginning professional and managerial positions in small businesses are reported to be more challenging and satisfying than similar posts in large firms. Small companies can't afford to train young graduates on unproductive jobs, so they put them to work on important tasks immediately. Nonetheless, five to ten years into careers, the views reverse: middle managers in large organizations report their jobs as more challenging and rewarding than those in small firms, who mention frustration and pressure for conformity. In the large organizations, middle-level jobs apparently carry more autonomy and authority than do similar level positions in small firms where the top can dominate everything.[5]

Incompetent First Supervisor

A first boss plays a disproportionate role in a young person's career.[6] The impact of an incompetent first supervisor can be especially unfortunate because the early experience tends to be perpetuated. What operates is a kind of self-fulfilling prophecy. If a superior doesn't expect much of his young subordinates, he doesn't challenge them and many don't perform well.[7] Even worse, if the incompetent supervisor doesn't set high standards for himself, almost everyone's performance deteriorates.[8] The word spreads that other managers don't want people from the group; the young person can be stuck in a dead end.

Ambitious young specialists and managers want visibility and exposure—opportunity to show higher-level executives how well they can perform and to understand executive problems and objectives. A fearful intermediate supervisor, however, can block such opportunity by relaying all communications himself and not allowing his subordinates to see higher levels. Handing a report to your immediate boss with no opportunity to argue in its favor and never hearing what happens to it can be very disturbing (especially if you discover later that your name on the cover was replaced by your superior's).

Organizations should institute policies to ensure that young specialists and managers enjoy the opportunity to communicate with and be evaluated by several higher executives and not just by their immediate supervisors. And young managers should fight for the right to go along with reports.

Resignation may be the best answer to an untenable position under an incompetent supervisor, but short of this step, understanding the situation may allow an individual to set higher personal standards than the boss does. He or she may be able to perform better than others in a demoralized department — even only slightly better may bring the attention of other executives who are not blind to the difficulty of performing well in that setting. The organization, of course, would be better off if young graduates were assigned mainly to the best supervisors, and many firms do this.

INSENSITIVITY AND PASSIVITY

All human organizations are political. This is neither condemnation nor praise, merely fact. For an organization to be effective, its managers must engage in the politics by which power is directed to problems and solutions implemented. Unfortunately, many young managers are insensitive to or even resentful of the political aspects of organizations.[9] This hurts them personally because they are passive about their careers, and it hurts the organization because it hinders development of power coalitions necessary for effective results.

Insensitivity to Political Environment

Managers who climb hierarchies rapidly tend to be proteges of successful higher executives.[10] These sponsor-protege linkages move together because members come to respect and trust each other. They personalize organization life and make it more predictable. When a manager has a problem, he prefers to consult someone whom he knows, not just an anonymous occupant of a bureaucratic position. To be sure, the criteria for inclusion in the group are often arbitrary and undemocratic in devotion to old-school tie and proper religion, race, or sex, but they are important nonetheless.

The importance of political relationships to the organization is that they form the power coalitions necessary to make and implement decisions.[11] Very few organizations are autocratically ruled by one omnipotent person; even fewer are pure democracies where the majority dominates. Most require a skillful minority coalition able to lead the majority through competent argument and common action. Without strong coalitions, power remains fractionated, actions are divisive, and the organization drifts willy-nilly.

A common complaint about young business school graduates is that they overemphasize analytical tools and rational decision making to the detriment of human understanding.[12] In spite of their desire to be treated as unique individuals, some observers note, they treat others as objects to be manipulated. Thus, the new graduates apparently are more Machiavellian in their managerial attitudes and more willing to use coercion than are practicing managers.[13] As one corporation vice president puts it, "It takes us a couple of years to show our business school graduates that an organization is composed of people with whom they must develop personal relationships."

Personal Passivity

Insensitivity to political environment is frequently accompanied by personal passivity and inadequate probing of the world around the young manager.[14] Such a person fears what he may discover about himself or assumes that virtue guarantees reward, so that good intentions will ensure that people will think he is doing a fine job. One man's experience as committee chairman illustrates such a common career mishap. Dave Seymour was assistant administrative manager of a regional office of a large company. He reported to the regional administrative manager responsible for office operations. Shortly after Dave assumed the post, the regional vice president personally requested that he become chairman of a committee to find ways to improve office efficiency. The committee was composed of various junior managers whom the vice president appointed. Dave accepted the job with alacrity because he saw it as an opportunity to prove his managerial potential.

Unfortunately, two years passed and nothing happened except meetings and collection of hundreds of pages of data and recommendations. None were implemented by district or regional managers. Dave hadn't known what to do; the vice president never inquired and Dave couldn't make up his mind to raise the issue with him. Dave had been flattered to be appointed chairman and figured it was an opportunity to distinguish himself. Months later he found that he had made no impact. Details differ, but the pattern is common.

Dave's first mistake was that he accepted the assignment without analyzing his political position and the attitudes toward change among the executives who would actually implement any improvements. Second, he did not clarify his personal power or the committee's authority. What were they to do? Issue orders directly to managers and try to persuade them to adopt the changes? Or just gather information in case anyone ever asked for it? The third mistake was that Dave did nothing to avoid his fate as time passed. He did not initiate action to modify the political environment or to better define his authority.

When accepting a delegated task, it is important that a subordinate try to clarify the nature of the delegation by asking certain questions.

- After I look into the problem, should I give you all the facts so that you can decide?
- Should I let you know the alternatives available with the advantages and disadvantages of each so you can decide which to select?
- Should I recommend a course of action for your approval?
- Should I select the alternative, let you know what I intend to do, and wait for your approval?
- Should I take action, let you know what I did, and keep you informed of results?
- Should I take action and communicate with you only if it is unsuccessful?

Dave did not ask these questions of his vice president. Worse, he didn't inform his superior that no changes were being made. No doubt this is one of the most difficult acts in management, but sometimes a subordinate must inform a superior that he (the subordinate) is powerless and that nothing will improve unless the superior acts. At times you must push your boss to make a decision.

It is often easier to drift with the times and hope things will work out for the best, but this is not a recipe for managerial success. The paradox is that the most promising young staff specialists may be the ones who find it easiest to drift. To be in demand is a mark of status and being busy gives a feeling of importance. Consequently, a good young person might allow himself to be dominated by others' desires, to be overcommitted to a narrow specialty, and to remain in a staff position too long. If you think of the organization as a cone, the staff tends to be on the outer surface, while line management is closer to the central power axis.[15] In his or her thirties, a young person may find himself making too much money to accept the pay of a lower line position, which is farther away from the top but has a more direct route to it. Young managers should take time to explore and probe the organizational environment and to understand people's attitudes, develop relationships, and clarify their own positions.

Ignorance of Real Evaluative Criteria

A central rule for managerial success is "please your boss." Unfortunately, what pleases him or her is not always clear so that insensitive and passive young managers don't know the real criteria by which performance is being evaluated. Business is often less structured and more ambiguous than the authoritarian stereotype that many young people bring with them. Of course, managers highly value good performance, as measured by profits, sales, productivity, and so on. Subordinates who occupy positions where results can be easily measured in these terms tend to report greater satisfaction and autonomy in their jobs than those in posts where performance cannot be evaluated quantitatively.[16] People in positions measured only by subjective evaluation tend to be less satisfied and to feel greater pressure for conformity in dress, thought, and action. In the absence of other criteria, these people may be measured by how closely they fit the superior's prejudices rather than by actual results.

Most people are biased by their own successes or failures in making judgments. We like others to be like ourselves, especially successful others because they verify our own correctness. Superiors tend to rate more highly those subordinates who are like them in appearance and managerial style.[17] Hence, hair length, speech habits, and clothes do affect how personnel are evaluated, with some superiors seeing mustaches and mod suits as signs of immaturity and radicalism while others perceive them as showing creativity and vitality.

The same is true for evaluation on the basis of managerial style. However, since the predominant style in the past has been authoritarian, many superiors more highly value subordinate managers who demonstrate authoritarian leadership. Even in the absence of corroborating performance data, authoritarian managers may be more highly rated than those who are participative or abdicative. One study indicated that a "permissive" manager whose division had good performance and much higher morale was rated as having no promotability, while a parallel authoritarian division manager with equal performance and lower morale was cited for excellent potential.[18]

A manager who desires to utilize a less directive style that is ill-suited to his superior's expectation is in a difficult position. If his boss is a hard-driving authoritarian manager, he may expect good subordinate managers to be similar to himself. By asking frequent questions and demanding reports, he makes it difficult for the subordinate to be anything but authoritarian.

A courageous, tough, and independent manager in the middle may serve as a buffer between his superior and his subordinates. By absorbing the pressure coming from above and not passing it on immediately to his people, he allows them enough autonomy to proceed collaboratively. Such leadership requires demonstrable success to survive.

Tension Between Older and Younger Managers

Tension between older and younger professionals and managers is very common. It may be exacerbated by individual personalities, but basically it stems from differences in life and career stages. A recently graduated specialist or manager understandably relies on what he or she knows best — academic knowledge. He or she is at least somewhat familiar with statistics, psychology, and economics, and these can be very valuable. Unfortunately, they can also hinder his working relationships with older managers.

Armed with an arsenal of analytical techniques, the young manager looks for problems to which they can be applied. But frequently the problems which the textbook solves are not the important ones. He may even talk to older personnel in the arcane vocabulary of "stochastic variables," "break-even points," and "self-actualizing opportunities." Such talk can be very threatening to an older person to whom it is unfamiliar. He may perceive the younger person as endeavoring to manipulate him.

In some cultures, older persons are automatically respected for age and assumed wisdom, but in the United States the young may respond to the older person's skepticism with veiled contempt. Because the older manager doesn't know the new techniques, the young specialist or manager erroneously infers that he is not as competent or important. But this can be a career-crippling mistake, because organizational contribution and influence have little to do with technical knowledge. An offended older executive can oppose the younger person's future advancement.

A young person should recognize that some older managers will see him or her as a threat (although the managers will deny it, even to themselves). The threat is not to position, but one of obsolescence and a reminder of human mortality.[19] Tension can arise even when the older person likes the younger. The young specialist should endeavor to show respect for the older, to frame his vocabulary appropriately, and to avoid condescension. As the young person comes to recognize the importance of political influence and intuitive judgment, he can develop the vertical coalitions helpful to both older and younger.

LOYALTY DILEMMAS

Loyalty is a popular but vague concept that is subject to both praise and scorn. There is little doubt, however, that most people in authority value subordinates' loyalty. But what is this quality? Some of the various unspoken views on loyalty that superiors expect of subordinates are: obey me; work hard; be successful whatever it takes; protect me and don't let me look bad; and tell me the truth. All of these concepts of loyalty are partially valid and contribute to organizational effectiveness. Unfortunately, all can also be distorted to the detriment of people and organization.

Loyalty as Obedience

The superior can equate loyalty with subordinates' doing what they are told. All managers have a right to expect general obedience, but excessive emphasis on it enshrines the "yes man" philosophy as organizational religion. It is understandable that a subordinate's willful disobedience would be construed as disloyalty, but equating loyalty and obedience assumes that authoritarian management is the only valid style while it ignores the possibility that loyalty may sometimes reside in not doing what the boss has ordered because disaster could follow.[20]

Loyalty as Effort

Young specialists and managers are rightly expected to work hard in the interest of the organization. Executives are skeptical of the intentions of young people who make a minimal commitment to their work. Yet when effort and hours worked are equated with loyalty, people will put in excessive hours without real effort or contribution. Consider the comments of some young managers in the home office of an insurance company:

"The officers are the first here in the morning and the last to leave at night; they are always here Saturdays and many Sundays."

"They set the pace and, at least implicitly, it is the pace we must accept and follow."

"If you want to get ahead this is the pattern you must accept. Contribution tends to be judged in terms of time spent in the office, not things accomplished."

"If you want to get ahead, you come in on Saturdays regardless of whether it is necessary or not. The cafeteria and offices are sometimes filled with people who just feel they can't afford not to come in on Saturday."

Thus, behavior can become a game to convince others that you are loyal even when it contributes nothing to organizational effectiveness.

Loyalty as Success

The superior can see loyalty as synonymous with reliability and successful performance whatever it takes (and don't bother him if it entails shady things he shouldn't know about). It is reasonable to expect honest effort, but this version of loyalty can be tough because it adds a moral criterion to judgment of competence. Thus, not all young managers who miss deadlines are disloyal. The task may simply be impossible within legal or ethical limits. A superior who judges all people and performance from a loyalty perspective will discourage honest communication and encourage illicit managerial practice.

Loyalty as Protection

The superior expects the subordinate to protect him and the organization from ridicule or adverse evaluation by others. Subordinates who only follow their superior's instructions to the exact letter *are* disloyal if they don't exercise common sense and fill obvious gaps. This version of loyalty has particular relevance where the superior is a generalist over specialist subordinates who know more than he does in their areas of expertise. In return for subordinate concern and protection, he implicitly promises to look out for their personal and political interests.

This loyalty concept sometimes includes an injunction to subordinates never to disagree with the superior in public when the boss's boss or outsiders are present. This makes sense, but it can become exaggerated when a sharp distinction is made between "us," to whom we owe loyalty, and "them," to whom we don't. The efforts of coalitions to conceal, contain, or cover up their mistakes reflect this view of loyalty. Violation through "leaks" and overly candid communication with outsiders is one of the most heinous organizational crimes because it threatens the security of the hierarchical system.[21] There is little that managers fear more than subordinates' trying to make them look bad in order to get their positions. Unfortunately, an insecure superior will sometimes attribute this motivation to a young manager when it really doesn't exist.

Loyalty as Honesty

This view of loyalty exalts truth over harmony. The superior expects the subordinate to warn him of potential failure before the control system picks it up or others find out. This can be particularly hard on a young manager because it tells him to report his own mistakes. To do so is threatening because the bearer of bad tidings is sometimes confused with the tidings. The Turks have an old proverb that warns, "he who delivers bad news should have one foot in the stirrup." Most of us would prefer not to report impending failure in the hope that it will go away or that no news will be interpreted as good news. One of America's most dynamic companies fights this by pushing the dictum, "don't let us be surprised by unpleasant news." Not reporting failure before it produces adverse results is worse than the failure itself.

The Dilemma

The young manager's problem is that sometimes he doesn't know what version of loyalty is expected by the organization or superior. He may even discover that a boss entertains several simultaneously contradictory views: that he expects strict obedience, but will be angry if obedience leads to poor performance; or that he interprets mistakes as disloyalty but still expects advance warning of impending failure. Loyalty expectations may violate the young manager's personal values if there is no excuse for failure and the hierarchy must be protected at all costs. Under such unhappy circumstances, the role-conflict-resolution tactics possible include conformance to power or authority, selectively ignoring what he can get away with, attempting to modify the superior's expectations, or departure.

PERSONAL ANXIETY

With time, promotions, and increased rewards, job satisfaction improves for most managers. The daily task becomes more challenging, yet new concerns crop up for many young managers — anxiety about personal integrity, organizational commitment, and dependence on others.

Anxiety About Integrity and Commitment

People admire different qualities at different stages of life. High school students place high value on independence as they struggle to become adults; college students stress individuality as they endeavor to find their uniqueness; older executives admire decisiveness that would allow them to bear the burdens of high office more easily. Young middle managers especially admire conviction and integrity in the person who remains his own man but believes in what he or she is doing. As they are rewarded by the organization, many persons begin to question the fundamental value of their jobs.[22] As one young brand manager for a major food company put it, "I'm a success, [I earn a good income], and I get a big kick from my job and seeing the climbing sales chart, but sometimes I wonder if getting 'Colonel Zoom' cereal on every breakfast table is really that important!" (Especially since it is being attacked by nutritional experts as having little food value.)

This questioning can be difficult for a young manager to understand. After years of apprenticeship, he is reaping the rewards of effort — autonomy, discretionary authority, and opportunity to achieve. Job morale is high. But for some it is not enough, because questions nag. "Am I really selling out to the organization?" "Have I forgotten to ask the important question of what I'm contributing to society?" If he or she concludes that the answers are more affirmative than negative, the young manager is faced with a dilemma — what to do?

Open complaint about the organization's activities may cause others to view the complainer as disloyal, hindering present security and future promotability. Associates and superiors will subtly suggest to the displeased young manager that he keep quiet, work his way upward, and then change company policy if he desires to. This is not bad advice, but the young manager might find being an executive so satisfying that he forgets what it was that he wanted to change. He might alleviate his dissonance by changing his personal values to agree with the dominant view. This facilitates total commitment to the organization and promotes the certainty that most of us desire. Such a solution may work for the individual, but it may ultimately harm society.

No entirely satisfactory answer exists for this dilemma. If the organization's mission and policy are in violent disagreement with personal values, the best course is resignation and perhaps a new career.[23] But premature departure can also be a cop-out, a flight from difficult moral choices. If the decision is to stay, the young manager should strive to keep alive his values, to apply them to small matters which he controls, and to remember them when he has the power to affect policy.

Attitudes toward commitment are ambivalent. A sense of certainty about career is desired because it simplifies one's life and stills the restlessness about whether one is in the right place. Nonetheless, many young people also fear commitment because it means closing doors and giving up the pleasant illusion that they can still do anything they wish. Yet maturity means facing reality and deepening interests. Therefore, a central facet of all careers is balancing commitment to the organization with maintaining a sense of independence.[24] Pure rebellion which rejects all organizational values and norms can end only in departure; pure conformity which accepts everything means loss of self. Creative individualism accepts pivotal values and norms, but searches for ways to have individual impact.

The occasion for loss of integrity is often a person's first failure. After a history of success in school and work, a young manager with a weak sense of identity can be overwhelmed by destruction of his illusions that he cannot fail, that he is immune to career crisis, and that he enjoys widespread social support. The current generation of young people may be especially vulnerable in this area because they are the progeny of prosperity. Success has grown, unchecked by fear of economic deprivation.[25]

Anxiety About Dependence

One aspect of the struggle for maturity is to declare psychological independence of home and parental authority while identifying oneself as an individual. Dependence on others is difficult to handle shortly after successfully establishing one's independence. Thus, undergraduate students tend to dislike team projects in which their grades can be lowered by others' mistakes. Nonetheless, total independence is impossible in real organizations. Superiors are dependent on subordinates' performance, subordinates are dependent on their superior's judgment and effective representation, and middle managers are dependent in both directions.

All of this dependence can provoke anxiety. For example, many junior military officers have suffered from psychosomatic illness because they bear the responsibility for their unit's safety and performance when they don't have as much experience or technical knowledge as their senior enlisted personnel. They cannot solve their problems by denying their dependence, but these problems can be reduced by learning the technical details of subordinates' duties. In the long run, however, young supervisors must recognize interdependence and strive to facilitate subordinate performance while representing their interests upward.

Most young adults are aware of their fear of being dependent on others, but they usually are not conscious of anxiety about having others dependent on them.[26] As they acquire spouse, family, job status, and community position, they receive increasing demands to give financial, temporal, and emotional support to more and more people and organizations. This sense of others' dependency can be gratifying, but time and energy are limited. Independent and self-reliant managers are sometimes disturbed to discover that they feel dominated by the needs of people dependent on them. If and when the burden becomes too great, they must establish life priorities that balance demands of family, organization, and community in a way that may fully satisfy none, but allows relations to continue with all.[27]

ETHICAL DILEMMAS

Few young people begin their careers with the strategic intention of being unethical as a means to success. And few managers are unethical as a matter of policy. Yet the majority share a problem of determining what is ethical or unethical when faced with unexpected dilemmas.[28] Many people believe that ethical means "what my feelings tell me is right." Unfortunately, feelings are very subjective phenomena, so one person may think that misleading advertising is all right while another believes it is wrong.

Others argue that ethical means religious beliefs or the golden rule, law and common behavior, or what contributes to the most people. Clearly, no single view of ethics is always correct or incorrect. A manager should assess his decisions from a variety of useful perspectives.[29]

Ethics as Economic Self-Interest

When a young manager in a high-technology firm was offered a position by a competitor, his employer sought a court injunction to prevent his moving. On the witness stand it was suggested that there was a matter of loyalty and ethics involved in leaving with the knowledge and expertise he had derived from his employment. The young man's response was, "Loyalty and ethics have their price; as far as I am concerned, my new employer is paying the price."[30]

It is easy to criticize this manager for his ethics and choice of language, but he is expressing faith in the free market system — that scarce resources such as he should flow to the buyer who can utilize them most and who is willing to pay the highest price. Ability to pay theoretically reflects market demand and social interest, so he could best serve society by changing employers for more money.[31] In addition, his position reflects the temporary nature of his demand. Like the athlete, his technical skills are subject to obsolescence and he owes it to himself to gain the most from them while they last. Under this ethic, his only responsibility to his present employer is to give him the opportunity to match the offer.

Not everyone shares this faith in the free market system, however, because ability to pay could reflect raw monopoly power and not consumer wishes.[32] And even those who believe that the market should allocate resources in this way don't all agree that economic self-interest is a good criterion for ethical decisions at the individual level. Most people see no connection between "ethical" and "economic" or "self-interest."

Ethics as Law

When asked about kids' buying his pornographic magazines, a publisher and purveyor of "adult" material responded, "What's the matter, don't you like to look at pictures of . . . pretty girls and boys? I keep within the law. My magazines aren't meant for kids, but I can't keep them from buying them. That's the government's problem."

For this businessman, law is the criterion for decision making. If society thinks what he is doing is unethical, it is government's responsibility to legislate. In the absence of prohibition, he does what is allowed. Certainly managers bear responsibility as citizens to obey the law.[33] The young marketing managers in the electrical equipment industry who secretly met to fix prices and allocate markets violated the law, and in their case the law was relatively clear.[34]

Sometimes the law is not clear, though. Even the managers in the electrical conspiracy argued that the law was vague because it required competition and prohibited collusion, yet they believed that cessation of "cooperation" would lead to dominance by the giant firms and decreased competition.

Most people feel that adherence to law is a necessary but insufficient basis for ethics. Behaving legally so you won't be punished is merely being prudent, not ethical. Law imposes demands from outside, while ethics should come from inside.[35] Besides, if law constituted the only behavior limits, government and law enforcement would swell to overwhelming proportions. Big Brother would be everywhere and freedom to do either wrong or right would disappear.

Ethics as Religion

If government law is not sufficient, what about higher law? One business executive suggests that there should be no problem knowing what is proper: "If a man follows the Gospel he can't go wrong. Too many managers have let basic religious truth out of their sight. That's our trouble."

Most religions maintain that there are universal moral principles that should guide human behaviors[36] — that in almost all times and places, thou shalt not lie, steal, or murder, for example. Thus, advertisements that deceive customers and industrial espionage to discover a competitor's secrets are clearly proscribed by common religious principles. Nonetheless, only a minority of managers think such principles are the basic ethical criteria for their managerial decisions. The problem is that moral principles are often abstract and difficult to apply to specific cases.[37] To be sure, intentional lying is clearly wrong, but most businessmen sincerely believe they must hide information and distort public communication as protection against competitors or unions. And stealing seems wrong, but padding expense accounts or "borrowing" company tools doesn't seem so immoral when the employer knows and seemingly condones it (perhaps this is a form of supplemental compensation). Catholic theology holds that every employer has an obligation to pay at least a "living wage," but determining this is subject to debate. Perhaps it is just unrealistic to expect a guide to conduct developed in the Middle East 2000 years ago to have direct relevance to the complex conditions of modern managers.[38]

Pragmatists argue that religious teachings and the golden rule are not meant to apply to competitive business anyway, that management is more akin to a poker game than to the religious life.[39] If obfuscation and deception are part of the game and everyone knows it, then they are not sinful. Finally, many people subscribe to no religious beliefs and bitterly resent believers' attempts to impose their tenets on everyone. Clearly, religion as an ethical guide is helpful and good, but only to some people some of the time.

Ethics as Common Behavior

"But everyone does it" has been a popular guide and justification for behavior from time immemorial. Realists argue that if the majority engage in a certain activity, then it must be all right, regardless of what parents or policemen say. The young manager could make his judgments based upon the characteristic behavior of his boss and his organization or industry, not universal rules. Thus, the garment salesman argues that he couldn't possibly follow the strict custom against booze and sex as aids to selling. . . . His industry accepts such inducements and buyers expect them, so he feels he couldn't compete without them. Similarly, managers in fiercely competitive industries argue that they can't be as open about costs and policies as a monopoly such as telephone communications.

Every young manager will experience the pressure of others' behavior as determinant of his own.[40] Yet we have a paradox: most agree that others' behavior is not the most elevated criterion for individual decisions yet still maintain that their superior's behavior is the major reason they behave unethically. It is the top that sets the ethical tone in most organizations and this is one of the gravest obligations of high-level executives. Their behavior will be emulated and converted into institutionalized custom by lower managers.[41]

A young person caught in such an unhappy situation pursues one of several courses: he adjusts his personal beliefs and stays happily; he stays, but with a guilty conscience (hopefully to change things when he gains power), or he departs.

Ethics as Impact on People

Upon being asked about unethical managers, a former president of General Electric observed that unethical people are not the problem: "What we must fear is the honest businessman who doesn't know what he is doing." Thus, most companies that have polluted the air and despoiled the land did so out of ignorance, not immorality. Knowledge may assist managers in making decisions based upon what is best for the greatest number of people.

This is what schools of business administration and management have striven for — to make management a profession whose primary concern is social contribution, not narrow self-interest.[42] By teaching prospective managers how business, economy, society, and environment interact, the hope is that their graduates will take the broader picture into account when making decisions. No intelligent executive in the last quarter of the twentieth century can really believe that air and water are "free goods" to be used as he or she unilaterally deems most profitable for the firm. Even if the firm doesn't pay for them, his education should have shown him that society does.

No doubt ignorance has occasioned much apparently unethical behavior, and greater professional knowledge should be of great benefit to all. But unfortunately, some professionals who have taken the Hippocratic oath or sworn allegiance to the Constitution cheat clients, defraud the public, and rape the environment. It is naive to expect that education alone is a sufficient guide for ethical behavior. Besides, what contributes to the greatest number of people sometimes means exploitation of the few or even breaking laws. Some executives have violated various business laws in order to protect the jobs of employees on the grounds that no one is hurt by colluding with a competitor, but many would be out of work and collecting unemployment compensation if pure competition existed.

Beware of Cynicism

No single ethical criterion is sufficient. The young manager striving to be ethical should do more than depend on economic self-interest, obey the law, observe his religious principles, follow his superior, and obtain the greatest good for the most people. He will have to take all of these into account filtered through his subjective judgment of what is right. In making these judgments, however, he should guard against cynicism.

Many people attribute poorer motivation and more unethical behavior to others than themselves. Young people today seem to be very cynical about business ethics and managers. They tend to believe that practicing managers engage in more unethical behavior than they would and more than the managers themselves think they do. Thus, students attribute such activities as padding expense accounts, stealing trade secrets, and immoral cooperation to managers to a greater extent than the managers anonymously report that they do. Research suggests that the younger the person, the greater his cynicism about managers; the older the manager, however, the greater the optimism about others. Whether this reflects time or "the times" is unknown. Do people become less cynical as they become older and see that everyone isn't as unethical as they had once thought? If so, today's young people might become less cynical as they climb their organizational ladders. Or is today's cynicism actually justified because older managers forget what it is like at lower levels or delude themselves about actual practice?

Nonetheless, excessive cynicism encourages unethical behavior on the grounds that "I'd be a fool not to if everyone else is." Cynicism thus can be self-fulfilling prophecy. More likely, a young manager who believes everyone does it will discover that they don't and that if he does, his career may be ruined.

ADVICE ON CAREER MANAGEMENT

Advising young people on how to manage their careers is a risky proposition. It depends upon the individual's objectives and his or her definition of success: Climbing to the top? Maintaining integrity? Keeping job and home separate? Happiness? These are not mutually exclusive goals, but they can be competitive.[43]

Assuming that a young manager's objective is to climb to higher managerial ranks, the following suggestions have been offered by various people:[44]

- Remember that good performance that pleases your superiors is the basic foundation of success, but recognize that not all good performance is easily measured. Determine the real criteria by which you are evaluated and be rigorously honest in evaluating your own performance against these criteria.

- Manage your career; be active in influencing decisions, because pure effort is not necessarily rewarded.

- Strive for positions that have high visibility and exposure where you can be a hero observed by higher officials. Check to see that the organization has a formal system of keeping track of young people. Remember that high-risk line jobs tend to offer more visibility than staff positions like corporate planning or personnel, but also that visibility can sometimes be achieved by off-job community activities.

- Develop relations with a mobile senior executive who can be your sponsor. Become a complementary crucial subordinate with different skills than your superior.

- Learn your job as quickly as possible and train a replacement so you can be available to move and broaden your background in different functions.

- Nominate yourself for other positions; modesty is not necessarily a virtue. However, change jobs for more power and influence, not primarily for status or pay. The latter could be a substitute for real opportunity to make things happen.

- Before taking a position, rigorously assess your strengths and weaknesses, what you like and don't like. Don't accept a promotion if it draws on your weaknesses and entails mainly activities that you don't like.

- Leave at your convenience, but on good terms without parting criticism of the organization. Do not stay under an immobile superior who is not promoted in three to five years.

- Don't be trapped by formal, narrow job descriptions. Move outside them and probe the limits of your influence.

- Accept that responsibility will always somewhat exceed authority and that organizational politics are inevitable. Establish alliances and fight necessary battles, minimizing upward ones to very important issues.

- Get out of management if you can't stand being dependent on others and having them dependent on you.

- Recognize that you will face ethical dilemmas no matter how moral you try to be. No evidence exists that unethical managers are more successful than ethical ones, but it may well be that those who move faster are less socially conscious.[45] Therefore, from time to time you must examine your personal values and question how much you will sacrifice for the organization.

- Don't automatically accept all tales of managerial perversity that you hear. Attributing others' success to unethical behavior is often an excuse for one's own personal inadequacies. Most of all, don't commit an act which you know to be wrong in the hope that your superior will see it as loyalty and reward you for it. Sometimes he will, but he may also sacrifice you when the organization is criticized.

SUMMARY

Frustration and dissatisfaction in young graduates' early careers is widespread because of several factors: their job expectations are unrealistic; they find it difficult to change from school's short-range perspectives to work's long range view; many employers assign them boring tasks that don't challenge them; and they may begin under an incompetent first supervisor. As a result, turnover from first positions is substantial.

Many young specialists and managers are insensitive to the organization's political aspects so that they needlessly offend older managers and fail to develop alliances necessary to concentrate power on important issues. To compound their problems, some are passive in not asking questions to clarify what is expected of them and what authority they possess. They let their careers drift under the control of others without even knowing the real criteria by which superiors evaluate their performance.

Loyalty presents one of the most difficult dilemmas for many young managers; everyone values it, but its meaning varies. For some superiors loyalty is subordinates doing exactly what they are told. For some it is subordinate success whatever the means. For still others it is subordinates who protect the executives and organization from looking bad. Finally, for a few it is subordinates who communicate honestly what is going on. All of these conceptions of loyalty are partially valid; an organization should value obedience, effectiveness, effort, reliability, and honesty, but all can distort behavior if carried to excess.

With time's passage and achievement, many still young managers experience anxiety about personal integrity, commitment, and dependence. They worry that they are losing track of their personal values while being rewarded for their contributions. They wonder if they are really doing something worthwhile that justifies the doors they have closed and the opportunities passed by. And some feel they are so interdependent with others that they are losing control of their lives.

The occasion for personal anxiety about integrity and commitment is when young managers are faced with ethical dilemmas. Most think they should be guided by personal feelings, but this is extremely subjective and other criteria should also be examined: economics and self-interest, regulations and laws, religious principles, others' customary behavior, and impact on people. All of these criteria can be helpful in making decisions, but none alone is sufficient all the time. In making decisions, however, be wary of cynicism that assumes the worst in everyone else. It can lead to improper and inappropriate behavior.

Career advice includes admonitions to perform well, be active in managing your career, strive for visibility and exposure, develop relations with senior sponsors, learn quickly and train a subordinate, nominate yourself for new positions, rigorously assess your strengths and weaknesses, don't be trapped by narrow job descriptions, recognize that organizational politics are inevitable, and be prepared for ethical dilemmas.

REFERENCE NOTES

1. Over 50 percent of all MBA's leave their first employer within five years. J. A. De Pasquale and R. A. Lange, "Job-Hopping and the MBA," *Harvard Business Review* (November–December 1971), p.4ff. See also, J. A. De Pasquale, *The Young Executive: A Summary of the Career Paths of Young Executives in Business* (New York: MBA Enterprises, Inc., 1970); and G. F. Farris, "A Predictive Study of Turnover," *Personnel Psychology* (1971), pp. 328–331. When a young graduate joins an organization, a "psychological contract" is forged between individual and organization. If the organization doesn't live up to the individual's perception of the contract, he feels offended and leaves. Unfortunately, the specific terms of this implied contract are seldom discussed. J. P. Kotter, "The Psychological Contract: Managing the Joining-up Process," *California Management Review* (Spring 1973), pp. 91–99. The reasons why the relationship is initially vague lie in the implicit bargaining and selling that take place in the attraction and selection process. No one really wants to communicate "truth." See L. W. Porter, E. E. Lawler III, and J. R. Hackman, "Choice Processes: Individuals and Organizations Attracting and Selecting Each Other," in *Behavior in Organizations* (New York: McGraw-Hill, 1975), pp. 131–158.

2. Lawler argues that expectation of immediate gratification means that management should shorten periods between evaluations and award frequent small raises rather than yearly. E. E. Lawler, "Compensating the New Life-style Worker," *Personnel* (1971), pp. 19–25. See

also, T. F. Stroh, *Managing the New Generation in Business* (New York: McGraw-Hill, 1971).

3 In general, the younger the managers, the higher the level they expect to reach in their careers. Thus, virtually all are disappointed at some time. M. L. Moore, E. Miller, and J. Fossum, "Predictors of Managerial Career Expectations," *Journal of Applied Psychology* (January 1974), pp. 90–92. Some executives are highly skeptical of MBA's in particular. Here is a portion of a letter written to the editors of *Columbia Journal of World Business* (May–June 1968), p. 5.

"I can't agree completely with Mr. [T. Vincent] Learson's statement (Jan.–Feb. 1968) that the salvation of the business world is the "scientifically trained man that comes from the ranks of the graduate schools." I have found many of these people have no concept of the value of a dollar. They are theorists only and for the most part have no desire to learn the basic fundamentals of the business they are engaged in, but rather consider themselves above finding out the basic principles of the business by experience. They want everyone to hand them experience on a velvet pillow and are too concerned with taking over the presidency of an organization six months after they enter an organization. I do believe the scientifically trained graduate student does have his place in industry, but . . . ."

4 A. G. Athos, "Is the Corporation Next to Fall?" *Harvard Business Review* (January–February 1970), pp. 49–60. For more on characteristics and expectation of young managers and specialists, see J. Gooding, "The Accelerated Generation Moves into Management," *Fortune* (March 1971), p. 101ff.; and L. B. Ward and A. G. Athos, *Student Expectations of Corporate Life* (Boston: Graduate School of Business Administration, Harvard University, 1972).

5 L. M. Porter, "Where is the Organization Man?" *Harvard Business Review* (November–December 1963), pp. 53–61.

6 J. A. Livingston, "Pygmalion in Management," *Harvard Business Review* (July–August 1969), pp. 81–89.

7 D. E. Berlow and D. T. Hall, "The Socialization of Managers: Effects of Expectations on Performance," *Administrative Science Quarterly* (September 1966), pp. 207–223.

8 In general, a superior's stringent personal standards are associated with higher subordinate performance than lower personal standards. The superior's personal standards also seem to exert more influence on subordinate performance than subordinate's personal standards. The best performance, however, is where both superior and subordinates have high personal standards. J.P. Campbell, M. D. Dunnette, E. E. Lawler, and K. E. Weick, *Managerial Behavior, Performance and Effectiveness* (New York: McGraw-Hill 1970), pp. 447–451.

9 For some case studies of sensitive and insensitive young managers, see W. R. Dill, T. L. Hilton, and W. R. Reitman, *The New Managers* (Englewood Cliffs, N.J.: Prentice-Hall, 1962).

10 E. E. Jennings, *The Mobile Manager: A Study of the New Generation of Top Executives* (Ann Arbor: Graduate School of Business Administration, University of Michigan, 1967). For examples of the critical importance of sponsors or mentors for ambitious females, see Gail Sheehy, *Passages: Predictable Crises of Adult Life* (New York: E. P. Dutton, 1976) and J. Thompson, "Patrons, Rabbis, Mentors— Whatever You Call Them, Women Need Them, Too" *MBA* (February 1976), p. 26.

11 On the importance of power, McMurry writes: "The most important and unyielding necessity of organizational life is not better communications, human relations or employee participation, but power. . . . Without power there can be no authority; without authority there can be no discipline; without discipline there can be difficulty in maintaining order, system and productivity. An executive without power is, therefore, all too often a figurehead—or worse, headless. . . . If the executive owns the business, that fact may ensure his power. If he does not, and sometimes even when he does, his power must be acquired and held by means which are essentially political." — R. N. McMurry, "Power and the Ambitious Executive," *Harvard Business Review* (November–December 1973), p. 140.

12 J. S. Livingston, "Myth of the Well-Educated Manager," *Harvard Business Review* (January–February 1971), pp. 79–88. In general, Livingston argues that there is no relation between managerial success and school performance and that schools don't develop important attributes. That "wisdom" is the neglected attribute is maintained by L. Urwick, "What Have the Universities Done for Business Management?" *Management of Personnel Quarterly* (Summer 1967), pp 35–40.

13 One survey indicates that MBA students express more authoritarian and Machiavellian views than do practicing managers, but that business school professors were more Machiavellian than either! J. P. Siegel, "Machiavellianism, MBA's and Managers: Leadership Correlates and Socialization Effects," *Academy of Management Journal* (September 1973), pp. 404–411. A similar finding is in R. J. Burke, "Effects of Organizational Experience on Managerial Attitudes and Beliefs: A Better Press for Managers," *Journal of Business Research* (Summer 1973), pp. 21–30.

14 D. Moment and D. Fisher, "Managerial Career Development and the Generational Confrontation," *California Management Review* (Spring 1973), pp. 46–55. See also, D. Moment and D. Fisher, *Autonomy in Organizational Life* (Cambridge: Schenkman, 1975).

15　Three-dimensional cone model of organization from E. H. Schein, "The Individual, The Organization and The Career. A Conceptual Scheme," in D. A. Kolb, I. M. Rubin and J. M. McIntyre, *Organizational Psychology: A Book of Readings* (Englewood Cliffs, N.J.: Prentice-Hall, 1971), pp. 301–316.

16　Porter, op. cit.

17　Campbell et al., op. cit.

18　The study compared three regional managers of different styles — "authoritarian, " "permissive," and "recessive" (laissez-faire). Objective measurements indicated no difference in regional performance, but higher management consistently rated the authoritarian as most effective and promotable. J. H. Mullen, *Personality and Productivity in Management* (New York: Temple University Publications, Columbia University Press, 1966).

19　H. Levinson. "On Being a Middle-Aged Manager," *Harvard Business Review* (July–August 1969), pp 51–60.

20　That not obeying may be loyalty is demonstrated by D. Wise in *The Politics of Lying* (New York: Random House, 1973). Newton Minow, appointed head of the Federal Communications Commission by President John F. Kennedy, is quoted as saying that in April 1962, after a story that was highly critical of the President was broadcast on the NBC "Huntley-Brinkley Report," Kennedy called Minow. As Minow recalls the conversation, it went like this:
　　JFK: "Did you see that thing in 'Huntley-Brinkley'?"
　　Minow: "Yes."
　　JFK: "I thought they were supposed to be our friends. I want you to do something about that."
　　Minow says he did not do anything, instead calling a Kennedy aide the next morning and asking him to tell the President he was lucky to have an FCC chairman who doesn't do what the President tells him.

21　For a disturbing example of the retribution heaped on a manager who reported his firm's shortcomings to the press, see K. Vandivier, "The Aircraft Brake Scandal," *Harper's Magazine* (April 1972), pp. 45–52.

22　On changing career identities, see D. T. Hall, "A Theoretical Model of Career Subidentity Development in Organizational Settings," *Organizational Behavior and Human Performance* (January 1972), pp. 50–76; and J. F. Veiga, "The Mobile Manager at Mid-Career," *Harvard Business Review* (January–February 1973), p. 115ff.

23　Hirschman suggests that economists will tend to exaggerate the power of leaving while political scientists and sociologists conversely underrate it. A. Hirschman, *Exit, Voice, and Loyalty* (Cambridge, Mass.: Harvard University, 1970). On new careers see D. L. Hiestand,

Changing Careers after Thirty-Five (New York: Columbia University Press, 1971). Connor and Fielder recommend that firms pay for the reeducation of unhappy managers who could then move on to other careers. S. R. Connor and J. S. Fielder, "Rx for Managerial Shelf Sitters," *Harvard Business Review* (November–December 1973), pp. 113–120. See also, R. F. Pearse and B. P. Pelzer, *Self-Directed Change for the Mid-Career Manager* (New York: Amacom, 1975).

24 A. Zaleznik, G.W. Dalton, L. B. Barnes, and P. Laurin, *Orientation and Conflict in Career* (Boston: Graduate School of Business Administration, Harvard University, 1970). The authors suggest that many people never reconcile this conflict between personal identity and organizational values, yet those in conflict may be more effective than those who are "oriented" toward the organization. See also, E. H. Schein, "Organizational Socialization and the Profession of Management," in Kolb et al., *Organizational Psychology: A Book of Readings*, pp. 1–16. Stoess reports a study indicating that managers are relatively more conforming than the general population. A. E. Stoess, "Conformity Behavior of Managers and Their Wives," *Academy of Management Journal* (September 1973), pp. 433–441.

25 E. E. Jennings, *Executive Success: Stresses, Problems and Adjustments* (New York: Appleton-Century-Crofts, 1967): and E. E. Jennings, *The Executive in Crisis* (East Landing Graduate School of Business Administration, Michigan State University, 1965).

26 E. Fromm, *The Art of Loving* (New York: Harper & Row, 1956).

27 J. Steiner, "What Price Success," *Harvard Business Review* (March–April 1972), pp. 69–74. For optimistic advice on how open communication between husbands and wives can help to solve many of the conflicts at home caused by an executive's commitment to career, see E. J. Walker, " 'Til Business Us Do Part?" *Harvard Business Review* (January–February 1976), pp. 94–101.

28 The conceptions of ethics are from R. Baumhart *Ethics in Business* (New York: Holt, Rinehart and Winston, 1968). See also S. H. Miller, "The Tangle of Ethics," *Harvard Business Review* (January–February 1960), pp. 59–62; J. W. Towle (ed.), *Ethics and Standards in American Business* (Boston: Houghton Mifflin, 1964); T. M. Garrett, *Business Ethics* (New York: Appleton-Century-Crofts, 1966); C. C. Walton, *Ethos and the Executive* (Englewood Cliffs, N.J.: Prentice-Hall, 1969).

29 G. F. F. Lombard, "Relativism in Organizations," *Harvard Business Review* (March–April 1971), pp. 55–65; J. F. Fletcher, *Situation Ethics* (Philadelphia: Westminster Press, 1966); J. F. Fletcher, *Moral Responsibility: Situation Ethics at Work* (Philadelphia: Westminster Press, 1967).

30 M. S. Baram, "Trade Secrets: What Price Loyalty," *Harvard Business Review* (November–December 1968), pp. 66–74. On various horror

stories of managers who supposedly put profits over ethics, see F. J. Cook, *The Corrupted Land* (New York: Macmillan, 1966) and R. L. Heilbroner, et al., *In the Name of Profit* (Garden City, N.Y.: Doubleday, 1972).

31 M. Freedman, *Capitalism and Freedom* (Chicago: University of Chicago Press, 1962). Carr argues that it is dangerous to a manager's career to act purely upon personal beliefs, but he can help his organization if he can show how unethical policies actually harm economic performance. A.Z. Carr, "Can an Executive Afford a Conscience?" *Harvard Business Review* (July–August 1970), pp. 58-64. Thus, Carr is both pessimistic and optimistic — pessimistic that only economics guides business behavior, but optimistic that many dilemmas may be converted to economic terms where economics and public interest correspond. That good ethics is good economics and good business is argued by G. Gilman, "The Ethical Dimension in American Management," *California Management Review* (Fall 1964), pp. 45-52.

32 J. K. Galbraith, *The New Industrial State* (Boston: Houghton Mifflin, 1967).

33 A. Chayes, "The Modern Corporation and the Rule of Law," in E. S. Mason (ed.), *The Corporation in Modern Society* (Cambridge, Mass.: Harvard University Press, 1959), p. 25ff.

34 C. C. Walton and F. W. Cleveland, Jr., *Corporations on Trial: The Electrical Cases* (Belmont, Calif.: Wadsworth, 1967).

35 A former chairman of the Chase Manhattan Bank writes about ethical problems:

> "Government's response to the problem, characteristically, has been that 'there oughta be a law.' In the first session of this Congress, more than 20,000 bills and resolutions were introduced, 20 percent more than in the first session of the previous Congress. The same approach has been in evidence on the state and local levels. The objective seems to be to hold together our fractured moral structure by wrapping it in endless layers of new laws—a kind of LSD trip by legislation. Yet it should be clear by now, even to busy lawmakers, that the great lesson to be learned from our attempts to legislate morality is that it can't be done. For morality must come from the heart and the conscience of each individual." George Champion, "Our Moral Deficit," *The MBA* (October 1968), p. 39.

36 H. L. Johnson, "Can the Businessman Apply Christianity?" *Harvard Business Review* (September–October 1957), pp. 68-76; J. W. Clark, *Religion and the Moral Standards of American Businessmen* (Cincinnati: South-Western, 1966).

37 T. F. McMahon, "Moral Responsibility and Business Management," *Social Forces* (December 1963), pp. 5-17.

38 See *Fortune* editorial in response to Pope Paul's encyclical "On the Development of Peoples" (May 1967), p. 115. The editors argue that the Church's view would hinder growth and harm the underdeveloped nations more than a few unethical companies do.

39 A. Z. Carr, "Is Business Bluffing Ethical?" *Harvard Business Review* (January–February 1968), pp. 143–153. In a similar vein, Levitt argues that advertising is like art: it is not reality, but illusion and everyone knows it. Therefore, some distortion is acceptable. T. Levitt, "The Morality of Advertising," *Harvard Business Review* (July–August 1970), pp. 84–92.

40 Baumhart, op. cit.

41 On the difficulties of managers who are confronted with accepting questionable conduct of their superiors, see J. J. Fendrock, "Crisis in Conscience at Quasar," *Harvard Business Review* (March–April 1968), pp. 112–120. For reader response to the situation, see J. J. Fendrock, "Sequel to Quasar Stellar," *Harvard Business Review* (September–October 1968), pp. 14–22. Ninety-eight percent said it was wrong to keep quiet, but 64 percent admitted they would be tempted to.

42 K. R. Andrews, "Toward Professionalism in Business Management," *Harvard Business Review* (March–April 1969), pp. 49–60. Some are skeptical about whether business schools really affect the ethics of their graduates. An executive observes, "They tend to get the notion up at Harvard that some things are more important than profits. But that doesn't affect them when they come here. They're not really contaminated. They're typical, intelligent, ambitious, greedy, grafting, ordinary American males." Quoted in S. Klaw, "Harvard's Degree in the Higher Materialism," *Esquire* (October 1965), p. 103. Schein argues that educational institutions tend to accept the values of the enterprises they prepare students for. E. H. Schein, "The Problems of Moral Education for the Business Manager," *Industrial Management Review* (Fall 1966), pp. 3–14.

43 On different career perspectives, see H. O. Prudent, "The Upward Mobile, Indifferent and Ambivalent Typology of Managers," *Academy of Management Journal* (September 1973), pp. 454–464.

44 Career advice is summarized in E. E. Jennings, *Routes to the Executive Suite* (New York: McGraw-Hill, 1971). See also, R. H. Buskirk, *Your Career: How to Plan It, Manage It, Change It* (Boston: Cahners, 1976). A summary of books on career planning may be found in K. Feingold, "Information Sources on Life Style/Career Planning," *Harvard Business Review* (January–February), p. 144ff.

45 B. M. Bass and L. D. Eldridge, "Accelerated Managers: Objectives in Twelve Countries," *Industrial Relations* (May 1973), pp. 158–170.

QUESTION

What are your career plans? Do you expect to go into management? If so, what problems do you foresee?

_____
_____
_____

Walter Cronkite at CBS

The 1952 Democratic convention was important in part because it brought a new face to the American people, a face that would be known in television history. The CBS team going to Chicago knew that it was going to be on the air live for endless hours and it needed someone to hold the broadcast together. The word for that in the trade, but not yet in the popular vernacular, was anchorman. Murrow himself, still at the peak of his influence, was not much interested. Nor were many of his colleagues. Walter Cronkite, however, was. Walter Cronkite was not one of the Murrow Boys. Cronkite in 1952 was perhaps the one rising star within the company who was outside the Murrow clique. There was a time in London during the war when he might have made the connection with Murrow. He was a United Press correspondent in London and a very good one. He was, in the eyes of Harrison Salisbury, the man then running the UP bureau and an exceptionally good judge of talent, the best on his beat. . . .

He finished the war with UP and there was no doubt of his excellence; the brass there thought highly of him and he was awarded, as a sign of his success, the Moscow bureau. Those were days of minimal creature comforts in Moscow, and he and his wife, Betsy, were warned that they had to bring everything to Moscow, which they did, and on the day they departed someone mentioned to Betsy Cronkite that she would do well to buy a lot of golf balls since there were none available in Moscow, which she immediately rushed out and did, buying hundreds and hundreds of them; an exceptional supply, considering that (a) Walter Cronkite did not play golf and (b) there were no golf courses at all in the Soviet Union. Moscow in 1946 was not very great fun, nor for that matter was United Press; the Russians were fast discontinuing their policy of limited friendship to brotherly Western correspondents, revoking the marginal privileges that had once existed; in addition, the financial generosity of United Press, which was always somewhat limited, seemed to diminish. The UP car was of antique proportions and did not run, and when, during one of the worst winters of recent Russian history, Cronkite asked for permission to buy a new car since even the Russians were complaining about the condition of his vehicle, his superiors suggested that he get a bicycle.

Source: The Powers That Be, *by David Halberstam. Copyright © 1979 by David Halberstam. Reprinted by permission of Alfred A. Knopf, Inc.*

Things like that often undermine a correspondent's confidence and Cronkite quickly asked to be brought out of Moscow. He came home to America for a year with a promise that he would soon return to Europe as the number-one man on the entire Continent. His salary was then a hundred and twenty-five dollars a week, and, with family obligations growing, he asked for more. The UP executives assured him, probably accurately, that he was already the highest-paid man on the staff. Which was fine except he still wanted more; yes, he said, he loved United Press, which he truly did, he loved scooping people and getting the story straight and clean and fast with no frills—even years later, reminiscing, there is a kind of love in his voice talking about the old UP days, how much he loved UP, how he liked the feel of dirt in his hands, he was not at home with a lot of commentary—but love or no, there had to be some money. So Earl Johnson, his superior, said that he thought it was time that he and Walter had a little talk, since Cronkite apparently did not understand the economic basis of United Press, an economic attitude which was legendary among most journalists and secret only to Cronkite. "No, I guess I don't understand it," Cronkite said, and so Johnson explained: "We take the best and the most eager young men we can find and we train them and we pay them very little and we give them a lot of room and then when they get very good they go elsewhere."

"Are you asking me to go somewhere else?" Cronkite asked.

"No, no," said Johnson, though adding that a hundred and twenty-five dollars a week is a lot of money for us, though probably not for you.

So Cronkite returned to Kansas City, whence he came, on a kind of extended leave, and while he was there he saw an old friend named Karl Koerper, who was a big local civic booster and the head of KMBC, which was a CBS affiliate. And Cronkite, who was disturbed by what he had found in Kansas City, told Koerper at lunch that Kansas City seemed to have died, there was no spirit and excitement any more. What had happened? Then he answered his own question, it was the death of the Kansas City *Journal*. You get monopoly journalism, he said, and something goes out of a city, a sense of excitement and competition. When a newspaper competition dies, something dies with it. Kansas City is a duller town now, Cronkite said.

"What do you mean?" Koerper said.

"It's your fault," Cronkite continued. "You radio guys cut the advertising dollars so much that you drove the newspapers out but you haven't replaced them. You have no news staff."

"We certainly do—we have eight men," said Koerper proudly.

"Do you know how many reporters the Kansas City *Star* has?" Cronkite asked.

"But that's their principal business," Koerper answered.

"There!" said Cronkite, seizing on it. "That's the answer!" So the upshot of the conversation was that Walter Cronkite was hired in 1948 by Karl Koerper to work as Washington correspondent for his station and a series of other Kansas and Missouri stations, which was the beginning of Walter Cronkite's career as a broadcaster. He was thirty-one years old, he was from the world of print, and more, he was from the highly specialized, fiercely competitive world of wire-service print. But he went to Washington; his salary was $250 a week and he was working for a string of midwestern radio stations. Somehow in the snobbery and pecking order of American journalism there was something slightly demeaning about seeing Walter Cronkite, who had been a big man during the war, hustling around Washington as a radio man for a bunch of small midwestern stations, although Cronkite did not find it demeaning since he liked the excitement of Washington and since he intended to return soon to Kansas City as general manager of the station.

He worked in Washington for about a year and a half, not entirely satisfied, but not all that restless, and then the Korean War broke out and he got a phone call from Ed Murrow asking whether he might be willing to go to Korea and cover the war for CBS. Would he? Well, Murrow better believe that he would, it was the kind of assignment he loved and wanted, it was exactly where he wanted to be. There was, Murrow said, no great problem with KMBC since it was a CBS affiliate and that type of thing would be easily straightened out. In the meantime, Cronkite should get himself ready to go overseas again. But there was some delay because one of his children was about to be born. Then in the middle of all this, the freeze on ownership of stations ended and CBS bought WTOP, which had been a locally owned Washington station, wanting it as a major outlet in the Washington area, a kind of political flagship. The station television news director asked Cronkite to do the Korean story every night, and inquired what he needed in the way of graphics, which turned out to be chalk and a blackboard. Everyone else was trying to make things more complicated and Cronkite, typically, was trying to make them more simple. He worked so hard in preparation for it, backgrounding himself, going to the Pentagon to develop independent sources, that his mastery and control of the subject were absolutely unique. He simply worked harder than everyone else, and in a profession as embryonic as television news, peopled as it frequently was in those days by pretty boys, he was an immediate success. He had that special quality that television demands, that audiences sense, and that is somehow intangible — he had *weight*, he projected a kind of authority. The people in the station knew that he was stronger and more professional than anyone else around and very soon he was asked to do the Korean War story twice a day, and then, very soon after that, the entire news show, and then two news shows a day. He was an immediate hit, a very good professional reporter on a new medium, and he soon began to do network feeds from Washington back to the network news show in New York. Korea began to slip away as an assignment.

Among those most aware of Cronkite's talents was Sig Mickelson, who was then in charge of television news at CBS. He was in effect the head of the stepchild section of CBS News, trying to build up television, but doing it very much against the grain, since in comparison with Murrow he had no bureaucratic muscle, and since all the stars of the News Department were in the Murrow group. Mickelson was quietly strengthening the rest of the News Department. He had known Cronkite in earlier incarnations and from the start he had seen Cronkite as the man around whom he could build the future television staff. As the 1952 convention approached, radio was still bigger than television, although the convention itself would help tip the balance in favor of television. The Mickelson group wanted a full-time correspondent who would sit there all day long and all night long and hold the coverage together, not get tired, and have great control over his material. Mickelson asked for Murrow, Sevareid, or Collingwood, the big radio stars. But the radio people told Mickelson to get lost. Instead, negotiating through Hubbell Robinson, they offered a list of reporters who were ostensibly second-stringers. On the list was precisely the name that Mickelson wanted, that of Walter Cronkite.

The Murrow group had never really considered Cronkite one of them and there was a certain snobbery about it all; Cronkite was somehow different from the others; it was not just that they had been stars longer than he, they were of a different cast and a different type and it would be crucial in the difference between television news reporting and radio news reporting. Cronkite was then, and he remained some twenty-five years later, almost consciously a nonsophisticate, and he is even now, much as he was then, right out of the Midwest, and there was a touch of *The Front Page* to him, he was almost joyously what he had always been, a lot of gee whiz, it was all new and fresh even when surely he had seen much of it before, and it was as if he took delight in not having been changed externally by all that he had seen. He was above all *of* the wire services — get it fast and get it straight and make it understandable and do not agonize over the larger questions that it raises. The Murrow men — Sevareid, Howard Smith, Collingwood, Shirer, Schoenbrun — were notoriously cerebral and had been picked for that reason; they had been encouraged to think and analyze, not just to run as sprinters. They had dined with the great and mighty of Europe and they had entered the great salons and taken on the mannerisms of those salons; they were, whether they wanted to be or not (and most of them wanted to be), sophisticates. If they had once worked for organizations like UP, they were glad to have that behind them and they did not romanticize those years. Sevareid, for example, came from Velva, North Dakota, which was smaller than St. Joseph, Missouri, where Cronkite came from, but Sevareid had left Velva behind long ago and there was a part of Cronkite which had never left St. Joe, and which he quite consciously projected.

Cronkite had come to the 1952 convention knowing that it was his big chance. He had come thoroughly prepared, he knew the weight of each delegation and he was able to bind the coverage together at all times. He was, in a field very short of professionalism, incredibly professional, and in a job that required great durability, he was the ultimate durable man. By the end of the first day, in the early morning, the other people in the control booth just looked at each other, they knew they had a winner, and a new dimension of importance for television; they knew it even more the next day when some of the Murrow people began to drift around to let the television staff know they were, well, available for assignment.

Cronkite himself had little immediate sense of it, he was so obsessed by the action in front of him that he had no awareness of the growing reaction to his performance. It was true that people kept coming up and congratulating him on his work and it was true that there seemed to be a new attitude on the part of his colleagues, but he still did not realize what had happened. On the last morning of the convention, when it was all over, he went for an early morning walk with Sig Mickelson along Michigan Avenue. Mickelson said that his life was going to change, he was going to want to renegotiate his contract and he would need a lot more money.

"Do you have an agent?" Mickelson asked.

"No," said Cronkite.

"Well, you better get one," Mickelson said. "You're going to need one."

"No, I won't," Cronkite said.

"Yes, you will," Mickelson said. . . .

Sig Mickelson and some of the other news executives had been looking to replace Doug Edwards as the anchorman of the evening news as early as the mid-fifties. Edwards was the original CBS anchorman, he had been given the job during the embryonic days of television. He had been fine standing off the "Camel News Caravan" of NBC's John Cameron Swayze ("Let's hopscotch the world"), but the rise of Huntley-Brinkley was a serious challenge. Edwards did not project the kind of weight that Mickelson and the others wanted, he simply did not seem strong and solid enough a personality to anchor a new modern news show. Douglas Edwards might close the evening news by saying, "And that's the way it is," but people might not necessarily believe that that was the way it was. . . . The job was the most prestigious that CBS had, but it was also not a commentator's job, television was simply too powerful for that kind of personal freedom. For the correspondents in their regular nightly appearances were an interesting combination, part wire-service men (in terms of the narrow spectrum of personal expression and the brevity of their reports) and part superstar, known to the entire country, as recognizable on a presidential campaign and often as sought out by the public as many candidates themselves. But the power was so great and the time on camera so limited that the reporters themselves often seemed underemployed. They were often serious and intelligent and sophisticated, and they seemed more knowledgeable than their nightly reports. The difference between the insight of the CBS reporting team on a brief spot on the news program and its performance at a national convention or during a Watergate special seemed enormous. Even a half-hour show was like trying to put *The New York Times* on a postage stamp, and there was a standing insider's joke at CBS that if Moses came down from the mountain the evening news lead would be: "Moses today came down from the mountain with the Ten Commandments, the two most important of which are. . .".

Sevareid and Collingwood might be the disciples of Murrow, and Cronkite might be the outsider who had never crashed the insider's club, but his style was now more compatible with what the show needed. His roots were in the wire service, he was the embodiment of the wire-service man sprung to life, speed, simplicity, scoop, a ten-minute beat; Hildy Johnson with his shirt sleeves rolled up. He came through to his friends and to his listeners alike as straight, clear, and simple, more interesting in hard news than analysis; the viewers could more readily picture Walter Cronkite jumping into a car to cover a ten-alarm fire than they could visualize him doing cerebral commentary on a great summit meeting in Geneva. From his earliest days he was one of the hungriest reporters around, wildly competitive, no one was going to beat Walter Cronkite on a story, and as he grew older and more successful, the marvel of it was that he never changed, the wild fires still burned. . . .

In addition, he had enormous physical strength and durability. Iron pants, as they say in the trade. He could sit there all night under great stress and constant pressure and never wear down, never blow it. And he never seemed bored by it all, even when it was in fact boring, When both Blair Clark and Sig Mickelson recommended him for the job, the sheer durability, what they called the farm boy in him, was a key factor. He was the workhorse. After all, the qualities of an anchorman were not necessarily those of brilliance, he had to synthesize others. There were those who felt that Sevareid had simply priced himself out of the market intellectually. Eric was too interested in analysis and opinion and thus not an entirely believable transmission belt for straight information. He was an intellectual, he wrote serious articles in serious magazines, and yet he wanted to be an anchorman as well, and there was those who thought this a contradiction in terms. When he found out that Cronkite was getting the job he was furious. "After all I've done for the company," he protested to Blair Clark.

The casting of Cronkite was perfect. He looked like Middle America, there was nothing slick about his looks (he was the son of a dentist in St. Joe, Missouri, and his accent was midwestern). He was from the heartland, and people from the Midwest are considered trustworthy, they are of the soil rather than of the sidewalks, and in American mythology the soil teaches real values and the sidewalks teach shortcuts. Though he had been a foreign correspondent and a very good one, in his television incarnation he had been definitely American, in those less combative, less divisive days of the late fifties and early sixties; Good Guy American. He had covered conventions which were very American, and space shots, which were big stories where no one became very angry. When there was an Eisenhower special to do, Walter did it; he was seen with Eisenhower, and that too was reassuring. Ike and Walter got along, shared values, it spoke well for both of them. (Among those not comforted was John F. Kennedy, who, shortly after his election to the presidency in 1960, took CBS producer Don Hewitt aside. "Walter Cronkite's a Republican, isn't he?" Kennedy asked. No, said Hewitt, he didn't think so. "He's a Republican," said Kennedy, "I know he's a Republican." Again Hewitt said he didn't think so, and indeed he suspected that Cronkite had voted for Eisenhower over Stevenson and Kennedy over Nixon. "He's always with Eisenhower," insisted Kennedy. "Always having his picture taken with Eisenhower and going somewhere with him.")

Cronkite was careful not to be controversial, disciplining himself severely against giving vent to his own personal opinion and prejudices, and this would be an asset for CBS in the decade to come. He represented in a real way the American center, and he was acutely aware when he went against it. To him editorializing was going against the government. He had little awareness, nor did his employers want him to, of the editorializing which he did automatically by unconsciously going along with the government's position. He was never precipitous. His wire-service background gave him a very strong innate sense of the limits to which a correspondent should go, a sense that blended perfectly with what management now deemed to be the role of the anchorman and the news show itself. He represented a certain breed and he was by far the best of the breed. He was wise and decent enough to be uneasy with his power, and the restraints the job required were built into him. And so he was chosen to anchor the half-hour news show — a mass figure who held centrist attitudes for a mass audience.

He became an institution. His influence, if not his power, rivaled that of Presidents. . . .

Robert Kintner had brought NBC News alive, and in doing so strengthened the entire network. He was a driving, difficult man with a great instinct for excellence and a great feel for what television was, for the excitement it could project; *and* he knew that the quickest and the cheapest way to create excitement was through an expanded news organization. The news organization could be the sinews of the network, could hold it together, and a great news organization would make a reputation for NBC and thus for Bob Kintner as well. He loved the sheer electricity of news, and he delighted in instant specials (in 1964 when Lyndon Johnson had a heavy cold there were constant bulletins throughout the day about Lyndon's health, interrupting the NBC programming schedule and blowing up the cold to massive proportions). In addition, he had come up with the Huntley-Brinkley team, which was an almost perfect anchor: Huntley, from Montana, Cronkitelike in his rock steadiness; David Brinkley, from North Carolina, the tart, slightly rebellious younger brother who could by deft tonal inflection imply a disbelief and an irreverence that the medium with its inherent overseriousness badly needed. Backing them was a team of fine floor reporters. In 1956 NBC had challenged CBS's supremacy for the first time; 1956 was the Huntley-Brinkley Democratic convention and as it went on, hour after hour, much too long, journalistic overkill, ultimately picking the same two candidates who had run in 1952, it had become a fine showcase for Brinkley's dry humor.

The sudden surge in the NBC ratings had subsequently scared CBS, indeed terrified the news executives, and Don Hewitt, the CBS producer, had panicked and had gone to Mickelson and suggested teaming Cronkite, who was then doing the anchor, with Murrow. The two big guns of CBS against the upstarts of NBC. A sure winner on paper. Ruth and Gehrig on the same team. It was a disaster. They were both the same man, playing the same role — two avunculars for the price of one. They did not play to each other or against each other as Huntley and Brinkley did. The chemistry was bad: Cronkite liked to work alone, and Murrow was not a good ad-libber.

By 1960 Huntley-Brinkley was number one in the ratings. For the first time, Paley, who loved to be number one, took notice and began to complain to his news executives — not about content but about ratings. Kintner loved it; he ordered the NBC people to close the nightly news with a statement saying that this program had the largest audience in the world. Bill Paley was Number Two! It grated on him terribly, but not so terribly that he would change the schedules of the five CBS-owned and -operated — O and O — stations (the five stations the FCC allowed each network to own outright, and indeed the richest source of network income) and put the Cronkite news on at 7 P.M. instead of 6:30, when it was then showing. NBC, of course, was showing Huntley-Brinkley at 7 on its O and O stations. Seven was the better hour, more people were at home then. The pleas of the CBS News Division that they be allowed to broadcast at seven, too, fell on deaf ears. It was a galling problem for the news people, it taught them how little muscle and prestige they really had in the company. Paley was adamant. Somewhere deep in the bowels of CBS, the news people were sure, there was a very smart accountant who was beating them on this issue.

It was in general a bad time for CBS News. The reason was simple: the rest of CBS was so successful, so dominant under Aubrey, that any interference with entertainment by public affairs lost money, real money; NBC, by contrast, not only was fielding an excellent news team at the peak of its ability, it was weaker in programming and had less to lose by emphasizing news, by interrupting programs, by promoting its apparent love of public affairs. Every NBC program seemed to bear some reminder that the way to watch the 1964 conventions was with Huntley-Brinkley. . . .

In 1964 NBC's success was awesome. A debacle for CBS. At one point in San Francisco NBC seemed to have submerged the entire opposition. Kintner, of course, loved it. He had a booth of his own with a special telephone to call his subordinates — it rang on their desks when he picked it up. Julian Goodman was in charge of listening on the phone, but at one point Goodman was out of the room and the job handling Kintner and his phone fell to a producer named Shad Northshield. The phone rang.

"Northshield," said Northshield.

"The news ratings we've got are eighty-six," said Kintner's gravelly voice.

"That's great," said Northshield.

Kintner hung up immediately. A second later the phone rang again.

"Did you get that straight — eighty-six percent?" Kintner said, and hung up.

Seconds later the phone rang again.

"It seems to me that you could give me more of a reaction," Kintner said.

"Well, what do you want, a hundred percent?" asked Northshield.

"Yes," said Kintner. Bang went the phone. . . .

The difference between the NBC and the CBS coverage of the convention was not great; NBC was in command with a good team, and CBS with a younger floor team and highly frenetic new level of executive leadership was less experienced. But there were not that many stories missed, because there were not that many stories to miss. The real difference was in the ratings, and it was an immense difference. Someone would have to pay. Long, long afterward, Walter Cronkite was still bothered, not just by the fact that he had been scapegoated, but because his superiors, in their discussion of what had gone wrong, never mentioned the coverage itself. He for one did not think that the coverage was very good, he thought that he hadn't done a particularly good job. But no one, when the crunch came, ever mentioned his weaknesses. And no one, certainly, thought of blaming the people who had failed to support the news program, Aubrey and Paley.

Paley had seemed irritable and restless at the Republican convention, and when Friendly and Bill Leonard, his deputy, returned to New York, that small media capital where everyone was talking only about NBC's triumph, they found his irritability had hardened. Paley now wanted drastic and immediate changes in the convention team, he was not about to remain number two. Friendly and Leonard tried to explain the performance in San Francisco, they pointed out that this was a young team, that time was now on their side, and that besides it was simply too late to change the team for the Democratic convention. They had compromised themselves slightly in their talks with Paley by mentioning innocently that Cronkite had talked a little too much during the convention. They realized their mistake immediately. Paley had seized on the comment: Yes, Cronkite was talking too much. Suddenly it was clear to them that Cronkite was going to be the fall guy, as far as Paley was concerned. Why was Cronkite on the air so much? Why did he dominate the others? Why did he talk too much? He had to go. There would be a new anchor. Paley and Stanton — usually it was Stanton who brought down the word from the corporate level but this time Paley was there as well — asked what changes the News Department was recommending. This was an ominous word, *recommending*. Friendly and Leonard said they planned to do nothing. Do you recommend, said Paley, that we get rid of Cronkite? Absolutely not, said Friendly. Then Paley told them to come back with specific recommendations in a few days. The corporation, it seemed, was about to confront the News Department. Friendly and Leonard met with Ernie Leiser, who was Cronkite's producer, and after much soul searching they recommended that it was impractical to do anything about the convention team. NBC was going to dominate at Atlantic City as it had in San Francisco and there was nothing that could be done about it. The best thing was simply to take your lumps and plan for the future.

It was not what Paley wanted to hear. This time the suggestion was a little less of a suggestion, more of a command. Come back and bring with you the names of the correspondents with whom you intend to replace Cronkite. Now they were meeting almost every day. At the next session

Friendly and Leonard were still trying to hold the line, but Paley now had his own suggestion. Mudd. This terrific young correspondent Roger Mudd. Mudd, he said, was a born anchorman. (Which was perhaps true, particularly for a team that had been beaten by David Brinkley, for there was a touch of Brinkley in Roger Mudd, he was intelligent and wry and slightly irreverent, he seemed not to be overwhelmed by the gravity of occasions which, as a matter of fact, were rarely grave.) And now Paley became enthusiastic, there was nothing like this young fellow Mudd, he was terrific. And, with Mudd, said Paley, how about Bob Trout? If Mudd was young and from the world of television, Trout was senior and a word man, Trout could really describe things. Trout, of course, was a famous radio man who could go on for hours with lingering descriptions of events. A Mudd-Trout anchor, that was Paley's idea. The great thing about being Bill Paley, thought one of his aides, was that he could put the hook to Cronkite for Mudd-Trout, and then a few months later, when Mudd-Trout had failed, he could wonder aloud why he had allowed Friendly and Leonard to force such a weak team upon him.

In all this there was no talk of substance, no talk of missed coverage or bad reporting, it was all of image and ratings. Friendly found himself caught between his ambition and his News Department, and what bothered friends of his in those days, as he talked his dilemma out, was that he seemed or at least half seemed to accept management's right to make nonnews judgments on news questions. A sacred line was being crossed without protest. Telling Dick Salant, his predecessor on the job, of the pressure and of the case Paley was building against Cronkite, Friendly said he did not know what to do. He just did not know which way to go. Salant answered: Fred, is it just ratings or is there a professional case against Cronkite? And Friendly answered, inadequately, that it was their candy store, that it all belonged to Paley. Knowing that he was being ordered to fire Cronkite, Friendly warned Paley that Cronkite would not stand for it and would quit if he lost his anchor, and Friendly was shocked by Paley's response: "Good, I hope he does." Finally Friendly gave in. It was a shocking failure, a classic example of what serious journalists had always feared about television, that the show-biz part would ultimately dominate the serious part. Among CBS working reporters Friendly's decision was not accepted; two years later, when Friendly resigned over the CBS failure to televise the Fulbright hearings, most members of his own staff thought he had chosen the wrong issue at the wrong time, that the real issue had been the yanking of Cronkite.

Friendly and Leonard flew out to California to break the news to Cronkite, who was vacationing. There was some talk of the possibility of a Mudd-Cronkite anchor, but Cronkite, a wildly proud man, wanted no part of it, he did not want to share his role with Mudd, and he knew CBS did not want him in the booth. Cronkite in his hour of crisis behaved very well. He did not dump on the company. He was properly loyal. Privately, talking with friends, he protected the company and the institution of television, saying that as a newspaper had a right to change editors if it wanted to, so too did a network have a right to change anchors. Then he held a public news conference and said yes, he thought the company had a right to change anchormen. No, he was not going to worry about it. He did not complain, nor did he agree to the suggestion of the CBS PR man who asked him to pose by a television set for an ad that was to say: *Even Walter Cronkite Listens to Mudd-Trout;* his loyalty to CBS did not extend to fatuousness. At Atlantic City he happened, by chance, to enter an elevator that contained Bob Kintner of NBC. Reporters spotted them coming out and thereupon wrote that Cronkite was going to NBC, a rumor that helped him in his next CBS contract negotiations. All in all it could have been worse for him; he was buttressed by an inner and quite valid suspicion that a Mudd-Trout was likely to be an endangered species.

When Friendly returned from his trip to California, he called Stanton to let him know that the preeminent figure of television had been separated from his most important job, and Stanton had said (it made Friendly feel like a sinister character in a Shakespeare play—yes, the deed had been done, sire), "Good, the chairman will be delighted." Mudd-Trout duly appeared. They were a total failure. NBC routed CBS even more dramatically at Atlantic City (some Cronkite fans going over to NBC in anger), and there was one moment during the convention (which, of course, was not a convention so much as it was a coronation) that remained engraved on the minds of the two news teams. It was the night that Johnson was to accept the nomination. Sander Vanocur of NBC had known Johnson and knew his style, and what he was likely to be feeling like, so he positioned himself near the entrance and waited and waited, guessing that Johnson at this moment might just be in an expansive mood, and then Johnson appeared and Vanocur popped up and had him. Yes, Johnson was in a marvelous, rich, anecdotal mood and—perhaps because Vanocur was regarded as a Kennedy man, what better way to vanquish the ghosts—he had gone on and on. With no one from CBS there at all. It was a marvelous exclusive and Kintner ran it and ran it all night, and when the CBS people saw it come over they were appalled. There was no one near at hand and so Bill Leonard, who was the head of the election unit and not a reporter at all, put on an electronic backpack and went rushing over, panting, and Vanocur, his exclusive done and by now running on the air for the third time, a great scoop in a scoopless convention, turned with a small smile of comfortable charity (which might later have cost him a job at CBS) and said to the President of the United States, "Mr. President, you know Bill Leonard of CBS—he's a good man." Victory at Atlantic City. The end of the Mudd-Trout.

Friendly had worked hard to keep Cronkite from quitting outright to persuade him to stay with the evening news. Cronkite did stay, and that fall CBS put together a magnificent election unit that ran far ahead of NBC up through election eve and that gave CBS the major share of the ratings. Cronkite was, of course, immediately rehabilitated; at the same time, the Huntley-Brinkley format was slipping, it had played for eight years and that was, given the insatiable greed of television, a very long time. The Cronkite show, aided by what was to be exceptional coverage of the Vietnam War by a team of talented young reporters, regained its prestige. But there are two footnotes to the tensions of the 1964 convention.

The first deals with the question of being number one. Paley had wanted to be number one without paying the price, while Friendly and the others had argued for the change in evening time slots that would allow Cronkite to come in at the better hour. But Paley had never listened. Then the dismal ratings of San Francisco stirred him, and one night during the convention, when all the indicators were absolutely terrible, Frank Stanton flew from New York to San Francisco and gathered Leiser, Friendly, and Leonard for dinner. He had, he said, some very good news. And so with that marvelous delicacy which marks the way things are done in corporations (no admission that perhaps the News Department was right and that Paley had changed his mind — chairmen do not change their minds), Stanton said that if Friendly called the people at the local stations in New York and Philadelphia he might be able to argue them into letting Cronkite come on at seven o'clock. So Friendly made the calls, and lo and behold, his marvelous persuasive powers worked and Cronkite got just enough of a boost from the time change to regain his rating.

The second footnote deals with the man himself. For the Walter Cronkite who came back to work was a somewhat different man from the one he had been before being humiliated in public. As the next few years passed and he became even more the dominant figure of the industry, his pride intensified. In 1968 during the Democratic convention the delegates were voting on the peace plank. And suddenly, as sometimes happens at conventions, Cronkite and everyone else started using — overusing — a single word to refer to a situation. The word this time was *erosion*, which had obviously replaced *slippage*, the last convention's word. The vote came to Alabama and Cronkite mentioned that there was an erosion of two votes. He was broadcasting live and suddenly someone passed him a scribbled note: "Tell Walter not to use the word 'erosion'!" Cronkite, without missing a beat in the commentary, answered with his own note: "Who says?" Back came another note: "Stanton." Suddenly it was as if there were fire coming out of Cronkite's nostrils, and even as he continued the delegate count he wrote one more note: "I quit." So someone handed a note to pass to the brass saying: "Walter quits." And this was passed back and even as it was being passed back Cronkite was standing up and taking off his headset and reaching for his jacket. It was an electric moment. And suddenly someone was yelling, "For God's sake tell him to get back down there, don't let him leave. They're not trying to censor him. They just don't like the word 'erosion.' " So he sat down, and continued his broadcast. They might mess with him once, but no one messed with Walter Cronkite a second time.

QUESTION

What lessons do you get from this article about the world of business; about your own career? Discuss.

_____
_____
_____

The Peter Principle

When I was a boy I was taught that the men upstairs knew what they were doing. I was told, "Peter, the more you know, the further you go." So I stayed in school until I graduated from college and then went forth into the world clutching firmly these ideas and my new teaching certificate. During the first year of teaching I was upset to find that a number of teachers, school principals, supervisors and superintendents appeared to be unaware of their professional responsibilities and incompetent in executing their duties. For example, my principal's main concerns were that all window shades be at the same level, that classrooms should be quiet and that no one step on or near the rose beds. The superintendent's main concerns were that no minority group, no matter how fanatical, should ever be offended and that all official forms be submitted on time. The children's education appeared farthest from the administrator mind.

At first I thought this was a special weakness of the school system in which I taught, so I applied for certification in another province. I filled out the special forms, enclosed the required documents and complied willingly with all the red tape. Several weeks later, back came my application and all the documents!

No, there was nothing wrong with my credentials; the forms were correctly filled out; an official department stamp showed that they had been received in good order. But an accompanying letter said, "The new regulations require that such forms cannot be accepted by the Department of Education unless they have been registered at the Post Office to ensure safe delivery. Will you please remail the forms to the Department, making sure to register them this time?"

I began to suspect that the local school system did not have a monopoly on incompetence.

As I looked further afield, I saw that every organization contained a number of persons who could not do their jobs.

Source: Chapters 1 and 2 in The Peter Principle by Dr. Laurence J. Peter and Raymond Hull. Copyright © 1969 by William Morrow and Company, Inc. Reprinted with permission.

A UNIVERSAL PHENOMENON

Occupational incompetence is everywhere. Have you noticed it? Probably we all have noticed it.

We see indecisive politicians posing as resolute statesmen and the "authoritative source" who blames his misinformation on "situational imponderables." Limitless are the public servants who are indolent and insolent; military commanders whose behavioral timidity belies their dreadnaught rhetoric, and governors whose innate servility prevents their actually governing. In our sophistication, we virtually shrug aside the immoral cleric, corrupt judge, incoherent attorney, author who cannot write and English teacher who cannot spell. At universities we see proclamations authored by administrators whose own office communications are hopelessly muddled; and droning lectures from inaudible or incomprehensible instructors.

Seeing incompetence at all levels of every hierarchy — political, legal, educational and industrial — I hypothesized that the cause was some inherent feature of the rules governing the placement of employees. Thus began my serious study of the ways in which employees move upward through a hierarchy, and of what happens to them after promotion.

For my scientific data hundreds of case histories were collected. Here are three typical examples.

Municipal Government File, Case No. 17

J.S. Minion* was a maintenance foreman in the public works department of Excelsior City. He was a favorite of the senior officials at City Hall. They all praised his unfailing affability.

"I like Minion," said the superintendent of works. "He has good judgment and is always pleasant and agreeable."

This behavior was appropriate for Minion's position: he was not supposed to make policy, so he had no need to disagree with his superiors.

The superintendent of works retired and Minion succeeded him. Minion continued to agree with everyone. He passed to his foreman every suggestion that came from above. The resulting conflicts in policy, and the continual changing of plans, soon demoralized the department. Complaints poured in from the Mayor and other officials, from taxpayers and from the maintenance-workers' union.

Minion still says "Yes" to everyone, and carries messages briskly back and forth between his superiors and his subordinates. Nominally a superintendent, he actually does the work of a messenger. The maintenance department regularly exceeds its budget; yet fails to fulfill its program of work. In short, Minion, a competent foreman, became an incompetent superintendent.

---

*Some names have been changed in order to protect the guilty.

Service Industries File, Case No. 3

E. Tinker was exceptionally zealous and intelligent as an apprentice at G. Reece Auto Repair Inc., and soon rose to journeyman mechanic. In this job he showed outstanding ability in diagnosing obscure faults, and endless patience in correcting them. He was promoted to foreman of the repair shop.

But here his love of things mechanical and his perfectionism became liabilities. He will undertake any job that he thinks looks interesting, no matter how busy the shop may be. "We'll work it in somehow," he says.

He will not let a job go until he is fully satisfied with it.

He meddles constantly. He is seldom to be found at his desk. He is usually up to his elbows in a dismantled motor and while the man who should be doing the work stands watching, other workmen sit around waiting to be assigned new tasks. As a result the shop is always overcrowded with work, always in a muddle, and delivery times are often missed.

Tinker cannot understand that the average customer cares little about perfection—he wants his car back on time! He cannot understand that most of his men are less interested in motors than in their pay checks. So Tinker cannot get on with his customers or with his subordinates. He was a competent mechanic, but is now an incompetent foreman.

Military File, Case No. 8

Consider the case of the late renowned General A. Goodwin. His hearty, informal manner, his racy style of speech, his scorn for petty regulations and his undoubted personal bravery made him the idol of his men. He led them to many well-deserved victories.

When Goodwin was promoted to field marshall he had to deal, not with ordinary soldiers, but with politicians and allied generalissimos.

He would not conform to the necessary protocol. He could not turn his tongue to the conventional courtesies and flatteries. He quarreled with all the dignitaries and took to lying for days at a time, drunk and sulking, in his trailer. The conduct of the war slipped out of his hands into those of his subordinates. He had been promoted to a position that he was incompetent to fill.

AN IMPORTANT CLUE!

In time I saw that all such cases had a common feature. The employee had been promoted from a position of competence to a position of incompetence. I saw that, sooner or later, this could happen to every employee in every hierarchy.

Hypothetical Case File, Case No. 1

Suppose you own a pill-rolling factory, Perfect Pill Incorporated. Your foreman pill roller dies of a perforated ulcer. You need a replacement. You naturally look among your rank-and-file pill rollers.

Miss Oval, Mrs. Cylinder, Mr. Ellipse, and Mr. Cube all show various degrees of incompetence. They will naturally be ineligible for promotion. You will choose — other things being equal — your most competent pill roller, Mr. Sphere, and promote him to foreman.

Now suppose Mr. Sphere proves competent as foreman. Later, when your general foreman, Legree, moves up to Works Manager, Sphere will be eligible to take his place.

If, on the other hand, Sphere is an incompetent foreman, he will get no more promotion. He has reached what I call his "level of incompetence." He will stay there till the end of his career.

Some employees, like Ellipse and Cube, reach a level of incompetence in the lowest grade and are never promoted. Some, like Sphere (assuming he is not a satisfactory foreman), reach it after one promotion.

E. Tinker, the automobile repair-shop foreman, reached his level of incompetence on the third stage of the hierarchy. General Goodwin reached his level of incompetence at the very top of the hierarchy.

So my analysis of hundreds of cases of occupational incompetence led me on to formulate *The Peter Principle:*

> *In a Hierarchy Every Employee Tends*
> *to Rise to His Level of Incompetence*

A NEW SCIENCE

Having formulated the Principle, I discovered that I had inadvertently founded a new science, hierarchiology, the study of hierarchies.

The term "hierarchy" was originally used to describe the system of church government by priests graded into ranks. The contemporary meaning includes any organization whose members or employees are arranged in order of rank, grade or class.

Hierarchiology, although a relatively recent discipline, appears to have great applicability to the fields of public and private administration.

THIS MEANS YOU

My Principle is the key to an understanding of all hierarchal systems, and therefore to an understanding of the whole structure of civilization. A few eccentrics try to avoid getting involved with hierarchies, but everyone in business, industry, trade-unionism, politics, government, the armed forces, religion and education is so involved. All of them are controlled by the Peter Principle.

Many of them, to be sure, may win a promotion or two, moving from one level of competence to a higher level of competence. But competence in that new position qualifies them for still another promotion. For each individual, for *you*, for *me*, the final promotion is from a level of competence to a level of incompetence.*

So, given enough time—and assuming the existence of enough ranks in the hierarchy—each employee rises to, and remains at, his level of incompetence. Peter's Corollary states:

In time, every post tends to be occupied by an employee who is incompetent to carry out its duties.

WHO TURNS THE WHEELS?

You will rarely find, of course, a system in which *every* employee has reached his level of incompetence. In most instances, something is being done to further the ostensible purposes for which the hierarchy exists.

Work is accomplished by those employees who have not yet reached their level of incompetence.

* * *

A study of a typical hierarchy, the Excelsior City school system, will show how the Peter Principle works within the teaching profession. Study this example and understand how hierarchiology operates within every establishment.

Let us begin with the rank-and-file classroom teachers. I group them, for this analysis, into three classes: competent, moderately competent and incompetent.

Distribution theory predicts, and experience confirms, that teachers will be distributed unevenly in these classes: the majority in the moderately competent class, minorities in the competent and incompetent class. This graph illustrates the distribution:

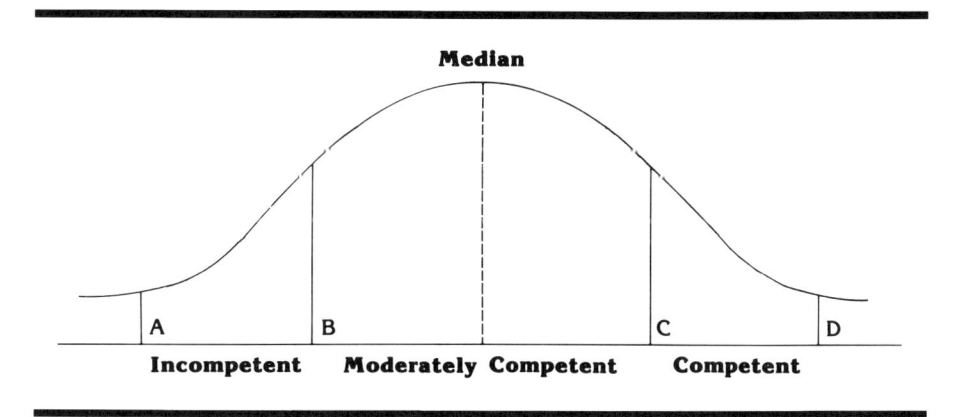

```
                    Median
                      |
              .-------|-------.
            /         |         \
           /          |          \
          /           |           \
         /            |            \
        /             |             \
   ___/               |               \___
   A       B          |          C        D
 Incompetent  Moderately Competent   Competent
```

---

*The phenomena of "percussive sublimation" (commonly referred to as "being kicked upstairs") and of "the lateral arabesque" are not, as the casual observer might think, exceptions to the Principle. They are only pseudo-promotions. . . .

THE CASE OF THE CONFORMIST

An incompetent teacher is ineligible for promotion. Dorothea D. Ditto, for example, had been an extremely conforming student in college. Her assignments were either plagiarisms from textbooks and journals, or transcriptions of the professors' lectures. She always did exactly as she was told, no more, no less. *She was considered to be a competent student.* She graduated with honors from the Excelsior Teachers' College.

When she became a teacher, she taught exactly as she herself had been taught. She followed precisely the textbook, the curriculum guide and the bell schedule.

Her work goes fairly well, except when no rule or precedent is available. For example, when a water pipe burst and flooded the classroom floor, Miss Ditto kept on teaching until the principal rushed in and rescued the class.

"Miss Ditto!" he cried. "In the Name of the Superintendent! There are three inches of water on this floor. Why is your class still here?"

She replied. "I didn't hear the emergency bell signal. I pay attention to those things. You know I do. I'm certain you didn't sound the bell." Flummoxed before the power of her awesome *non sequitur*, the principal invoked a provision of the school code giving him emergency powers in an extraordinary circumstance and led her sopping class from the building.

So, although she never breaks a rule or disobeys an order, she is often in trouble, and will never gain promotion. Competent as a student, *she has reached her level of incompetence as a classroom teacher, and will therefore remain in that position throughout her teaching career.*

THE ELIGIBLE MAJORITY

Most beginning teachers are moderately competent or competent — see the area from B to D on the graph — and *they will all be eligible for promotion.* Here is one such case.

A Latent Weakness

Mr. N. Beeker had been a competent student, and became a popular science teacher. His lessons and lab periods were inspiring. His students were cooperative and kept the laboratory in order. Mr. Beeker was not good at paper work, but this weakness was offset, in the judgment of his superiors, by his success as a teacher.

Beeker was promoted to head of the science department where he now had to order all science supplies and keep extensive records. *His incompetence is evident!* For three years running he has ordered new Bunsen burners, but no tubing for connecting them. As the old tubing deteriorates, fewer and fewer burners are operable, although new ones accumulate on the shelves.

Beeker is not being considered for further promotion. *His ultimate position is one for which he is incompetent.*

Higher up the Hierarchy

B. Lunt had been a competent student, teacher, and department head, and was promoted to assistant principal. In this post he got on well with teachers, students and parents, and was intellectually competent. He gained a further promotion to the rank of principal.

Till now, he had never dealt with school-board members, or with the district superintendent of education. It soon appeared that he lacked the required finesse to work with these high officials. *He kept the superintendent waiting* while he settled a dispute between two children. Taking a class for a teacher who was ill, *he missed a curriculum revision committee meeting* called by the assistant superintendent.

He worked so hard at running his school that *he had no energy for running community organizations.* He declined offers to become program chairman of the Parent-Teacher Association, president of the Community Betterment League and consultant to the Committee for Decency in Literature.

His school lost community support and he fell out of favor with the superintendent. Lunt came to be regarded, by the public and by his superiors, as an incompetent principal. When the assistant superintendent's post became vacant, the school board declined to give it to Lunt. He remains, and will remain till he retires, unhappy and incompetent as a principal.

The Autocrat

R. Driver, having proved his competence as student, teacher, department head, assistant principal and principal, was promoted to assistant superintendent. Previously he had only to interpret the school board's policy and have it efficiently carried out in his school. Now, as assistant superintendent, he must participate in the policy discussions of the board, using democratic procedures.

But Driver dislikes democratic procedures. He insists on his status as an expert. He lectures the board members much as he used to lecture his students when he was a classroom teacher. He tries to dominate the board as he dominated his staff when he was a principal.

The board now considers Driver an incompetent assistant superintendent. He will receive no further promotion.

Soon Parted

G. Spender was a competent student, English teacher, department head, assistant principal and principal. He then worked competently for six years as an assistant superintendent — patriotic, diplomatic, suave and well liked. He was promoted to superintendent. Here he was obliged to enter the field of school finance, in which he soon found himself at a loss.

From the start of his teaching career, Spender had never bothered his head about money. His wife handled his pay check, paid all household accounts and gave him pocket money each week.

Now Spender's incompetence in the area of finance is revealed. He purchased a large number of teaching machines from a fly-by-night company which went bankrupt without producing any programs to fit the machines. He had every classroom in the city equipped with television, although the only programs available in the area were for secondary schools. Spender has found his level of incompetence.

ANOTHER PROMOTION MECHANISM

The foregoing examples are typical of what are called "line promotions." There is another mode of upward movement: the "staff promotion." The case of Miss T. Totland is typical.

Miss Totland, who had been a competent student and an outstanding primary teacher, was promoted to primary supervisor. She now has to teach, not children, but teachers. Yet *she still uses the techniques which worked so well with small children.*

Addressing teachers, singly or in groups, she speaks slowly and distinctly. She uses mostly words of one or two syllables. She explains each point several times in different ways, to be sure it is understood. She always wears a bright smile.

Teachers dislike what they call her false cheerfulness and her patronizing attitude. Their resentment is so sharp that, instead of trying to carry out her suggestions, they spend much time devising excuses for *not* doing what she recommends.

Miss Totland has proved herself incompetent in communicating with primary teachers. She is therefore ineligible for further promotion, *and will remain as primary supervisor, at her level of incompetence.*

YOU BE THE JUDGE

You can find similar examples in any hierarchy. Look around you where you work, and pick out the people who have reached their level of incompetence. You will see that in every hierarchy *the cream rises until it sours.* Look in the mirror and ask whether . . .

QUESTIONS

1. Have you ever seen the Peter Principle at work? Discuss.

   _____
   _____
   _____

2. If you were the president of an organization, what would you do to prevent the Peter Principle from occurring? Explain.

   _____
   _____
   _____

That Urge to Achieve

Most people in this world, psychologically, can be divided into two broad groups. There is that minority which is challenged by opportunity and willing to work hard to achieve something, and the majority which really does not care all that much.

For nearly twenty years now, psychologists have tried to penetrate the mystery of this curious dichotomy. Is the need to achieve (or the absence of it) an accident, is it hereditary, or is it the result of environment? Is it a single, isolatable human motive, or a combination of motives—the desire to accumulate wealth, power, fame? Most important of all, is there some technique that could give this will to achieve to people, even whole societies, who do not now have it?

While we do not yet have complete answers for any of these questions, years of work have given us partial answers to most of them and insights into all of them. There is a distinct human motive, distinguishable from others. It can be found, in fact tested for, in any group.

Let me give you one example. Several years ago, a careful study was made of 450 workers who had been thrown out of work by a plant shutdown in Erie, Pennsylvania. Most of the unemployed workers stayed home for a while and then checked back with the United States Employment Services to see if their old jobs or similar ones were available. But a small minority among them behaved differently: the day they were laid off, they started job-hunting.

They checked both the United States and the Pennsylvania Employment Offices; they studied the "Help Wanted" sections of the papers; they checked through their union, their church, and various fraternal organizations; they looked into training courses to learn a new skill; they even left town to look for work, while the majority when questioned said they would not under any circumstances move away from Erie to obtain a job. Obviously the members of that active minority were differently motivated. All the men were more or less in the same situation objectively: they needed work, money, food, shelter, job security. Yet only a minority showed initiative and enterprise in finding what they needed. Why? Psychologists, after years of research, now believe they can answer that question. They have demonstrated that these men possessed in greater

Source: David C. McClelland, "That Urge to Achieve," Think (1966). Reprinted with permission.

degree a specific type of human motivation. For the moment let us refer to this personality characteristic as "Motive A" and review some of the other characteristics of the men who have more of the motive than other men.

Suppose they are confronted by a work situation in which they can set their own goals as to how difficult a task they will undertake. In the psychological laboratory, such a situation is very simply created by asking them to throw rings over a peg from any distance they may choose. Most men throw more or less randomly, standing now close, now far away, but those with Motive A seem to calculate carefully where they are most likely to get a sense of mastery. They stand nearly always at moderate distances, not so close as to make the task ridiculously easy, nor so far away as to make it impossible. They set moderately difficult, but potentially achievable goals for themselves, where they objectively have only about a 1-in-3 chance of succeeding. In other words, they are always setting challenges for themselves, tasks to make them stretch themselves a little.

But they behave like this only if *they* can influence the outcome by performing the work themselves. They prefer not to gamble at all. Say they are given a choice between rolling dice with one in three chances of winning and working on a problem with a one-in-three chance of solving in the time allotted, they choose to work on the problem even though rolling the dice is obviously less work and the odds of winning are the same. They prefer to work at a problem rather than leave the outcome to chance or to others.

Obviously they are concerned with personal achievement rather than with the rewards of success *per se*, since they stand just as much chance of getting those rewards by throwing the dice. This leads to another characteristic the Motive A men show—namely, a strong preference for work situations in which they get concrete feedback on how well they are doing, as one does, say in playing golf, or in being a salesman, but as one does not in teaching, or in personnel counseling. A golfer always knows his score and can compare how well he is doing with par or with his own performance yesterday or last week. A teacher has no such concrete feedback on how well he is doing in "getting across" to his students.

THE *n* ACH MEN

But why do certain men behave like this? At one level the reply is simple: because they habitually spend their time thinking about doing things better. In fact, psychologists typically measure the strength of Motive A by taking samples of a man's spontaneous thoughts (such as making up a story about a picture they have been shown) and counting the frequency with which he mentions doing things better. The count is objective and can even be made these days with the help of a computer program for content analysis. It yields what is referred to technically as an individual's *n* Ach score (for "need for Achievement"). It is not difficult to understand why people who think constantly about "doing better" are more apt to do better at job-hunting, to set moderate, achievable goals for themselves, to dislike gambling (because they get no achievement satisfaction from success), and to prefer work situations where they can tell easily whether they are improving or not. But why some people and not others come to think this way is another question. The evidence suggests it is not because they are born that way, but because of special training they get in the home from parents who set moderately high achievement goals but who are warm, encouraging and nonauthoritarian in helping their children reach these goals.

Such detailed knowledge about one motive helps correct a lot of commonsense ideas about human motivation. For example, much public policy (and much business policy) is based on the simpleminded notion that people will work harder "if they have to." As a first approximation, the idea isn't totally wrong, but it is only a half-truth. The majority of unemployed workers in Erie "had to" find work as much as those with higher n Ach, but they certainly didn't work as hard at it. Or again, it is frequently assumed that *any* strong motive will lead to doing things better. Wouldn't it be fair to say that most of the Erie workers were just "unmotivated"? But our detailed knowledge of various human motives shows that each one leads a person to behave in *different ways*. The contrast is not between being "motivated" or "unmotivated" but between being motivated toward A or toward B or C, etc.

A simple experiment makes the point nicely: subjects were told that they could choose as a working partner either a close friend or a stranger who was known to be an expert on the problem to be solved. Those with higher n Ach (more "need to achieve") chose the experts over their friends, whereas those with more n Aff (the "need to affiliate with others") chose friends over experts. The latter were not "unmotivated"; their desire to be with someone they liked was simply a stronger motive than their desire to excel at the task. Other such needs have been studied by psychologists. For instance, the need for Power is often confused with the need for Achievement because both may lead to "outstanding" activities. There is a distinct difference. People with a strong need for Power want to command attention, get recognition, and control others. They are more active in political life and tend to busy themselves primarily with controlling the channels of communication both up to the top and down to the people so that they are more "in charge." Those with high n Power are not as concerned with improving their work performance daily as those with high n Ach.

It follows, from what we have been able to learn, that not all "great achievers" score high in n Ach. Many generals, outstanding politicians, great research scientists do not, for instance, because their work requires other personality characteristics, other motives. A general or a politician must be more concerned with power relationships, a research scientist must be able to go for long periods without the immediate feedback the person with high n Ach requires, etc. On the other hand, business executives, particularly if they are in positions of real responsibility or if they are salesmen, tend to score high in *n* Ach. This is true even in a Communist country like Poland: apparently there, as well as in a private enterprise economy, a manager succeeds if he is concerned about improving all the time, setting moderate goals, keeping track of his or the company's performance, etc.

MOTIVATION AND HALF-TRUTHS

Since careful study has shown that commonsense notions about motivation are at best half-truths, it also follows that you cannot trust what people tell you about their motives. After all, they often get their ideas about their own motives from common sense. Thus a general may say he is interested in achievement (because he has obviously achieved), or a businessman that he is interested only in making money (because he has made money), or one of the majority of unemployed in Erie that he desperately wants a job (because he knows he needs one); but a careful check of what each one thinks about and how he spends his time may show that each is concerned about quite different things. It requires special measurement techniques to identify the presence of *n* Ach and other such motives. Thus what people say and believe is not very closely related to these "hidden" motives which seem to affect a person's "style of life" more than his political, religious or social attitudes. Thus *n* Ach produces enterprising men among labor leaders or managers, Republicans or Democrats, Catholics or Protestants, capitalists or Communists.

Wherever people begin to think often in *n* Ach terms, things begin to move. Men with higher *n* Ach get more raises and are promoted more rapidly, because they keep actively seeking ways to do a better job. Companies with many such men grow faster. In one comparison of two firms in Mexico, it was discovered that all but one of the top executives of a fast-growing firm had higher *n* Ach scores than the highest scoring executive in an equally large but slow-growing firm. Countries with many such rapidly growing firms tend to show above-average rates of economic growth. This appears to be the reason why correlations have regularly been found between the *n* Ach content in popular literature (such as popular songs or stories in children's textbooks) and subsequent rates of national economic growth. A nation which is thinking about doing better all the time (as shown in its popular literature) actually does do better economically speaking. Careful quantitative studies have shown this to be true in Ancient Greece, in Spain in the Middle Ages, in England from 1400–1800, as well as among contemporary nations, whether capitalist or Communist, developed or underdeveloped.

Contrast these two stories for example. Which one contains more *n* Ach? Which one reflects a state of mind which ought to lead to harder striving to improve the way things are?

Excerpt from story A (4th grade reader): "Don't Ever Owe a Man — The world is an illusion. Wife, children, horses and cows are all just ties of fate. They are ephemeral. Each after fulfilling his part in life disappears. So we should not clamour to have any attachments and just think of God. We have to spend our lives without trouble, for is it not time that there is an end to grievances? So it is better to live knowing the real state of affairs. Don't get entangled in the meshes of family life."

Excerpt from story B (4th grade reader): "How I Do Like to Learn—I was sent to an accelerated technical high school. I was so happy I cried. Learning is not very easy. In the beginning I couldn't understand what the teacher taught us. I always got a red cross mark on my papers. The boy sitting next to me was very enthusiastic and also an outstanding student. When he found I could not do the problems he offered to show me how he had done them. I could not copy his work. I must learn through my own reasoning. I gave his paper back and explained I had to do it myself. Sometimes I worked on a problem until midnight. If I couldn't finish, I started early in the morning. The red cross marks on my work were getting less common. I conquered my difficulties. My marks rose. I graduated and went on to college."

Most readers would agree, without any special knowledge of the *n* Ach coding system, that the second story shows more concerns with improvement than the first, which comes from a contemporary reader used in Indian public schools. In fact the latter has a certain Horatio Alger quality that is reminiscent of our own McGuffey readers of several generations ago. It appears today in the textbooks of Communist China. It should not, therefore, come as a surprise if a nation like Communist China, obsessed as it is with improvement, tended in the long run to outproduce a nation like India, which appears to be more fatalistic.

The *n* Ach level is obviously important for statesmen to watch and in many instances to try to do something about, particularly if a nation's economy is lagging. Take Britain, for example. A generation ago (around 1925) it ranked fifth among 25 countries where children's readers were scored for *n* Ach—and its economy was doing well. By 1950 the *n* Ach level had dropped to 27th out of 39 countries—well below the world average—and today, its leaders are feeling the severe economic effects of this loss in the spirit of enterprise.

ECONOMICS AND *n* ACH

If psychologists can detect *n* Ach levels in individuals or nations, particularly before their effects are widespread, can't the knowledge somehow be put to use to foster economic development? Obviously detection or diagnosis is not enough. What good is it to tell Britain (or India for that matter) that it needs more *n* Ach, a greater spirit of enterprise? In most such cases, informed observers of the local scene know very well that such a need exists, though they may be slower to discover it than the psychologist hovering over *n* Ach scores. What is needed is some method of developing *n* Ach in individuals or nations.

Since about 1960, psychologists in my research group at Harvard have been experimenting with techniques designed to accomplish this goal, chiefly among business executives whose work requires the action characteristics of people with high n Ach. Initially, we had real doubts as to whether we could succeed, partly because like most American psychologists we have been strongly influenced by the psychoanalytic view that basic motives are laid down in childhood and cannot really be changed later, and partly because many studies of intensive psychotherapy and counseling have shown minor if any long-term personality effects. On the other hand we were encouraged by the nonprofessionals: those enthusiasts like Dale Carnegie, the Communist ideologue or the Church missionary, who felt they could change adults and in fact seemed to be doing so. At any rate we ran some brief (7 to 10 days) "total push" training courses for businessmen, designed to increase their n Ach.

FOUR MAIN GOALS

In broad outline the courses had four main goals: (1) They were designed to teach the participants how to think, talk and act like a person with high n Ach, based on our knowledge of such people gained through 17 years of research. For instance, men learned how to make up stories that would code high in n Ach (i.e., how to think in n Ach terms), how to set moderate goals for themselves in the ring toss game (and in life). (2) The courses stimulated the participants to set higher but carefully planned and realistic work goals for themselves over the next two years. Then we checked back with them every six months to see how well they were doing in terms of their own objectives. (3) The courses also utilized techniques for giving the participants knowledge about themselves. For instance, in playing the ring toss game, they could observe that they behaved differently from others—perhaps in refusing to adjust a goal downward after failure. This would then become a matter for group discussion and the man would have to explain what he had in mind in setting such unrealistic goals. Discussion could then lead on to what a man's ultimate goals in life were, how much he cared about actually improving performance v. making a good impression or having many friends. In this way the participants would be freer to realize their achievement goals without being blocked by old habits and attitudes. (4) The courses also usually created a group *esprit de corps* from learning about each other's hopes and fears, successes and failures, and from going through an emotional experience together, away from everyday life, in a retreat setting. This membership in a new group helps a man achieve his goals, partly because he knows he has their sympathy and support and partly because he knows they will be watching to see how well he does. The same effect has been noted in other therapy groups like Alcoholics Anonymous. We are not sure which of these course "inputs" is really absolutely essential—that remains a research question—but we were taking no chances at the outset in view of the general pessimism about such efforts, and we wanted to include any and all techniques that were thought to change people.

The courses have been given: to executives in a large American firm, and in several Mexican firms; to underachieving high school boys; and to businessmen in India from Bombay and from a small city—Kakinada in the state of Andhra Pradesh. In every instance save one (the Mexican case), it was possible to demonstrate statistically, some two years later, that the men who took the course had done better (made more money, got promoted faster, expanded their business faster) than comparable men who did not take the course or who took some other management course.

Consider the Kakinada results, for example. In the two years preceding the course 9 men, 18 percent of the 52 participants, had shown "unusual" enterprise in their business. In the 18 months following the course 25 of the men, in other words nearly 50 percent, were unusually active. And this was not due to a general upturn of business in India. Data from a control city, some forty-five miles away, show the same base rate of "unusually active" men as in Kakinada before the course—namely, about 20 percent. Something clearly happened in Kakinada: the owner of a small radio shop started a chemical plant; a banker was so successful in making commercial loans in an enterprising way that he was promoted to a much larger branch of his bank in Calcutta; the local political leader accomplished his goal (it was set in the course) to get the federal government to deepen the harbor and make it into an all-weather port; plans are far along for establishing a steel rolling mill, etc. All this took place without any substantial capital input from the outside. In fact, the only costs were for four 10-day courses plus some brief follow-up visits every six months. The men are raising their own capital and using their own resources for getting business and industry moving in a city that had been considered stagnant and unenterprising.

The promise of such a method of developing achievement motivation seems very great. It has obvious applications in helping underdeveloped countries, or "pockets of poverty" in the United States, to move faster economically. It has great potential for businesses that need to "turn around" and take a more enterprising approach toward their growth and development. It may even be helpful in developing more n Ach among low-income groups. For instance, data show that lower-class Negro Americans have a very low level of n Ach. This is not surprising. Society has systematically discouraged and blocked their achievement striving. But as the barriers to upward mobility are broken down, it will be necessary to help stimulate the motivation that will lead them to take advantage of new opportunities opening up.

EXTREME REACTIONS

But a word of caution. Whenever I speak of this research and its great potential, audience reaction tends to go to opposite extremes. Either people remain skeptical and argue that motives can't really be changed, that all we are doing is dressing Dale Carnegie up in fancy "psychologese," or they become converts and want instant course descriptions by return mail to solve their local motivational problems. Either response is unjustified. What I have described here in a few pages has taken 20 years of patient research effort, and hundreds of thousands of dollars in basic research costs. What remains to be done will involve even larger sums and more time for development to turn a promising idea into something of wide practical utility.

ENCOURAGEMENT NEEDED

To take only one example, we have not yet learned how to develop n Ach really well among low-income groups. In our first effort — a summer course for bright underachieving 14-year-olds — we found that boys from the middle class improved steadily in grades in school over a two-year period, but boys from the lower class showed an improvement after the first year followed by a drop back to their beginning low grade average (see the accompanying chart). Why? We speculated that it was because they moved back into an environment in which neither parents nor friends encouraged achievement or upward mobility. In other words, it isn't enough to change a man's motivation if the environment in which he lives doesn't support at least to some degree his new efforts. Negroes striving to rise out of the ghetto frequently confront this problem; they are often faced by skepticism at home and suspicion on the job, so that even if their n Ach is raised, it can be lowered again by the heavy odds against their success. We must learn not only to raise n Ach but also to find methods of instructing people how to manage it, to create a favorable environment in which it can flourish.

Many of these training techniques are now only in the pilot testing stage. It will take time and money to perfect them, but society should be willing to invest heavily in them in view of their tremendous potential for contribution to human betterment.

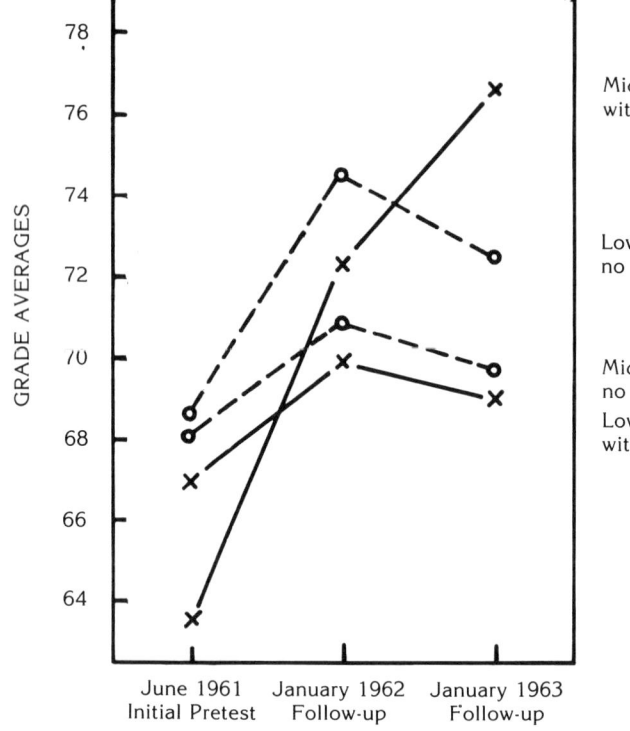

                                                                Middle-class boys
                                                                with training

                                                                Lower-class boys
                                                                no training

                                                                Middle-class boys
                                                                no training
                                                                Lower-class boys
                                                                with training

      June 1961   January 1962   January 1963
      Initial Pretest   Follow-up   Follow-up

In a Harvard study, a group of underachieving 14-year-olds was given a six-week course designed to help them do better in school.

Some of the boys were also given training in achievement motivation, or *n* Ach (solid lines). As graph reveals, the only boys who continued to improve after a two-year period were the middle-class boys with the special *n* Ach training.

Psychologists suspect the lower-class boys dropped back, even with *n* Ach training, because they returned to an environment in which neither parents nor friends encouraged achievement.

QUESTIONS

1. Evaluate yourself. Do you have the urge to achieve? Discuss.

   _____

   _____

   _____

2. What are the advantages and disadvantages of the social need for achievement? How does this need affect individuals; how does it influence society?

   _____

   _____

   _____

What Makes a Top Executive?

SENIOR EXECUTIVE: At one time, Jim was the leading, perhaps the only, candidate for chief executive officer. And then he ran into something he'd never faced before—an unprofitable operation. He seemed to go on a downward spiral after that, becoming more remote each day, unable to work with key subordinates.
INTERVIEWER: Why do you think he derailed?
SENIOR EXECUTIVE: Some of it was bad luck, because the business was going down when he inherited it. Some of it was surrounding himself with specialists, who inevitably wear the blinders of their particular field. And some of it was that he had never learned to delegate. He had no idea of how to lead by listening.

The case of Jim is by no means unusual. Many executives of formidable talent rise to very high levels, yet are denied the ultimate positions. The quick explanations for what might be called their derailment are the ever-popular Peter Principle—they rose past their level of competence—or, more darkly, they possessed some fatal flaw.

The grain of truth in these explanations masks the actual complexity of the process. So we learned from a study that we recently did here at the Center for Creative Leadership, a nonprofit research and educational institution in Greensboro, North Carolina, formed to improve the practice of management.

When we compared 21 derailed executives—successful people who were expected to go even higher in the organization but who reached a plateau late in their careers, were fired, or were forced to retire early—with 20 "arrivers"—those who made it all the way to the top—we found the two groups astonishingly alike. Every one of the 41 executives possessed remarkable strengths, and every one was flawed by one or more significant weaknesses.

Insensitivity to others was cited as a reason for derailment more often than any other flaw. But it was never the only reason. Most often, it was a combination of personal qualities and external circumstances that put an end to an executive's rise. Some of the executives found themselves in a changed situation, in which strengths that had served them well earlier in their careers became liabilities that threw them off track. Others found that weaknesses they'd had all along, once outweighed by assets, became

Source: Morgan W. McCall, Jr., and Michael M. Lombardo. Reprinted with permission from Psychology Today *magazine. Copyright © 1983 American Psychological Association.*

crucial defects in a new situation requiring particular skills to resolve some particular problem.

Our goal was to find out what makes an effective executive, and our original plan was to concentrate on arrivers. But we soon realized that, paradoxically, we could learn a lot about effectiveness by taking a close look at executives who had failed to live up to their apparent potential.

We and our associate, Ann Morrison, worked with several Fortune-500 corporations to identify "savvy insiders"—people who had seen many top executives come and go and who were intimately familiar with their careers. In each corporation one of us interviewed several insiders, usually a few of the top 10 executives and a few senior "human resources professionals," people who help to decide who moves up. We asked them to tell both a success story and a story of derailment.

FATAL FLAWS

Asked to say what had sealed the fate of the men (they were all men) who fell short of ultimate success, our sources named 65 factors, which we boiled down to 10 categories:

1. Insensitive to others; abrasive, intimidating, bullying style.
2. Cold, aloof, arrogant.
3. Betrayal of trust.
4. Overly ambitious; thinking of next job, playing politics.
5. Specific performance problems with the business.
6. Overmanaging: unable to delegate or build a team.
7. Unable to staff effectively.
8. Unable to think strategically.
9. Unable to adapt to boss with different style.
10. Overdependent on advocate or mentor.

No executive had all the flaws cited; indeed, only two were found in the average derailed executive.

As we have noted, the most frequent cause for derailment was insensitivity to other people. "He wouldn't negotiate; there was no room for countervailing views. He could follow a bull through a china shop and still break the china," one senior executive said of a derailed colleague.

Under stress, some of the derailed managers became abrasive and intimidating. One walked into a subordinate's office, interrupting a meeting, and said, "I need to see you." When the subordinate tried to explain that he was occupied, his boss snarled, "I don't give a. . . . I said I wanted to see you now."

Others were so brilliant that they became arrogant, intimidating others with their knowledge. Common remarks were: "He made others feel stupid" or "He wouldn't give you the time of day unless you were brilliant too."

In an incredibly complex and confusing job, being able to trust others absolutely is a necessity. Some executives committed what is perhaps management's only unforgivable sin: They betrayed a trust. This rarely had anything to do with honesty, which was a given in almost all cases. Rather, it was a one-upping of others, or a failure to follow through on promises that wreaked havoc in terms of organizational efficiency. One executive didn't implement a decision as he had promised to do, causing conflicts between the marketing and the production divisions that reverberated downward through four levels of frustrated subordinates.

Others, like Cassius, were overly ambitious. They seemed to be always thinking of their next job, they bruised people in their haste, and they spent too much time trying to please upper management. This sometimes led to staying with a single advocate or mentor too long. When the mentor fell from favor, so did they. Even if the mentor remained in power, people questioned the executive's ability to make independent judgments. Could he stand alone? One executive had worked for the same boss for the better part of 15 years, following him from one assignment to another. Then top management changed, and the boss no longer fit in with the plans of the new regime. The executive, having no reputation of his own, was viewed as a clone of his boss and was passed over as well.

A series of performance problems sometimes emerged. Managers failed to meet profit goals, got lazy, or demonstrated that they couldn't handle certain kinds of jobs (usually new ventures or jobs requiring great powers of persuasion). More important in such cases, managers showed that they couldn't change; they failed to admit their problems, covered them up, or tried to blame them on others. One executive flouted senior management by failing to work with a man specifically sent in to fix a profit problem.

After a certain point in their careers, managers must cease to do the work themselves, and must become executives who see that it is done. But some of the men we studied never made this transition, never learning to delegate or to build a team beneath them. Although overmanaging is irritating at any level, it can be fatal at the executive level. When executives meddle, they are meddling not with low-level subordinates but with other executives, most of whom know much more about their particular area of expertise than their boss ever will. One external-affairs executive who knew little about government regulation tried to direct an expert with 30 years' experience. The expert balked, and the executive lost a battle that should never have begun.

Others got along with their staff, but simply picked the wrong people. Sometimes they staffed in their own image, choosing, for instance, an engineer like themselves when a person with marketing experience would have been better suited for the task at hand. Or sometimes they simply picked people who later bombed.

Inability to think strategically — to take a broad, long-term view — was masked by attention to detail and a miring in technical problems, as some executives simply couldn't go from being doers to being planners. Another common failure appeared as a conflict of style with a new boss. One manager who couldn't change from a go-getter to a thinker/planner eventually ran afoul of a slower-paced, more reflective boss. Although the successful managers sometimes had similar problems, they didn't get into wars over them, and rarely let the issues get personal. Derailed managers exhibited a host of unproductive responses—got peevish, tried to shout the boss down, or just sulked.

In summary, we concluded that executives derail for four basic reasons, all connected to the fact that situations change as one ascends the organizational hierarchy:

1. *Strengths become weaknesses.* Loyalty becomes overdependence, narrowness, or cronyism. Ambition is eventually viewed as politicking and destroys an executive's support base.

2. *Deficiencies eventually matter.* If talented enough, a person can get by with insensitivity at lower levels, but not at higher ones, where subordinates and peers are powerful and probably brilliant also. Those who are charming but not brilliant find that the job gets too big and problems too complex to get by on interpersonal skills.

3. *Success goes to their heads.* After being told how good they are for so long, some executives simply lose their humility and become cold and arrogant. Once this happens, their information sources begin to dry up and people no longer wish to work with them.

4. *Events conspire.* A few of the derailed apparently did little wrong. They were done in politically, or by economic upheavals. Essentially, they just weren't lucky.

While conducting the interviews, we heard few stories about water-walkers. In fact, the executive who came closest to fitting that category, the one "natural leader," derailed precisely because everyone assumed that he could do absolutely anything. At higher levels of management, he became lost in detail, concentrated too much on his subordinates, and seemed to lack the intellectual ability to deal with complex issues. Still, no one helped him; it was assumed that he would succeed regardless.

In short, both the arriver and those who derailed had plenty of warts, although these generally became apparent only late in the men's careers. The events that exposed the flaws were seldom cataclysmic. More often, the flaws themselves had a cumulative impact. As one executive put it, "Careers last such a long time. Leave a trail of mistakes and you eventually find yourself encircled by your past."

In general, the flaws of both the arrivers and the derailed executives showed up when one of five things happened to them: 1) They lost a boss who had covered, or compensated for, their weaknesses. 2) They entered a job for which they were not prepared, either because it entailed much greater responsibility or because it required the executives to perform functions that were new to them. Usually, the difficulties were compounded by the fact that the executives went to work for a new boss whose style was very different from that of his newly promoted subordinate. 3) They left behind a trail of little problems or bruised people, either because they handled them poorly or moved through so quickly that they failed to handle them at all. 4) They moved up during an organizational shake-up and weren't scrutinized until the shake-down period. 5) They entered the executive suite, where getting along with others is crucial.

One or more of these events happened to most of the executives, so the event itself was telling only in that its impact began to separate the two groups. How one person dealt with his flaws under stress went a long way toward explaining why some men arrived and some jumped the tracks just short of town. A bit of dialogue from one interview underscores this point.

SENIOR EXECUTIVE: Successful people don't like to admit that they make big mistakes, but they make whoppers nevertheless. I've never known a CEO [chief executive officer] who didn't make a least one big one and lots of little ones, but it never hurt them.
INTERVIEWER: Why?
SENIOR EXECUTIVE: Because they know how to handle adversity.

Part of handling adversity lies in knowing what *not* to do. As we learned, lots of different management behavioral patterns were acceptable to others. The key was in knowing which ones colleagues and superiors would find intolerable.

As we said at the beginning, both groups were amazingly similar: incredibly bright, identified as promising early in their careers, outstanding in their track records, ambitious, willing to sacrifice — and imperfect. A closer look does reveal some differences, however, and at the levels of excellence characteristic of executives, even a small difference is more than sufficient to create winners and losers.

THE ARRIVERS AND THE DERAILED COMPARED

In the first place, derailed executives had a series of successes, but usually in similar kinds of situations. They had turned two businesses around, or managed progressively larger jobs in the same function. By contrast, the arrivers had more diversity in their successes — they had turned around *and* successfully moved from line to staff and back, or started a new business from scratch *and* completed a special assignment with distinction. They built plants in the wilderness and the Amazonian jungle, salvaged disastrous operations, resolved all-out wars between corporate divisions without bloodshed. One even built a town.

Derailed managers were often described as moody or volatile under pressure. One could control his temper with top management he sought to impress, but was openly jealous of peers he saw as competitors. His too-frequent angry outbursts eroded the cooperation necessary for success, as peers began to wonder whether he was trying to do them in. In contrast, the arrivers were calm, confident, and predictable. People knew how they would react and could plan their own actions accordingly.

Although neither group made many mistakes, all of the arrivers handled theirs with poise and grace. Almost uniformly, they admitted the mistake, forewarned others so they wouldn't be blind-sided by it, then set about analyzing and fixing it. Also telling were two things the arrivers didn't do. They didn't blame others, and once they had handled the situation, they didn't dwell on it.

Moreover, derailed executives tended to react to failure by going on the defensive, trying to keep it under wraps while they fixed it, or, once the problem was visible, blaming it on someone else.

Although both groups were good at going after problems, arrivers were particularly single-minded. This "What's the problem?" mentality spared them three of the common flaws of the derailed: They were too busy worrying about their present job to appear overly eager for their next position; they demanded excellence from their people in problem-solving; and they developed many contacts, saving themselves from the sole-mentor syndrome. In fact, almost no successful manager reported having a single mentor.

Lastly, the arrivers, perhaps due to the diversity of their backgrounds, had the ability to get along with all types of people. They either possessed or developed the skills required to be outspoken without offending people. They were not seen as charming-but-political or direct-but-tactless, but as direct-and-diplomatic. One arriver disagreed strongly with a business strategy favored by his boss. He presented his objections for his concerns as well as the alternative he preferred. But when the decision went against him, he put his energy behind making the decision work. When his boss turned out to be wrong, the arriver didn't gloat about it; he let the situation speak for itself without further embarrassing his boss.

One of the senior executives we interviewed made a simple but not simplistic distinction between the two groups. Only two things, he said, differentiated the successful from the derailed: total integrity, and understanding other people.

Integrity seems to have a special meaning to executives. The word does not refer to simple honesty, but embodies a consistency and predictability built over time that says, "I will do exactly what I say I will do when I say I will do it. If I change my mind, I will tell you well in advance so you will not be harmed by my actions." Such a statement is partly a matter of ethics, but, even more, a question of vital practicality. This kind of integrity seems to be the core element in keeping a large, amorphous organization from collapsing in its own confusion.

Ability—or inability—to understand other people's perspectives was the most glaring difference between the arrivers and the derailed. Only 25 percent of the derailed were described as having a special ability with people; among arrivers, the figure was 75 percent.

Interestingly, two of the arrivers were cold and asinine when younger, but somehow completely changed their style. "I have no idea how he did it," one executive said, "It was as if he went to bed one night and woke up a different person." In general, a certain awareness of self and willingness to change characterized the arrivers. That same flexibility, of course, is also what is needed to get along with all types of people.

A final word—a lesson, perhaps, to be drawn from our findings. Over the years, "experts" have generated long lists of critical skills in an attempt to define the complete manager. In retrospect it seems obvious that no one, the talented executive included, can possess all of those skills. As we came to realize, executives, like the rest of us, are a patchwork of strengths *and* weaknesses. The reasons that some executives ultimately derailed and others made it all the way up the ladder confirm what we all know but have hesitated to admit: There is no one best way to succeed (or even to fail). The foolproof, step-by-step formula is not just elusive; it is, as Kierkegaard said of truth, like searching a pitch-dark room for a black cat that isn't there.

QUESTIONS

1. Consider whether you possess any of the fatal flaws of derailed executives. What are your potential problems? What are your strengths?

2. If you were trying to develop effective executives (arrivers), what would you do? How would you select them? How would you train them? Discuss.

How to Manage Your Time: Everybody's No. 1 Problem

Whenever a senior executive — whether in business, government, or the academic world — tells me that he controls more than half of his work hours, I am reasonably certain that he actually has no idea where his time goes. For "discretionary time" is one of the scarcest and most precious of commodities. It is the time which an executive has at his own disposal, to spend according to his own judgment on matters that are truly important. In working with dozens of businessmen, I have seldom found a senior officer who controls as much as 25 percent of his time. And the higher up in the organization an executive is, the larger the share of his time which is *not* under his control, and is not spent productively.

Most executives don't know this. One company chairman, for example, was absolutely certain that he divided his working hours into three roughly equal parts — one-third spent with his senior officers, another with his important customers, and the rest devoted to community activities. But when a secretary was assigned to make a detailed record of what he actually did during a six-week period, he discovered that he spent almost no time on any of these areas. In fact, the record showed that he spent most of his time as a kind of auxiliary dispatcher, keeping track of orders from customers he knew personally and bothering the plant with phone calls about them. (Most of these orders were going through all right anyhow, and his intervention merely wasted the plant's time as well as his own.) When he first saw the time log he refused to believe it, and called the girl a liar. It took two more logs to convince him that memory cannot be trusted when it comes to the use of time.

This case is by no means unusual. I am constantly surprised to find executives deceiving themselves about the way they budget their time, even though it obviously is their most important resource. Time is altogether unique because its supply is totally inelastic. For most large organizations, money is usually fairly plentiful, manpower can be hired, raw materials and plant space can be increased somehow — but time is the one thing that no manager can rent, hire, buy, or store.

Source: "How to Manage Your Time" (Harpers', December 1966) adapted from Chapter 2 in The Effective Executive *by Peter F. Drucker. Copyright © 1966, 1967 by Peter F. Drucker. Reprinted by permission of Harper & Row, Publishers, Inc.*

Moreover, much of the working day of every executive is inevitably wasted. He is under constant pressure to use his time in unproductive ways—and these pressures increase with the size of the organization. Many of them are irresistible. When a company's best customer calls up, the sales manager can't say, "I'm busy." He has to listen, even if the customer wants to talk about nothing more than last night's bridge game or his daughter's chances of getting into the right college. Unless a hospital administrator attends the meetings of every one of his staff committees, the physicians, the nurses, or the technicians may feel slighted. And every government administrator has to pay attention when a Congressman calls to ask for information that he could get more quickly out of a standard reference book. Such time wasters consume a large part of every manager's life.

The truly effective executive understands this; consequently he is notable for his tender loving care of that part of his working day which he can control himself. He will have discovered that there are only three things he can do to make sure that his disposable time is used to the best advantage. These three devices sound simple, but they are not easy to apply. When they are used properly, however, they are immensely effective—in any kind of enterprise, from a bank to a civic organization, a law firm, a government agency, or a factory. This holds true, incidentally, not only in our capitalist society, but in a socialist state—or for that matter in the Cosa Nostra.

The first step is for the executive to make sure that he knows *from a written record* how his time is actually used. Some executives keep such a time log themselves. Others have secretaries do it for them. The important thing is that the record must be made throughout the working day, noting each activity at the time it actually takes place, rather than later on from memory.

A good many executives keep such a log all the time and examine it critically every month. Others make a record for three or four weeks at a stretch at regular six-month intervals. After each sampling of their time use, they reappraise and rework their schedules. But six months later they invariably find that they have drifted, once again, into wasting more time than they had realized.

Once he has got into the habit of recording and appraising his use of time, the executive is then ready for the second step: the systematic management of his working hours. He can best approach this by asking himself a series of diagnostic questions:

(a) "What am I doing that really does not need to be done at all—by me or anyone else?" He should look at every single activity on his time log and figure out what would happen if he dropped it and nobody else picked it up. It is amazing how many things busy people are doing that never will be missed. The head of a very large company once told me that in two years as chief executive officer he had eaten out every evening except on Christmas Day and New Year's Day. All the dinners were "official" functions—called to honor an employee retiring after fifty years of service or the Governor of one of the states in which the company was doing business—and he felt he had to be there and dine graciously. When he analyzed these dinners, however, he found that at least one-third would proceed just as well without anyone from the company's senior management. In fact, he discovered somewhat to his chagrin that many of his hosts had invited him as a polite gesture, fully expecting him to decline. They did not know quite what to do with him when he turned up.

(b) *"Which of the activities on my time log could be handled by somebody else just as well, if not better?"* The dinner-eating executive found, for instance, that another third of the dinners could be delegated to any senior executive of the company; all the occasion demanded was the company's name on the guest list.

Every manager, whatever his organization, has been exhorted for years to be a better "delegator." Most have themselves given this sermon, and more than once. I have yet to see any results from all the preaching, however, and the reason no one listens is simple: as it is usually presented, delegation makes little sense. If it means that somebody else ought to do part of my *"my work,"* it is wrong. And if it implies that the laziest manager is the best manager, it is not only nonsense; it is immoral nonsense.

But the first look at the time log makes it abundantly clear that the only way an executive can get to the important things is by pushing on others anything that can be done by them at all. For example, a great many trips have to be made; but a junior can make most of them. Travel is still a novelty for him. He is still young enough to get a good night's rest in a hotel bed and he will therefore do a better job than the more experienced, perhaps better-trained, but tired superior. Unloading whatever can be done by somebody else so that one can really get to one's own work—that means a major improvement in effectiveness.

(c) *"What do I do that wastes the time of others?"* Effective executives ask this question systematically and without coyness. The senior administrator of a large government agency learned from his subordinates that meetings in his office wasted a lot of their time. This man asked all his direct subordinates to every meeting—whatever the topic. As a result, the meetings were far too large. And because everyone felt that he had to "show interest," everybody asked at least one question—usually irrelevant. The meetings stretched on endlessly. The administrator had feared that any uninvited men would feel slighted, but when he found out that everyone felt the meetings a waste, he began sending out a printed form which reads:

> I have asked (Messrs. Smith, Jones, and Robinson) to meet with me (Wednesday at 3:00) to discuss (next year's capital appropriations budget). Please come if you think that you need the information or want to take part in the discussion. In any event, you will immediately receive a full

summary of the discussion and of any decisions reached, together with a request for your comments.

Where formerly two dozen people met all afternoon, four men and a secretary now get the matter over with in an hour or so.

DIAGNOSING THE CALENDAR

Many executives know all about the unproductive time demands I have discussed here. Yet they don't prune them because they are afraid of cutting out something important, by mistake. If one prunes too harshly one finds out soon enough to make speedy corrections. But, in fact, we tend to overrate our importance. Even very effective executives still think far too many things can be done only by them. The best proof that overpruning is not a real danger is the extraordinary effectiveness so often attained by severely handicapped people. Harry Hopkins, President Roosevelt's confidential adviser in World War II, was a dying man for whom every step was an intolerable strain. He could only work a few hours every other day or so. As a result, he became—in Churchill's words—"Lord Heart of the Matter," and he accomplished more than almost anyone else in wartime Washington.

These three diagnostic questions should be considered by every executive. Managers must be concerned, in addition, with time wasting that results from poor management and deficient organization. Their first task is to identify the time wasters which follow from lack of system or foresight. The symptom to look for is the recurrent "crisis." Such a crisis can be prevented or reduced to a routine which clerks can manage, for a routine makes unskilled people with no judgment at all capable of doing what it took near-genius to do before.

A fairly large company I once studied ran into a crisis every year around the first of December. In a highly seasonal business, with the last quarter usually the year's low, fourth-quarter sales and profits were not easily predictable. Management, however, made an earnings prediction at the end of the second quarter. Three months later, there were company-wide emergency actions to live up to management's forecast. It took only one stroke of the pen to prevent this crisis; instead of predicting a definite year-end figure, top management is now predicting results within a range.

Prior to Robert McNamara's appointment as Secretary of Defense, a similar crisis always shook the entire American defense establishment toward the end of the government's year. Every bureau chief tried desperately to find ways to spend what was left of the money appropriated by Congress for that year. Otherwise, he was afraid, he would have to give the money back. This crisis was totally unnecessary, as Mr. McNamara immediately saw. The law had always permitted placing unspent, but needed, sums in an interim account.

ARE ALL THOSE MEETINGS NECESSARY?

Years ago, when I started work as a consultant, I had to learn how to tell a well-managed industrial plant from a poorly managed one — without any production knowledge. A well-managed plant, I learned, is dull. Nothing exciting happens in it because the "crises" have been anticipated and converted into routines.

The recurrent crisis is by far the most common symptom of poor management, but overstaffing also wastes a great deal of time. My first-grade arithmetic primer asked, "If it takes two ditchdiggers two days to dig a ditch, how long would it take four ditchdiggers?" In the first grade, the correct answer is "One day." In executives' work, however, the right answer is probably "Four days," if not "Forever."

There is a fairly reliable symptom of overstaffing. If the senior people in the group spend more than about one-tenth of their time on problems of "human relations," then the work force is almost certainly too large. People have become an impediment to performance rather than a means thereto. The excuse for overstaffing is always, "But we have to have a thermodynamicist (or a patent lawyer or an economist) on the staff." He is not used much. He may not be used at all. But he always has to be "familiar with our problem" and "part of the group from the start." Specialists who may be needed once in a while should always remain outside. It is infinitely cheaper to consult them on a fee basis than to have them in the group — both in terms of money and in terms of the impact an underemployed but overskilled man will have on the group's effectiveness.

A third common managerial time waster is malorganization. Its symptom is an excess of meetings. One cannot meet and work at the same time. Organizations will always require meetings because the knowledge and experience needed in specific situations are never available in one head; they have to be pieced together out of the knowledge and experience of several people. But wherever a time log shows the fatty degeneration of meetings — wherever, for instance, people find themselves in meetings a quarter of the time or more — the system needs to be corrected. Work spread over several jobs or components should be in one job or component. Responsibility should be consolidated and information should be addressed only to the people who need it.

The last managerial time problem has to do with malfunction in information. The administrator of a large hospital was plagued for years by phone calls from doctors asking him to find beds for patients who had to be hospitalized. The admissions people "knew" there were no empty beds. Yet the administrator almost invariably found a few. The floor nurse was aware of them and so were the people in the front office who presented departing patients with their bills. The admissions people, however, were relying on a "bed count" made every morning at five o'clock—while the great majority of the patients were sent home in midmorning after doctors had made rounds. All that was needed to put this right was an extra carbon copy of the chit the floor nurse sent the front office.

Even more wasteful, but equally common, is information in the wrong form. Manufacturing businesses typically suffer because production figures have to be "translated" before operating people can use them. They report "averages"—which the accountants use. Operating people, however, usually need ranges and extremes. To get them, they either spend hours each day adapting the figures or they build their own secret accounting organizations. The accountant has all the figures they need, only no one has thought of asking him for them.

USING TIME IN LARGE CHUNKS

The executive who has recorded and analyzed all his time and attempted to prune time wasters can then turn to his discretionary time. Unfortunately he is never going to have a great deal. One of the most accomplished time managers I ever met was the president of a big bank. I saw him once a month for two years. My appointment was always for an hour and a half, and there was never more than one item on the agenda. When I had been with him for an hour and twenty minutes, the president would turn to me and say, "Mr. Drucker, I believe you'd better sum up now and outline what we should do next." And an hour and thirty minutes after I had been ushered into his office, he was at the door saying goodbye to me. I finally asked him why conferences always took an hour and a half. He answered, "That's easy. I have found that my attention span is about an hour and a half. If I work on any topic longer than this, I begin to repeat myself. But I have also found that nothing of importance can really be tackled in much less time."

While I was in his office, the telephone never rang and his secretary never stuck her head through the doorway to announce that an important man wanted to see him urgently. One day I asked him about this. He said, "My secretary has strict instructions not to put anyone through except the President of the United States and my wife. The President very rarely calls and my wife knows better. When we have finished our conference, I take half an hour to return every call. I have yet to come across a crisis which could not wait ninety minutes." But even this disciplined man had to resign himself to having at least half his working time taken up by things of minor importance and dubious value.

The effective executive, however, knows that as little as one quarter of the day, if consolidated in large time units, is usually enough to get the important things done. There are a good many ways of consolidating time. Some people, usually very senior men, work at home one day a week; this method is particularly popular with editors and research scientists. Other men schedule all operating work—meetings, reviews, problem sessions, and so on—on two days a week and set aside the mornings of the remaining days for consistent, continuing work on major issues. Another fairly common method is to schedule a daily work period at home in the morning. Even if this means waking very early so as to get to the office on time, it is preferable to the more popular way of getting to important work—taking it home in the evening. By that time, most executives are too tired to do a good job. And the reason working at home at night is so popular is actually its worst feature: it enables an executive to avoid tackling his time and its management during the day.

The method one uses to consolidate discretionary time is far less important than the approach. Most people try to push the secondary matters together, thus clearing a free space between them. This way, one still gives priority in one's mind and in one's schedule to the less important things. As a result, each new time pressure is likely to be satisfied at the expense of the discretionary time.

Effective executives start out by estimating how much time they can realistically call their own. Then they put aside continuous blocks of time and set appropriate deadlines for themselves. Most of their tasks require fairly large quantums of time for minimum effectiveness. To write a report may, for instance, require six to eight hours. It is pointless to give seven hours to the task by spending fifteen minutes on it twice a day for three weeks. But if one can lock the door, disconnect the telephone, and wrestle with the report for five or six hours without interruption, one may come up with what I call a "zero draft"—the one before the first. Then one can rewrite section by section in small blocks of time.

Similarly, working with people demands large segments of time. The more people there are in an organization, the more often a decision about them arises. But fast personnel decisions are likely to be wrong. Among the effective executives I have observed are some who generally make decisions relatively quickly and some who make decisions rather slowly. Without exception, both groups make *personnel* decisions slowly, and they make them several times before they commit themselves. Alfred P. Sloan, Jr., former head of General Motors, always made a tentative decision the first time a personnel question came up, and even that took several hours, although Sloan was not normally a patient man. A few days later, he tackled the problem again as if he had never seen it before. Only when he came up with the same name two or three times in a row was he willing to go ahead. Sloan had a deserved reputation for the winners he picked. General George C. Marshall, U.S. Army Chief of Staff in World War

II, otherwise very different from Sloan in the way he operated, followed exactly the same procedure. He too was known as a great judge of men.

PLANNING TIME, NOT WORK

Few executives make personnel decisions as important as these. But all effective executives I have observed have learned that they have to give several hours of uninterrupted thought to decisions on people if they hope to come up with the right ones. The director of a medium-sized government research institute found this out when one of his senior administrators had to be removed. The man was in his fifties and had been with the institute all his working life. Suddenly, he had begun to deteriorate. He could not be dismissed or demoted; the institute owed him consideration and loyalty. Yet his shortcomings were sapping the whole organization. The director and his deputy had been over this situation many times without seeing a way out. But when they sat down for a quiet evening of uninterrupted discussion, the "obvious" solution finally emerged. It was so simple that neither man could explain why he had not seen it before. It got the employee into another job which needed to be done, but which did not require the administrative abilities he no longer had.

Executives are forever being exhorted to plan their work. This sounds eminently plausible—the only thing wrong with it is that it rarely works. The plans tend to remain on paper, tend to remain good intentions. Those executives who really get things done don't start with their work. They start with their time. Executives are also forever being urged to acquire new skills, to learn new things—from mathematics to art appreciation—and to work on developing themselves, their knowledge, and their methods. But the executives who show the most startling growth in effectiveness are the ones who work on acquiring a little more discretionary time. Time management takes perseverance and self-discipline. But no other investment on the market pays higher dividends in terms of achievement and performance.

QUESTIONS

1. What are your biggest time wasters? Discuss.

   _____
   _____
   _____

2. What steps could you take to manage your time more effectively? Explain.

_____

_____

_____

Planning on the Left Side
and Managing on the Right

In the folklore of the Middle East, the story is told about a man named Nasrudin, who was searching for something on the ground. A friend came by and asked: "What have you lost, Nasrudin?"

"My key," said Nasrudin.

So, the friend went down on his knees, too, and they both looked for it. After a time, the friend asked: "Where exactly did you drop it?"

"In my house," answered Nasrudin.

"Then why are you looking here, Nasrudin?"

"There is more light here than inside my own house."

This "light" little story is old and worn, yet it has some timeless, mysterious appeal, one which has much to do with the article that follows. But let me leave the story momentarily while I pose some questions—also simple yet mysterious—that have always puzzled me.

First: Why are some people so smart and so dull at the same time, so capable of mastering certain mental activities and so incapable of mastering others? Why is it that some of the most creative thinkers cannot comprehend a balance sheet, and that some accountants have no sense of product design? Why do some brilliant management scientists have no ability to handle organizational politics, while some of the most politically adept individuals cannot seem to understand the simplest elements of management science?

Second: Why do people sometimes express such surprise when they read or learn the obvious, something they already must have known? Why is a manager so delighted, for example, when he reads a new article on decision making, every part of which must be patently obvious to him even though he has never before seen it in print?

Third: Why is there such a discrepancy in organizations, at least at the policy level, between the science and planning of management on the one hand, and managing on the other? Why have none of the techniques of planning and analysis really had much effect on how top managers function?

Source: Reprinted by permission of the Harvard Business Review. "Planning on the Left Side and Managing on the Right" by Henry Mintzberg (July/August 1976). Copyright © 1976 by the President and Fellows of Harvard College; all rights reserved.

What I plan to do in this article is weave together some tentative answers to these three questions with the story of Nasrudin around a central theme, namely, that of the specializaton of the hemispheres of the human brain and what that specialization means for management.

THE TWO HEMISPHERES OF THE HUMAN BRAIN

Let us first try to answer the three questions by looking at what is known about the hemispheres of the brain.

Question One

Scientists—in particular, neurologists, neurosurgeons, and psychologists—have known for a long time that the brain has two distinct hemispheres. They have known, further, that the left hemisphere controls movements on the body's right side and that the right hemisphere controls movements on the left. What they have discovered more recently, however, is that these two hemispheres are specialized in more fundamental ways.

In the left hemisphere of most people's brains (left-handers largely excepted) the logical thinking processes are found. It seems that the mode of operation of the brain's left hemisphere is linear; it processes information sequentially, one bit after another, in an ordered way. Perhaps the most obvious linear faculty is language. In sharp contrast, the right hemisphere is specialized for simultaneous processing; that is, it operates in a more holistic, relational way. Perhaps its most obvious faculty is comprehension of visual images.

Although relatively few specific mental activities have yet been associated with one hemisphere or the other, research is proceeding very quickly. For example, a recent article in *The New York Times* cites research which suggests that emotion may be a right-hemispheric function.[1] This notion is based on the finding that victims of right-hemispheric strokes are often comparatively untroubled about their incapacity, while those with strokes of the left hemisphere often suffer profound mental anguish.

What does this specialization of the brain mean for the way people function? Speech, being linear, is a left-hemispheric activity, but other forms of human communication, such as gesturing, are relational rather than sequential and tend to be associated with the right hemisphere. Imagine what would happen if the two sides of a human brain were detached so that, for example, in reacting to a stimulus, a person's words would be separate from his gestures. In other words, the person would have two separate brains—one specialized for verbal communication, and the other for gestures—that would react to the same stimulus.

This "imagining," in fact, describes how the main breakthrough in the recent research on the human brain took place. In trying to treat certain cases of epilepsy, neurosurgeons found that by severing the corpus callosum, which joins the two hemispheres of the brain, they could "split the brain," isolating the epilepsy. A number of experiments run on these "split-brain" patients produced some fascinating results.

In one experiment doctors showed a woman epileptic's right hemisphere a photograph of a nude woman. (This is done by showing it to the left half of each eye.) The patient said she saw nothing, but almost simultaneously blushed and seemed confused and uncomfortable. Her "conscious" left hemisphere, including her verbal apparatus, was aware only that something had happened to her body, but not of what had caused the emotional turmoil. Only her "unconscious" right hemisphere knew. Here neurosurgeons observed a clear split between the two independent consciousnesses that are normally in communication and collaboration.[2]

Now, scientists have further found that some common human tasks activate one side of the brain while leaving the other largely at rest. For example, a person's learning a mathematical proof might evoke activity in the left hemisphere of his brain, while his conceiving a piece of sculpture or assessing a political opponent might evoke activity in his right.

So now we seem to have the answer to the first question. An individual can be smart and dull at the same time simply because one side of his or her brain is more developed than the other. Some people—probably most lawyers, accountants, and planners—have better developed left-hemispheric thinking processes, while others—artists, sculptors, and perhaps politicians—have better developed right-hemispheric processes. Thus an artist may be incapable of expressing his feelings in words, while a lawyer may have no facility for painting. Or a politician may not be able to learn mathematics, while a management scientist may constantly be manipulated in political situations.

Eye movement is apparently a convenient indicator of hemispheric development. When asked to count the letters in a complex word such as *Mississippi* in their heads, most people will gaze off to the side opposite their most developed hemisphere. (Be careful of lefties, however.) But if the question is a specialized one—for example, if it is emotionally laden, spatial, or purely mathematical—the number of people gazing one way or another will change substantially.

Question Two

A number of word opposites have been proposed to distinguish the two hemispheric modes of "consciousness," for example: explicit versus implicit; verbal versus intuitive; and analytic versus gestalt.

I should interject at this point that these words, as well as much of the evidence for these conclusions, can be found in the remarkable book entitled *The Psychology of Consciousness* by Robert Ornstein, a research psychologist in California. Ornstein uses the story of Nasrudin to further the points he is making. Specifically, he refers to the linear left hemisphere as synonymous with lightness, with thought processes that we know in an explicit sense. We can *articulate* them. He associates the right hemisphere with darkness, with thought processes that are mysterious to us, at least "us" in the Western world.

Ornstein also points out how the "esoteric psychologies" of the East (Zen, Yoga, Sufism, and so on) have focused on right-hemispheric consciousness (for example, altering pulse rate through meditation). In sharp contrast, Western pyschology has been concerned almost exclusively with left-hemispheric consciousness, with logical thought. Ornstein suggests that we might find an important key to human consciousness in the right hemisphere, in what to us in the West is the darkness. To quote him:

> Since these experiences [transcendence of time, control of the nervous system, paranormal communication, and so on] are, by their very mode of operation, not readily accessible to casual explanation or even to linguistic exploration, many have been tempted to ignore them or even to deny their existence. These traditional psychologies have been relegated to the "esoteric" or the "occult," the realm of the mysterious—the word most often employed is "mysticism." It is a taboo area of inquiry, which has been symbolized by the Dark, the Left side [the right hemisphere] of ourselves, the Night.[3]

Now, reflect on this for a moment. (Should I say meditate?) There is a set of thought processes—linear, sequential, analytical—that scientists as well as the rest of us know a lot about. And there is another set—simultaneous, relational, holistic—that we know little about. More importantly, here we do not "know" what we "know" or, more exactly, our left hemispheres cannot articulate explicitly what our right hemispheres know implicitly.

So here is, seemingly, the answer to the second question as well. The feeling of revelation about learning the obvious can be explained with the suggestion that the "obvious" knowledge was implicit, apparently restricted to the right hemisphere. The left hemisphere never "knew." Thus it seems to be a revelation to the left hemisphere when it learns explicitly what the right hemisphere knew all along implicitly.

Now only the third question—the discrepancy between planning and managing—remains.

Question Three

By now, it should be obvious where my discussion is leading (obvious, at least, to the reader's right hemisphere and, now that I write it, to the reader's left hemisphere as well). It may be that management researchers have been looking for the key to management in the lightness of logical analysis whereas perhaps it has always been lost in the darkness of intuition.

Specifically, I propose that there may be a fundamental difference between formal planning and informal managing, a difference akin to that between the two hemispheres of the human brain. The techniques of planning and management science are sequential and systematic; above all, articulated. Planners and management scientists are expected to proceed in their work through a series of logical, ordered steps, each one involving explicit analysis. (The argument that the successful application of these techniques requires considerable intuition does not really change my point. The occurrence of intuition simply means that the analyst is departing from his science, as it is articulated, and is behaving more like a manager.)

Formal planning, then, seems to use processes akin to those identified with the brain's left hemisphere. Furthermore, planners and management scientists seem to revel in a systematic, well-ordered world, and many show little appreciation for the more relational, holistic processes.

What about managing? More exactly, what about the processes used by top managers? (Let me emphasize here that I am focusing this discussion at the policy level of organizations, where I believe the dichotomy between planning and managing is most sharp.) Managers plan in some ways, too (that is, they think ahead), and they engage in their share of logical analysis. But I believe there is more than that to the effective managing of an organization. I hypothesize, therefore, that *the important policy processes of managing an organization rely to a considerable extent on the faculties identified with the brain's right hemisphere.* Effective managers seem to revel in ambiguity; in complex, mysterious systems with relatively little order.

If true, this hypothesis would answer the third question about the discrepancy between planning and managing. It would help to explain why each of the new analytic techniques of planning and analysis has, one after the other, had so little success at the policy level. PPBS, strategic planning, "management" (or "total") information systems, and models of the company—all have been greeted with great enthusiasm; then, in many instances, a few years later have been quietly ushered out the corporate back door. Apparently none served the needs of decision making at the policy level in organizations; at that level other processes may function better.

MANAGING FROM THE RIGHT HEMISPHERE

Because research has so far told us little about the right hemisphere, I cannot support with evidence my claim that a key to managing lies there. I can only present to the reader a "feel" for the situation, not a reading of concrete data. A number of findings from my own research on policy-level processes do, however, suggest that they possess characteristics of right-hemisphere thinking.[4]

One fact recurs repeatedly in all of this research: the key managerial processes are enormously complex and mysterious (to me as a researcher, as well as to the managers who carry them out), drawing on the vaguest of information and using the least articulated of mental processes. These processes seem to be more relational and holistic than ordered and sequential, and more intuitive than intellectual; they seem to be most characteristic of right-hemispheric activity.

Here are ten general findings:

1. The five chief executives I observed strongly favored the verbal media of communciation, especially meetings, over the written forms, namely reading and writing. (The same result has been found in virtually every study of managers, no matter what their level in the organization or the function they supervised.) Of course verbal communication is linear, too, but it is more than that. Managers seem to favor it for two fundamental reasons that suggest a relational mode of operation.

    First, verbal communication enables the manager to "read" facial expressions, tones of voice, and gestures. As I mentioned earlier, these stimuli seem to be processed in the right hemisphere of the brain. Second, and perhaps more important, verbal communication enables the manager to engage in the "real-time" exchange of information. Managers' concentration on the verbal media, therefore, suggests that they desire relational, simultaneous methods of acquiring information, rather than the ordered and sequential ones.

2. In addition to noting the media managers use, it is interesting to look at the content of managers' information, and at what they do with it. The evidence here is that a great deal of the manager's inputs are soft and speculative—impressions and feelings about other people, hearsay, gossip, and so on. Furthermore, the very analytical inputs—reports, documents, and hard data in general—seem to be of relatively little importance to many managers. (After a steady diet of soft information, one chief executive came across the first piece of hard data he had seen all week—an accounting report—and put it aside with the comment, "I never look at this.")

    What can managers do with this soft, speculative information? They "synthesize" rather than "analyze" it, I should think. (How do you analyze the mood of a friend or the grimace someone makes in response to a suggestion?) A great deal of this information helps the manager understand implicitly his organization and its environment, to "see the big picture." This very expression, so common in management, implies a relational, holistic use of information. In effect, managers (like everyone else) use their information to build mental "models" of their world, which are implicit synthesized apprehensions of how their organizations and environments function. Then, whenever an action is contemplated, the manager can simulate the outcome using his implicit models.

    There can be little doubt that this kind of activity goes on all the time in the world of management. A number of words managers commonly use suggest this kind of mental process. For example, the word "hunch" seems to refer to the thought that results from such an implicit simulation. "I don't know why, but I have a hunch that if we do x, then they will respond with y." Managers also use the word *judgment* to refer to thought processes that work but are unknown to them. *Judgment* seems to be the word that the verbal intellect has given to the thought processes that it cannot articulate. Maybe "he has good judgment" simply means "he has good right-hemisphere models."

3. Another consequence of the verbal nature of the manager's information is of interest here. The manager tends to be the best informed member of his organization, but he has difficulty disseminating his information to his employees. Therefore, when a manager overloaded with work finds a new task that needs doing, he faces a dilemma: he must either delegate the task without the background information or simply do the task himself, neither of which is satisfactory.

    When I first encountered this dilemma of delegation, I described it in terms of time and of the nature of the manager's information; because so much of a manager's information is verbal (and stored in his head), the dissemination of it consumes much of his time. But now the split-brain research suggests that a second, perhaps more significant, reason for the dilemma of delegation exists. The manager may simply be incapable of disseminating some relevant information because it is removed from his verbal consciousness. (This suggests that we might need a kind of managerial psychoanalyst to coax it out of him!)

4. Earlier in this article I wrote that managers revel in ambiguity, in complex, mysterious systems without much order. Let us look at evidence of this. What I have discussed so far about the manager's use of information suggests that their work is geared to action, not reflection. We see further evidence for this in the pace of their work ("Breaks are rare. It's one . . . thing after another"); the brevity of their activities (half of the chief executives' activities I observed were completed in less than 9 minutes); the variety of their activities (the chief executives had no evident patterns in their workdays); the fact that they actively exhibit a preference for interruption in their work (stopping meetings, leaving their doors open); and the lack of routine in their work (only 7% of 368 verbal contacts I observed were regularly scheduled, only 1% dealt with a general issue that was in any way related to general planning).

    Clearly, the manager does not operate in a systematic, orderly, and intellectual way, puffing his pipe up in a mountain retreat, as he analyzes his problems. Rather, he deals with issues in the context of daily activities—the cigarette in his mouth, one hand on the telephone, and the other shaking hands with a departing guest. The manager is involved, plugged in; his mode of operating is relational, simultaneous, experiential, that is, encompassing all the characteristics of the right hemisphere.

5. If the most important managerial roles of the ten described in the research were to be isolated, *leader, liaison,* and *disturbance handler* would certainly be among them. (The other seven are

figurehead, monitor, disseminator, spokesman, negotiator, entrepreneur, and *resource allocator,* and the last two are also among the most important roles.) Yet these three are the roles least "known" about. *Leader* describes how the manager deals with his own employees. It is ironic that despite an immense amount of research, managers and researchers still know virtually nothing about the essence of leadership, about why some people follow and others lead. Leadership remains a mysterious chemistry; catchall words such as *charisma* proclaim our ignorance.

In the *liaison* role, the manager builds up a network of outside contacts, which serve as his or her personal information system. Again, the activities of this role remain almost completely outside the realm of articulated knowledge. And as a *disturbance handler* the manager handles problems and crises in his organization. Here again, despite an extensive literature on analytical decision making, virtually nothing is written about decision making under pressure. These activities remain outside the realm of management science, inside the realm of intuition and experience.

6. Let us turn now to strategic decision-making processes. There are 7 "routines" that seem to describe the steps involved in such decision making. These are *recognition, diagnosis, search, design, screening, evaluation/choice,* and *authorization.* Two of these routines stand out above the rest—the *diagnosis* of decision situations and the design of custom-made solutions—in that almost nothing is known of them. Yet these two stand out for another reason as well: they are probably the most important of the seven. In particular, diagnosis seems to be *the* crucial step in strategic decision making, for it is in that routine that the whole course of decision making is set.

   It is a surprising fact, therefore, that diagnosis goes virtually without mention in the literature of planning or management science. (Almost all of the later literature deals with the formal evaluation of given alternatives, yet this is often a kind of trimming on the process, insignificant in terms of determining actual outcomes.) In the study of the decision processes themselves, the managers making decisions mentioned taking an explicit diagnostic step in only 14 of the 25 decision processes. But all the managers must have made some diagnosis; it is difficult to imagine a decision-making process with no diagnosis at all, no assessment of the situation. The question is, therefore, *where* did diagnosis take place?

7. Another point that emerges from studying strategic decision-making processes is the existence and profound influence of what can be called the *dynamic factors.* Strategic decision-making processes are stopped by interruptions, delayed and speeded up by timing factors, and forced repeatedly to branch and cycle. These processes are, therefore, dynamic ones of importance. Yet it is the dynamic factors that the ordered, sequential techniques of analysis are least

able to handle. Thus, despite their importance, the dynamic factors go virtually without mention in the literature of management science.

Let's look at timing, for example. It is evident that timing is crucial in virtually everything the manager does. No manager takes action without considering the effect of moving more or less quickly, of seizing the initiative, or of delaying to avoid complications. Yet in one review of the literature of management, the authors found fewer than 10 books in 183 that refer directly to the subject of timing.[5] Essentially, managers are left on their own to deal with the dynamic factors, which involve simultaneous, relational modes of thinking.

8. When managers do have to make serious choices from among options, how do they in fact make them? Three fundamental modes of selection can be distinguished—analysis, judgment, and bargaining. The first involves the systematic evaluation of options in terms of their consequences on stated organizational goals; the second is a process in the mind of a single decision maker; and the third involves negotiations between different decision makers.

One of the most surprising facts about how managers made the 25 strategic decisions studied is that so few reported using explicit analysis; only in 18 out of 83 choices made did managers mention using it. There was considerable bargaining, but in general the selection mode most commonly used was judgment. Typically, the options and all kinds of data associated with them were pumped into the mind of a manager, and somehow a choice later came out. *How* was never explained. *How* is never explained in any of the literature either. Yehezkel Dror, a leading figure in the study of public policy making, is one of the few thinkers to face the issue squarely. He writes:

> Experienced policy makers, who usually explain their own decisions largely in terms of subconscious processes such as "intuition" and "judgment," unanimously agree, and even emphasize, that extrarational processes play a positive and essential role in policymaking. Observations of policymaking behavior in both small and large systems, indeed, all available description of decisional behavior, especially that of leaders such as Bismarck, Churchill, DeGaulle, and Kennedy, seem to confirm that policy makers' opinion.[6]

9. Finally, in the area of strategy formulation, I can offer only a "feel" for the results since my research is still in progress. However, some ideas have emerged. Strategy formulation does not turn out to be the regular, continuous, systematic process depicted in so much of the planning literature. It is most often an irregular, discontinuous process, proceeding in fits and starts. There are periods of stability in strategy development, but also there are periods of flux, of groping, of piecemeal change, and of global change. To my mind, a "strategy" represents the mediating force between a dynamic environment and a stable operating system. Strategy is

the organization's "conception" of how to deal with its environment for a while.

Now, the environment does not change in any set pattern. For example, the environment does not run on planners' five-year schedules; it may be stable for thirteen years, and then suddenly blow all to . . . in the fourteenth. And even if change were steady, the human brain does not generally perceive it that way. People tend to underreact to mild stimuli and overreact to strong ones. It stands to reason, therefore, that strategies that mediate between environments and organizational operations do not change in regular patterns, but rather, as I observed earlier, in fits and starts.

How does strategic planning account for fits and starts? The fact is that it does not (as planners were made so painfully aware of during the energy crisis). So again, the burden to cope falls on the manager, specifically on his mental processes—intuitional and experiential—that can deal with the irregular inputs from the environment.

10. Let me probe more deeply into the concept of strategy. Consider the organization that has no strategy, no way to deal consistently with its environment; it simply reacts to each new pressure as it comes along. This is typical behavior for an organization in a very difficult situation, where the old strategy has broken down beyond repair, but where no new strategy has yet emerged. Now, if the organization wishes to formulate a new strategy, how does it do so (assuming that the environment has stabilized sufficiently to allow a new strategy to be formulated)?

Let me suggest two ways (based on still tentative results). If the organization goes the route of systematic planning, I suggest that it will probably come up with what can be called a "mainline" strategy. In effect, it will do what is generally expected of organizations in its situation; where possible, for example, it will copy the established strategies of other organizations. If it is in the automobile business, for instance, it might use the General Motors strategy, as Chrysler and Ford have so repeatedly done.

Alternatively, if the organization wishes to have a creative, integrated strategy which can be called a "gestalt strategy," such as Volkswagen's one in the 1950s, then I suggest the organization will rely largely on one individual to conceptualize its strategy, to synthesize a "vision" of how the organization will respond to its environment. In other words, scratch an interesting strategy, and you will probably find a single strategy formulator beneath it. Creative, integrated strategies seem to be the products of single areas, perhaps of single right hemispheres.

A strategy can be made explicit, can be announced as what the organization intends to do in the future, only when the vision is fully worked out, if it ever is. Often, of course, it is never felt to be fully worked out, hence the strategy is never made explicit and remains the private vision of the chief executive. (Of course, in some situations the formulator need not be the manager. There is no reason why a manager cannot have a creative right-hand man — really a left-hand man — who works out his gestalt strategy for him, and then articulates it to him.) No management process is more demanding of holistic, relational, gestalt thinking than the formulation of a creative, integrated strategy to deal with a complex, intertwined environment.

How can sequential analysis (under the label *strategic planning*) possibly lead to a gestalt strategy?

Another "famous old story" has relevance here. It is the one about the blind men trying to identify an elephant by touch. One grabs the trunk and says the elephant is long and soft; another holds the leg and says it is massive and cylindrical; a third touches the skin and says it is rough and scaly. What the story points out is that —

> Each person standing at one part of the elephant can make his own limited, analytic assessment of the situation, but we do not obtain an elephant by adding "scaly," "long and soft," "massive and cylindrical" together in any conceivable proportion. Without the development of an overall perspective, we remain lost in our individual investigations. Such a perspective is a province of another mode of knowledge, and cannot be achieved in the same way that individual parts are explored. It does not arise out of a linear sum of independent observations.[7]

What can we conclude from these ten findings? I must first re-emphasize that everything I write about the two hemispheres of the brain falls into the realm of speculation. Researchers have yet to formally relate any management process to the functioning of the human brain. Nevertheless, the ten points do seem to support the hypothesis stated earlier: *the important policy-level processes required to manage an organization rely to a considerable extent on the faculties identified with the brain's right hemisphere.*

This conclusion does not imply that the left hemisphere is unimportant for policy makers. I have overstated my case here to emphasize the importance of the right. The faculties identified with the left hemisphere are obviously important as well for effective management. Every manager engages in considerable explicit calculation when he or she acts, and all intuitive thinking must be translated into the linear order of the left if it is to be articulated and eventually put to use. The great powers that appear to be associated with the right hemisphere are obviously useless without the faculties of the left. The artist can create without verbalizing; the manager cannot.

Truly outstanding managers are no doubt the ones who can couple effective right-hemispheric processes (hunch, judgment, synthesis, and so on) with effective processes of the left (articulateness, logic, analysis, and so on). But there will be little headway in the field of management if managers and researchers continue to search for the key to managing in the lightness of ordered analysis. Too much will stay unexplained in the darkness of intuition.

Before I go on to discuss the implications for management science and planning, I want to stress again that throughout this article I have been focusing on processes that managers employ at the policy level of the organization. It seems that the faculties identified with the right-hemispheric activities are most important in the higher levels of an organization, at least in those with "top-down" policy-making systems.

In a sense, the coupling of the holistic and the sequential reflects how bureaucratic organizations themselves work. The policy maker conceives the strategy in holistic terms, and the rest of the hierarchy — the functional departments, branches, and shops — implement it in sequence. Whereas the right-hemispheric faculties may be more important at the top of an organization, the left-hemispheric ones may dominate lower down.

IMPLICATIONS FOR THE LEFT HEMISPHERE

Let us return to practical reality for a final word. What does all I've discussed mean for those associated with management?

For Planners and Management Scientists

No, I do not suggest that planners and management scientists pack up their bags of techniques and leave the field of management, or that they take up basket-weaving or meditation in their spare time. (I haven't — at least not yet!) It seems to me that the left hemisphere is alive and well; the analytic community is firmly established, and indispensable, at the operating and middle levels of most organizations. Its real problems occur at the policy level. Here analysis must co-exist with — perhaps even take its lead from — intuition, a fact that many analysts and planners have been slow to accept. To my mind, organizational effectiveness does not lie in that narrow-minded concept called "rationality"; it lies in a blend of clear-headed logic *and* powerful intuition. Let me illustrate this with two points.

1. *First, only under special circumstances should planners try to plan.* When an organization is in a stable environment and has no use for a very creative strategy — the telephone industry may be the best example — then the development of formal, systematic strategic plans (and main-line strategies) may be in order. But when the environment is unstable or the organization needs a creative strategy, then strategic planning may not be the best approach to strategy formulation, and planners have no business pushing the organization to use it.

2. *Second, effective decision making at the policy level requires good analytical input; it is the job of the planner and management scientist to ensure that top management gets it.* Managers are very effective at securing soft information; but they tend to underemphasize analytical input that is often important as well. The planners and management scientists can serve their organizations effectively by carrying out ad hoc analyses and feeding the results to top management (need I say verbally?), ensuring that the very best of analysis is brought to bear on policy making. But at the same time, planners need to recognize that these inputs cannot be the only ones used in policy making, that soft information is crucial as well.

For the Teacher of Managers

If the suggestions in this article turn out to be valid, then educators had better revise drastically some of their notions about management education, because the revolution in that sphere over the last fifteen years — while it has brought so much of use — has virtually consecrated the modern management school to the worship of the left hemisphere.

Should educators be surprised that so many of their graduates end up in staff positions, with no intention of ever managing anything? Some of the best-known management schools have become virtual closed systems in which professors with little interest in the reality of organizational life teach inexperienced students the theories of mathematics, economics, and psychology as ends in themselves. In these management schools, management is accorded little place.

I am not preaching a return to the management school of the 1950s. That age of fuzzy thinking has passed, thankfully. Rather, I am calling for a new balance in our schools, the balance that the best of human brains can achieve, between the analytic and the intuitive. In particular, greater use should be made of the powerful new skill-development techniques which are experiential and creative in nature, such as role playing, the use of video-tape, behavior laboratories, and so on. Educators need to put students into situations, whether in the field or in the simulated experience of the laboratory, where they can practice managerial skills, not only interpersonal but also informational and decisional. Then specialists would follow up with feedback on the students' behavior and performance.

For Managers

The first conclusion for managers should be a call for caution. The findings of the cognitive psychologists should not be taken as license to shroud activities in darkness. The mystification of conscious behavior is a favorite ploy of those seeking to protect a power base (or to hide their intentions of creating one); this behavior helps no organization, and neither does forcing to the realm of intuition activities that can be handled effectively by analysis.

A major thrust of development in our organizations, ever since Frederick Taylor began experimenting in factories late in the last century, has been to shift activities out of the realm of intuition, toward conscious analysis. That trend will continue. But managers, and those who work with them, need to be careful to distinguish that which is best handled analytically from that which must remain in the realm of intuition, where, in the meantime, we should be looking for the lost keys to management.

REFERENCE NOTES

1 Richard Restak, "The Hemisphere of the Brain Have Minds of Their Own." *New York Times*, 25 January 1976.

2 Robert Ornstein, *The Psychology of Consciousness* (San Francisco: W. H. Freeman, 1975).

3 Ibid., p. 97.

4 These findings are based on (a) my observational study of the work of five chief executives reported in *The Nature of Managerial Work* (New York: Harper and Row, 1973) and in "The Manager's Job: Folklore and Fact" (HBR July–August 1975, p. 49); (b) a study of twenty-five strategic decision processes reported in "The Structure of 'Unstructured' Decision Processes," coauthored with Duru Raisinghani and Andre Theoret, to appear in a forthcoming issue of *Administrative Science Quarterly*; and (c) a series of studies carried out under my supervision at McGill University on the formation of organizational strategies over periods of decades, reported in "Patterns in Strategy Formation," Working Paper I.A.E., Aix-en-Provence, France, submitted for publication.

5 Clyde T. Hardwick, and Bernard R. Landuyt, *Administrative Strategy and Decision Making*, 2nd ed. (Cincinnati: South-Western, 1966).

6 Yehezkel Dror, *Public Policymaking Re-Examined* (Scranton: Chandler, 1968), p. 149.

7 Ornstein, p. 10.

QUESTIONS

1. In general, would you characterize yourself as left-brain dominant or right-brain dominant?

2. Discuss the special contributions of left-brain managers and right-brain managers.

　

3. Have you seen conflict between left-brain people and right-brain people? How would you handle such conflict?

The Fertile Tension between Discipline and Impulse

Some people can arrange paint or clay or words in ways that inspire us, while others find the process of artistic creation baffling. Faced with a painting, a novel, a sculpture, or a symphony, psychologists are unable to tell us how Picassos create works of art and why the rest of us can't.

Researchers have devised several tests of creativity. None of them differentiate between James Joyce and a writer of greeting-card verse, but they do divide us into creative and uncreative people. In one of these tests, a person is asked to supply as many uses as he can think of for ordinary objects. People differ markedly in their ability to come up with original uses for bananas, bricks, or paper clips. Extremely creative people produce long lists of imaginative, sometimes outlandish uses ("grind the brick into powder and use it as make-up for an Indian War Dance"), while others can list only the most mundane ("use the brick for a bookend").

This disparity in the ability to give free rein to the imagination indicates a basic difference in the way people think. The research of Liam Hudson at the University of Edinburgh shows that this difference affects many spheres of our lives and may help us to understand why some people can write poetry while others have difficulty reading it.

Hudson believes a creative achievement arises when a person attempts to resolve a tension between intuition and discipline or between impulse and caution. Creativeness is not simply the untrammeled expression of an artist's impulse; it flows from an internal negotiation between what seems to him intuitively correct and what the constraining forces of technique, of material, of tradition, of criticism, and of the marketplace require. Wherever one looks in art or in science, this same state of fertile tension appears. Hudson contends that exciting ideas come from the interplay of discipline and impulse. This idea of a generative tension helps him connect and understand four kinds of seemingly unrelated findings about people's minds and lives. One part of his evidence comes from mental tests; another from the sleep laboratory; another from children's stereotyped beliefs; and the last from studies of marriage and divorce.

Source: Daniel Coleman. reprinted with permission from Psychology Today *magazine. Copyright © 1976 American Psychological Association.*

When we look at different kinds of mental measurement, we find a difference that parallels the distinction Hudson draws between discipline and impulse. In IQ tests logic rather than whim produces high scores. Open-ended tests, on the other hand, reward impulse. A test that invites us to write down as many different uses as we can for an ordinary object demands an undisciplined response.

All of us possess both sorts of skill, but some show a marked preference for one rather than the other. Those who score higher on IQ tests than on open-ended tests are called *convergers;* those who do better on open-ended test are *divergers.* In the middle, there are the *all-rounders,* people who do as well—or as poorly—on one test as on the other.

Convergers and divergers differ in many ways. An especially telling difference may help us understand the mild-mannered person who shocks the community by an unexpected act of brutal violence. Convergers generally are conventional in their beliefs and show respect for authority. When they offer uses for objects, they are less likely than divergers to come up with violent ideas. This mildness among the convergers is what one would expect. But a close look at the responses reveals that while the convergers give fewer violent responses, those they do produce are likely to be *very* violent; from time to time they are positively sickening. . . .

CONTROLLED ERUPTIONS

Convergers are more specific than divergers in their suggestions, more likely to spell out the bloody details, and more concerned with the emotional undercurrents of family life. At the same time, the converger is skilled in close analytical argument. To achieve this, he must learn to control eruptions into his mind of non-rational thoughts. The diverger is more open to the nonrational, but the price he pays is an inability to concentrate on close, analytical argument.

In psychoanalytic language the converger is a repressor. He pushes alien thoughts out of his consciousness and guards his mind against their intrusion. For him, the nonrational seems to hold a heightened and focused threat.

The diverger, on the other hand, is an intellectualizer. Instead of repressing nonrational thought, he exploits it, and may even welcome its intrusion.

The most familiar kind of uncontrolled, nonrational thought is the dream. If Hudson's theory is correct, convergers repress not only their waking impulses, but their dreams as well. Three or four times a night, most of us enter a phase known as rapid-eye-movement sleep or REM sleep. Our eyes flicker intermittently, as though we were watching some private movie. If people are awakened during this phase, they usually say that they were dreaming.

Two of Hudson's graduate students, Mark Austin and Michael Holmes, put small groups of convergent and divergent students through the sleep laboratory at the University of Edinburgh. Divergers, they found, recalled their dreams when awakened; convergers either claimed they were not dreaming more often or else recalled that they had been dreaming but were unable to remember the contents of their dreams.

Paradoxically, though the convergers recalled less than the divergers, they showed physiological signs of dreaming more intensely. The convergers spent less time than the divergers in the REM phase of sleep, but within that phase, their bursts of eye movement were more profuse. Divergers' eye movements were, by contrast, diffuse.

What's more, Holmes found that the converger's weakness in dream recall was selective. He only found it if he woke the converger when his eyes were actually in movement. If awakenings were timed to occur in the brief intervals of calm between bursts of eye movement, the converger's recall was excellent, even better than the diverger's. Eye movements are associated with vivid, arbitrary images; the pauses between movements seem to be taken up with the sleeper's attempts to fit these arbitrary images into a sensible pattern. In other words, convergers are weak at recalling those arbitrary mental events that do not yet fit a rational, common-sense framework. From the viewpoint of Freudian thought, convergers appear to repress the nonrational, primary-process mode of thought, and recall the more logical secondary-process elaboration. These results from the sleep laboratory echo those from the mental tests.

SOFT AND WARM

The world is sorted into convergers and divergers, even by children. Hudson found this when he studied popular beliefs about various careers. To identify stereotypes, he used a test in which a person was asked to associate various professions in terms of pairs of adjectives: for instance, hard/soft, warm/cold, intelligent/stupid. Whether or not they know such people, almost everybody agrees that the scientist is hard and cold, whereas the poet is soft and warm. In addition to holding these stereotypes, most see the science graduate as working long hours and being faithful to his wife, while the arts graduate wears fashionable clothes, flirts with his secretary, and panics in emergencies.

These stereotypic beliefs reveal a sharp discontinuity between the values we attribute to each group. On these tests, students used the adjectives "valuable," "dependable," and "intelligent" together so often that they could be synonyms. Similarly with "warm," "exciting," and "imaginative." But in the students' minds these two clusters were quite separate. A warm, imaginative person excites us, but we value the intelligent, dependable person.

Stereotypes built around each of these clusters of values take shape at different ages. A common image of the scientist exists among British 13-year-olds; it begins to show up by age 11, although many 11-year-olds have had no formal science courses. All agree that the scientist is hard, cold, dull, intelligent, manly, dependable, and valuable. The image of the artist takes shape later. It is poorly etched in children's minds at 13, but within a few years it has become sharper than that of the scientist. By the time they are 17, students agree that the artist is soft, warm, exciting, imaginative, feminine, undependable, and lacking in value.

In preadolescence, the Swiss psychologist Jean Piaget tells us, children are sternly authoritarian in moral judgement. At the same time they are acquiring relatively primitive, basic intellectual skills. During this period the stereotype of the scientist develops, a figure that seems to personify the issues that preoccupy young schoolchildren.

Adolescence, on the other hand, is an age of emotional, personal discovery. Not until a person is well into adolescence and preoccupied with feelings of self-discovery does the stereotype of the artist come into being. In this model of intellectual development, the converger's frame of mind becomes set before adolescence, and the diverger becomes set later, during adolescence.

When Hudson studied British students he found that convergers, with their affinity for logic and control, tend to study the physical sciences, mathematics, and classics; divergers, with their link to emotions, are drawn by history, literature, and modern languages. Biology attracts convergers and divergers in roughly equal numbers. If the intellectual qualities of convergence and divergence are linked to personality, specialists in different academic fields should not only think differently, but also should lead different private lives.

With this in mind, Hudson and his wife gathered evidence from the 1969 edition of the British Who's Who. They also used the massive Carnegie Survey of American Academic Life. Restricting themselves to evidence about births, marriages, and social class, they found that there were indeed differences between the disciplines. Those in the humanities, for example, were less likely than scientists to marry and have children. No less than 41 percent of eminent British classicists had no children, either because they stayed single, or because they entered into childless marriages. Among physical scientists, only 15 percent were childless, while among biological scientists the rate dropped to eight percent.

In addition to these broad differences among disciplines, there are also differences within each discipline between creative and uncreative persons. But in terms of the stereotype, and in terms of statistics, most physicists are convergent. But a minority of the students who choose physics are divergers, and many of the convergers or all-rounders have considerable divergent abilities. Statistically, we must expect some of those in a convergent discipline like physics to have a talent for a more divergent style of thinking, should they feel inclined to exploit it.

The very act of entering a profession he sees as convergent — and therefore "safe" — may set the convergent person free to exercise the more divergent aspects of his personality. Our research suggests that shifts of this sort are likely because the amount of divergent ability an individual displays depends largely on the way he defines the situation, on his sense of what is allowable.

DIVORCE-PRONE SCIENTISTS

Successful biologists seem to be a case in point. They married more than their colleagues in other fields, but they also divorced more. Divorce, among members of the last generation, is an act that goes against the rules they learned as children. These biologists were between three and four times as likely to divorce as those in the humanities, and six times as likely to divorce as successful chemists or engineers.

Among these biologists, divorces were concentrated in a small group: those who had been educated at private schools, and who had been born in the first rather than the second decade of the century. These apparently odd facts made sense when we examined the names of these divorce-prone scientists. They were the ones who put the field of experimental biology on its feet.

Perhaps it is the free-ranging divergers who have the greatest impact on a field during its formative phase, when innovative concepts are at a premium. Participating in intellectual upheaval, in its turn, may make domestic upheaval more likely, leading more innovators to divorce. This evidence fits with the distinction between "normal" and "revolutionary" science made by Thomas Kuhn, the historian of science, in *The Structure of Scientific Revolutions*. It may be that convergers become famous through normal science, when research is ruled by an agreed-upon set of laws and assumptions, while divergers gain eminence in science's revolutionary phases, when the explanatory power of the established paradigm breaks down, and a new one must be found.

The converger controls impulse, preferring logic and order. The diverger acts on impulse and dips comfortably into fantasy. This difference parallels that between behavior dominated by the left and right halves of the brain. The left hemisphere generally is dominant during logical, linear thought, such as that required to solve a math problem. The right takes over during nonrational, nonlinear thought, such as composing music. While this line of thinking suggests that the converger operates primarily with his left hemisphere, the diverger with his right, psychologist Colin Martindale has found otherwise [see "What Makes Creative People Different," *Psychology Today*, July 1975].

It is not the way highly creative people use their right hemispheres that sets them apart, but their overall level of brain activity.

Martindale used the same test as Hudson did—original uses for ordinary objects—to identify highly creative people, and then compared them to medium-creative all-rounders and to uncreative convergers. The groups differed both in the midst of giving an imaginative answer and while relaxing.

RETREATING ARTIST

During relaxation, the diverger's brains produced fewer alpha waves than all-rounders or convergers, and they also showed higher levels of sweat, indicating that their brains were more active. What is more, both of the divergers' hemispheres were equally active. The divergers responded more intensely than others to their environment; they were more easily disturbed by noises; and they exaggerated sensations and the sizes of objects. Martindale's data bear out the stereotype of the sensitive artist who must retreat from the world in order to create.

Martindale also found telling differences between divergers and convergers during the act of creation. While thinking of original uses for a brick, divergers shifted to a lower level of arousal, while convergers at work on the same task showed increased brain activity. Divergers turned on alpha; convergers turned it off.

Creativity calls for letting the mind roam freely, exploring possibilities undreamed of during ordinary goal-oriented acts. This happens best when one is in a state of low arousal, for example, during the drowsy state between waking and falling asleep. Logical reasoning or goal-oriented behavior demands that one keep a tight rein on attention, and that requires a highly aroused brain.

Martindale found that divergers, when told to be original, immediately increased their production of alpha waves, indicating lowered arousal. All-rounders and convergers did not. The divergers, then, seem to pass freely between the dream world of imagination and fantasy, which Freud called primary-process thought and identified with the unconscious, and the orderly domain of rationality and reason — Freud's secondary-process thought. The converger rigorously patrols the border between these realms, staying firmly rooted in the rational. When primary process thought does break into the converger's awareness, it may do so with uncontrolled violence.

James Joyce, known for such stream-of-consciousness novels as Ulysses and Finnegan's Wake, once consulted analyst Carl Jung about Joyce's daughter, who had been diagnosed as schizophrenic. Since both he as a writer and his daughter while psychotic had free access to their unconscious, Joyce wondered what the difference was between them. Jung replied, "You dive, she falls."

Our ability to dive freely into primary-process thought influences many parts of our lives. Our ability to recall our dreams, the kind of marriages we have, our choice of careers, and how we contribute to our respective fields are all related to the way we maintain the boundary between rational and nonrational thought and how we manage impulse. Worthwhile, creative ideas emerge from the inner conflict between the realm of fantasy and the common sense world of fact.

QUESTIONS

1. Is your personality like that of the converger? Diverger? All-rounder? How did you get this way?

   _____
   _____
   _____

2. Does your job or career support the type of person you are? Discuss.

   _____
   _____
   _____

Following the Leader: How to Link Management Style to Subordinate Personalities

The successful manager has always led his or her subordinates, to a great extent, by examining and responding appropriately to their behaviors. This observation opens the possibility of developing a theory of "followership"—the other side of the leadership equation.

A followership theory would classify typical subordinate reactions to leaders into recognizable behavior patterns, just as there are identifiable leadership styles. This would help the leader develop appropriate behaviors of his own for interacting with subordinates. And, since we are all followers in some way, a followership theory can tell us more about ourselves.

THE ENHANCEMENT/PROTECTION CONFLICT

In managing others, the role of the leader is to convince followers that if they raise their incremental performances, they will receive some sort of identifiable reward, or increased security. Correspondingly, the basic dimensions of followership are the desire for job enhancement and recognition, and the desire to be protected from failure.

Both tendencies affect the follower's willingness to take risks. Unfortunately, they are difficult to measure because they are always in conflict; desire for enhancement increases one's willingness to take risks, and failure avoidance decreases it.

Enhancement of Self

The follower's desire for enhancement of self implies a wish to participate more in the organization's formal system of status and explicit rewards. Thus a follower would seek enhancement by assuming more responsibility and taking greater risk. Therefore, every follower has some

Source: Joesph A. Steger, George E. Manners, Jr., and Thomas W. Zimmerer. Reprinted, by permission of the publisher, from Management Review, *October 1982, copyright © 1982 American Management Association, New York. All rights reserved.*

desire to "solo"--to be a star. This, however, is tempered in varying degrees by desire for:

Protection of Self

Fear of failure—and desire to protect oneself from it—is one of the most pervasive explanatory motives in organizational behavior literature. (Moreover, individuals frequently fear social consequences of failure as much as they fear failure itself.)

Fear of failure, organizational researchers tell us, manifests itself in such worker tendencies as apathy, defensiveness, and aggression. Regardless of a follower's desire for enhancement, the protection-from-failure motive can be so strong as to cancel the enhancement motive altogether. When this happens, it is natural for the leader to ask: Who is responsible? The organization, via its track record in reacting to employees' failures? Or the leader may question whether he, himself, is at fault. Or is the protection-from-failure motive innate to the follower and therefore uncontrollable?

FOLLOWERSHIP DYNAMICS

We must next examine how the relative strengths of these two variables mold systematic *behaviors* of followers. Willingness to take risks, after all, is only one tendency; the actual nature of followership, and its implications for the leader, is far more dynamic.

Figure 1 classifies individual followership behaviors into nine categories (each will be examined below), characterized by low, medium, and high levels of enhancement desire and failure avoidance. (These behaviors may also be seen as representative of entire occupational roles or entire organizations.) They may be learned behaviors—acquired by followers prior to joining an organization—and so ingrained that the organization may not modify them but only deal with their implications. Or the behaviors may have been acquired since joining the organization (as a function of the system of rewards and punishments) and/or maturation. (Motives for enhancement and protection must be somewhat correlated with age, social history, and so on, regardless of leaders' actions.)

What implications do these categories have for leadership behavior? And, indeed, what implications do they have for followers, in understanding their impact on leaders and other members of the organization? In analyzing each followership style, emphasis will be placed on the manager's role and methods used to influence follower's behavior. Most followers can be effectively led if the leader is aware of what the followers want and what they fear.

The Game Player

One might assume that intense desire for enhancement in terms of formal status symbols and rewards and great desire for protection from

FIGURE 1

Followership Types Derived from the Enhancement/Failure Avoidance Conflict

Protection of Self and/or Extended Self*

	High	Medium	Low
Enhancement of Self and/or Extended Self — High	**The Game Player** Substitutes status for performance. Focuses on political cues. Defensive. Uses power relations to resist change.	**The Achiever** Productive, persistent goal setter. Needs feedback. Definite movement for change.	**The Kamikaze** High energy level. Productive. Organization change stressed. Occasional folly. Could be costly for the organization.
Medium	**The Bureaucrat** Productive. Enjoys status symbols but recognizes personal limits. Very low risk. Maintains status quo.	**The Super Follower** Productive. Average achiever. Some movement for change. The ultimate follower.	**The Artist** Productive. Positive attitude towards change. Must watch risk levels. Many times works for self-satisfaction but enjoys recognition.
Low	**The Apathetic** Nonproductive. Defensive. Withdrawn. Apathy actually represents fear.	**The Donkey** Low level of productivity. Has no interest in formal system of status and rewards. No movement unless pushed.	**The Deviant** Impossible to motivate. Could-not-care-less attitude. High turnover rate. Can be destructive.

*Extended self would apply primarily to one's family but, under some conditions, might also apply to one's work group.

---

failure would be incompatible. However, such is not always the case: The Game Player simply does not recognize the dissonance. This individual wants all the trappings of status and power but none of the risks. The Game Player actually substitutes, intellectually, symbols of performance for performance per se.

Game Players are sensitive to organizational politics and, if they acquire staying power, can be valuable to the leader. However, this individual is invariably defensive and resistant to change. This can be dangerous since the Game Player uses power and its symbols, often effectively, to marshal support for resistance, or to gain an optimal position in a conflict.

The weaker the leader, the more successful the Game Player. The good manager may not like the Game Player, but can always use him by effective manipulation of status symbols. A poor manager does not recognize that the game is being played, and cannot intellectually separate actual performance from the Game Player's symbols of performance.

Game Players avoid risk by predicting the "right side" of an issue based upon who supports it. Insecure managers—who are frequently Game Players themselves—find the Game Player to be a comfortable couch. These followers comprise the entourage that often surrounds the executive, and they derive much of their power from association with higher-level executives. They will use symbols of power to influence others to perform tasks they consider risky, then carry the successfully completed task forward under the illusion of being the producer.

The Game Player is easy to identify because of his desire for status. Photos with key executives, a wall full of awards and certificates, and the like create the continuing illusion of power and influence. The Game Player usually has formal education and degrees to aid his credibility.

Managers are better off without the Game Player. If Game Players are part of their followership, they are easily managed—but never loyal.

The Achiever

The individual who has a high desire for enhancement and is reasonably ready to accept the possibility of failure is the classic Achiever. He loves visible symbols of success and takes risks to get them, but he avoids really big risks. The Achiever is productive, is a goal setter, and desires a great deal of performance feedback.

To many managers, however, the Achiever is also annoying. He is too goal-oriented in an ambiguous world, too concerned with the social relativity of symbols of success, and constantly needs feedback. Yet, the Achiever is receptive to, and shows movement toward, organizational change.

The Achiever typically wishes to develop a close personal relationship between himself, the job, and his supervisor. The leader, in the mind of the Achiever, needs to know how to achieve results, or there is a quick loss of respect. This follower requires that the leader demonstrate technical knowledge *and* ability to deliver rewards.

In essence, managing the Achiever requires more excellence than with any other type of follower. An Achiever will not follow a poor manager for very long. The Achiever requires a manager who plans ahead, and is decisive and dynamic. Together they plan for new mountains to climb, execute the plan, and reap the rewards.

The Kamikaze

For this individual, fun, fame, and fortune are the goals — never mind the risks. In situations requiring significant organizational change, the Kamikaze can be a leader's delight. On the other hand, Kamikazes may get themselves, the leader, and the organization into serious trouble. They are typically immature, have little concept of extended self, have not become jaded enough to fear failure, and have tremendous need for symbols of success. Although they alienate those with a greater desire for protection, they are usually productive.

Although often innovative, the Kamikaze generally is not an effective problem solver. The Kamikaze sees a problem, jumps to the first conclusion, and charges forward. His energy and enthusiasm often carry the day. The Kamikaze can quickly create resentment among those he comes in contact with, because he employs politically insensitive methods to accomplish results. Thus, the Kamikaze's supervisor should expect to spend a great deal of time repairing the damage this individual creates.

A manager may effectively appoint a Kamikaze to complete some tasks that create flux in the organization. If the manager has a straightforward task that needs to be accomplished quickly and for which he can offer a visible reward, the Kamikaze is the person to assign.

The Kamikaze is easily managed at the start of a task; however, he is hard to control once underway. Thus, the manager should have some *a priori* plan for removing the Kamikaze from the task.

The Bureaucrat

Typically found in the administrative ranks, the Bureaucrat is the classic "organization man" (or woman). As a category of followership, however, one must remember that this term originated with the work of Max Weber *(The Theory of Social and Economic Organization)*, in which bureaucracy was viewed as an ideal form of organization. Thus the Bureaucrat is generally productive, because he enjoys status symbols and the trappings of power — yet understands his role's limitations.

On the other hand, this term has evolved to imply organizational members preoccupied with preserving the current structure. The Bureaucrat is a very low risk taker and, when change is necessary, can become indecisive and procrastinate since failure avoidance is so dominant.

In a slow-growth organization, Bureaucrats are often viewed by their superiors as excellent followers. Their work rate is constant, their behavior predictable. Leaders often find that followers who are predictable, dependable, and moderately productive are a joy to manage. Consequently, leaders create many of them.

But when external or internal threat creates a need for change, these managers offer little. If the leader can offer both a solution and a guarantee of protection, the Bureaucrat will then follow — but only then. These followers are administrators in the very sense of the word: They maintain administrative and bureaucratic systems; cannot tolerate ambiguity;

and constantly strive to maintain known environments within which to work.

Bureaucrats are apparently easy to manage, yet their own rigidity can become a severe problem for their leader. While acknowledging change, they do so only superficially and often frustrate the content or function of change.

The Super Follower

This is the ultimate form of followership. This individual desires rewards, although not as much as the Achiever. The Super Follower assumes a position of moderate risk. Thus he is usually quite productive to the organization. The history of great performances rarely includes organizations without members having a tremendous desire for personal enhancement — but that does not say that these organizations did not have plenty of Super Followers.

If there is a followership style that can maintain a high productivity level while remaining self-motivated to change, it is the Super Follower. He can be molded by the leader, yet can act independently in adapting to new situations — while retaining a positive commitment to the organization. He follows, yet does what is best for the organization, balancing personal gain against organizational gain.

Super Followers are easily managed because they are mature and open, and they have a sense of propriety not found in the Kamikaze or the Game Player. They are true assets and need to be rewarded, both short- and long-term.

The Artist

The Artist bases his decision of what work to pursue on personal and/or professional pleasure or achievement. Such behavior may involve a high level of risk in the eyes of others in the organization (and they may be right). Thus, Artists can be productive, although the leader must allocate time to monitor work direction and risk levels. In addition, the leader must be aware that Artists are also exhibitionists — which implies need for formal recognition by the organization.

The key to motivating an Artist is to find the proper work for him to do. When the leader has a chance to work with the Artist in identifying that "one best task," productivity from the Artist can be exceptional. Yet, the Artist works for the delight of the creation *per se*. He revels in the system or products of his work, not their outputs or efficiencies. This, then, requires the leader's practical hand and guidance.

The Artist poses another problem for the manager: Since he never sees his work as finished, he revises and revises. In the demanding work world, this can be a manager's nightmare.

The Artist is difficult to manage from the manager's plan-execute-results point of view. Artists make significant contributions, but their leaders require an electric management style.

The Apathetic

Some desire to participate in the formal system of rewards is necessary for followers' productivity. When the follower has no such desire, coupled with intense desire for protection from failure, he will exhibit insidious behavior — apathy.

Defensiveness, withdrawal, and so on accompany apathy. However, the history of the organization's (or leader's) distribution of rewards, as well as its reaction to failure, may to a certain degree justify this apathy. This may be particularly true when the individual's only preceived source of "protection" is another organization which may be in conflict with the formal organization (such as a union).

To break through the barriers the Apathetic employee constructs, the leader must redesign structural elements of the job that may have served as the source of apathy. Forced assumption of responsibility, training, and job change are some approaches.

This work redesign *must* be attempted, because the Apathetic is an organizational cancer. Not only does this follower not produce, but he hides in the woodwork of the system. Behind the scenes, he fights any changes which he feels may result in his being exposed. This is contagious: Other workers learn that you can beat the system even if you cannot be successful within it. Accountability and its associated visibility are the Apathetic's nemesis.

The Apathetic is difficult if not impossible to lead; the best remedy may be termination.

The Donkey

What distinguishes the Donkey from the Apathetic is the amount of power the organization (or leader) can exert over the individual. The Donkey will respond to change essentially because he has to, but rarely will the response be based on expectation of formal rewards. Thus, the Donkey is characterized by very little movement, unless he is pushed, and low productivity. Again, however, one must assess the organization's effect on these behavior patterns. Certainly, when McGregor defined Theory X (authoritarian management), he was thinking of leaders who *assumed* that their followers were Donkeys.

If you inherit a staff of Donkeys, you will be quite tired at the end of the day. Productivity is achieved by a continuous string of threats and the exercise of power. The Donkey does not want what you have to offer and, if he does, he does not expect to get it, given his incremental effort. Establishing credibility takes time (and control over rewards).

The manager's problem is that the Donkey thinks effort is performance. Therein lies a related problem: Donkeys expect rewards for effort regardless of outcome.

The Deviant

Since he has no desire to participate in the formal reward system, and is unafraid of the visibility of failure within the organization, the Deviant responds against the organization. This individual could not care less what the leader thinks, and is usually a high-turnover category of employee.

. . . Leaders should not believe that their job is one of a social worker. Time spent on changing this follower is not invested in enhancing of high-performing followers. If the manager finds he has Deviant followers, he had best look to the selection process that is providing them and change entry routes into the organization.

ORGANIZATIONAL PATTERNS

Since these categories of followership are so observable in organizations, they raise two important questions for leaders. First, what organizational/leadership behaviors create (or reinforce) followership categories? Second, how does an individual manager create motivation and change when dealing with specific types of followership?

How closely an organization ties its system of status symbols and rewards to incremental performance and the assumption of responsibility is obviously an important determinant of followership categories and their intensity. Concomitantly, how an organization responds to individual failure serves as a catalyst to developing various types of followers.

Let us deal first with the system of status symbols and rewards and its equitability in the organization. As a predictor of emerging followership categories, a careful distinction must be drawn between symbols and rewards associated with position (usually hierarchical level) and rewards associated with incremental performance within position. The "climate" created by variations in these two reward systems leads to certain followership types. This is outlined in Figure 2. Thus, reward distribution delineates the categories of followership illustrated in the first row of Figure 1—Game Player, Achiever, and Kamikaze.

Thus, to the extent that the reward system aids high-enhancement followers, the organizational pattern of reaction to failure and its tolerance of self-expression serve to separate medium- and low-enhancement followers. This is illustrated in Figure 3.

The last three categories of followership—Apathetic, Donkey, Deviant—can be placed in an organizational context by understanding the distribution of power. Since low-enhancement followers are predicted by (1) little relationship among performance and rewards, (2) high negative reactions to failure (by the organization), and (3) little tolerance for self-expression (by the organization), the amount of power that can be exercised by the organization becomes extremely important.

This is outlined in Figure 4. Our observation is that when there is high countervailing power, typically a union, Apathetics abound—often regardless of the extent of the formal organization's power. On the other hand, when countervailing power is low, the amount of power that can be exerted by the organization, or the leader, becomes the predictor of the emergence of the Donkey or Deviant.

FIGURE 2

Followership Types Emerging with Reward Distribution

	Rewards for incremental performance within position	
	Not High	High
Rewards for position: High	Game Player	Achiever
Rewards for position: Not high	?	Kamikaze

FIGURE 3

Followership Types Emerging with Failure Reactions and Tolerance of Self-Expression

	Tolerance of expression	
	High	Not High
Negative reactions to failure: High	Bureaucrat	?
Negative reactions to failure: Not High	Artist	Super Follower

CREATING MOTIVATION FOR CHANGE

The organization's nature and emergence of followership categories, although based on direct observation, is still tentative. Many other developmental factors external to the organization — social history, marital status (the extended self can be very important), predisposition to achievement motivation — may also predict emergence of follower stereotypes. Thus, no matter how these behaviors emerge, the leader's task is to deal with them as they exist. Introducing change is a critical motivational task facing the leader, relative to many follower categories.

FIGURE 4

Followership Types Emerging with Power Distribution

		Organizational power	
		High	Low
Countervailing power	High	Apathetic	Apathetic
	Low	Donkey	Deviant

When organizational change is made imperative by either internal or external events, each followership category, as previously discussed, is predisposed to support or resist a new set of behaviors. By identifying the follower's basic tendencies, the leader can more effectively develop a workable change strategy — either for individual or collective followers. We again stress that a manager is not a social worker; the situation may demand change, and the leader must be instrumental in its introduction and implementation.

Conceptually, there are three basic approaches to organizational change: (1) the direct-power approach, (2) the supportive, developmental approach, and (3) the devious, manipulative approach. In fact, all three approaches can be appropriate depending upon the severity of the change and the targeted followership category.

Figure 5 outlines the basic change approaches that we believe to be the best strategies for each followership category. Since the Super Follower, the Achiever, the Kamikaze, and the Artist are all willing to take risks and desire enhancement, a supportive and developmental strategy is preferred. Of course the nature of this support, as well as the extent of the leader's direct participation, must vary depending on the category. The Bureaucrat should also receive support, clarity, and development, although the leader should somewhat conceal the fact that change is imminent.

The greater the extent of self-protection, the greater the necessity for a manipulative change strategy — particularly where the Game Player is concerned. Also, the less the desire for enhancement, the greater the necessity for a direct power approach. When the follower does not want to participate in the formal reward system (or does not expect to), the leader usually has no other choice than direct power. When a countervailing power (presence of a union) is significant, a healthy dose of deviousness is usually also required.

FIGURE 5

Basic Change Approaches to Follower Categories

Protection of self or extended self

	High	Medium	Low
High	Game Player	Achiever	Kamikaze
Medium	Bureaucrat	Super Follower	Artist
Low	Apathetic	Donkey	Deviant

Enhancement of self or extended self

Direct power
Supportive and developmental
Devious and manipulative

Speaking specifically rather than conceptually, we have observed various techniques of introducing change that managers effectively use. These are listed in Figure 6. Of course, the three basic change approaches — direct power, support, manipulation — can be keyed to specific follower types as in Figure 5, thus providing a comprehensive strategy to introducing change among various follower categories.

We should stress that the way change is introduced is more crucial to success than actual implementation. Introductory techniques are what really address resistance, even among those willing to take risks.

RELATIONS AMONG FOLLOWER GROUPS

We are often asked: If leaders segment followers, and vary change strategies depending upon follower categories, will this not create dissatisfaction among some follower groups? The answer is yes — with two important caveats. First, previous success is the ultimate predictor of group satisfaction. Second, managing to motivate is substantively different than managing to minimize dissatisfaction. The former approach can work; the latter never will.

FIGURE 6

Examples of Specific Change Introduction Techniques

Change introduction technique	Direct power	Support	Manipulation
Dictate	✓		
Discussion/salesmanship	✓	✓	
Training	✓	✓	✓
Participation		✓	
Rumor			✓
Modeling			
Coworkers		✓	✓
Competition			✓
Create system failure	✓		✓
Surveys		✓	✓
Consultants	✓		✓
Manuals	✓		✓

Also, interactions take place among followers simultaneously with manager's actions. These second-order interactions, so to speak, are another set of complications for the manager to understand. These interactions are determined by the make-up of the group (number of different type of followers) and can enhance or detract from the manager's actions. Managers must study their followerships' make-up; develop strategies to motivate based on different followership types; and use followers' actions directed at each other to enhance their own strategy.

IMPLICATIONS OF FOLLOWERSHIP

Serious questions emerge throughout the study of followership that reflect on the leader: Can a manager adapt to a diversity of followers? Can management training provide the manager with these skills? Can managers learn new leadership approaches when moving to new levels and therefore new followerships?

Questions relating to organizational systems make the followership examination even more complex, such as: Does company policy allow managers flexibility in followership? Is the compensation system tied to performance so a manager may use it to manage?

Lastly, the study of followership leads to serious questions about selection and turnover. Those chosen today are not necessarily the right people for the organization tomorrow. Security and job longevity are more critical than ever. The need for this followership study reveals that companies often pay scant attention to the future when hiring and very little attention to strategic human resources planning and development.

Some commonly held cultural beliefs and organizational policies remove the organization's ability to optimize leader-followership relations. These policies, such as tenure in a university, remove one complete dimension—job security—of the motivational framework both leader and follower should work within. Moderate job security is one thing; complete employment guarantees regardless of contribution is another.

The followership framework outlined above requires a manager who understands his subordinates, works in a milieu that provides for diversity of management actions, and is allowed to reward his followers to enhance their motivation. Hopefully, more study of the manager-followership interface will lead to better organizational structure without undue concern for existing power relations. All power is a compromise, and the study of followership is aimed at optimizing this compromise so that all can win.

QUESTIONS

1. Use this article to evaluate your own followership style. Consider the degree of self-protective and self-enhancing behavior you exhibit.

2. Describe the leadership behaviors that bring out the best in your own morale and job performance.

3. Critique a current leader on the basis of versatility in dealing with different types of subordinates. Use examples.

CASES

Grandview Morning Press 252

The Dashman Company 254

The Paragon Printing and Lithography Company 257

A Talk with Kirkeby's Son 260

The Vice-President 263

The Reluctant Backhoe Operator 266

The Sales Meeting 268

The Puzzle Block Work Teams 271

Creativity Requires the Right Atmosphere 276

Emery Air Freight 280

Grandview Morning Press

The *Grandview Morning Press* is published seven days a week in the city of Grandview, an area that undergoes a huge increase in population every summer due to its fine scenery and excellent climate. Normally the paper consists of a single section with occasional advertising supplements. However, in the summer, a second, "Summer Living," section is added, and the number and frequency of advertising inserts increases drastically in an effort to profit as much as possible from the summer trade.

The insertion of the advertising supplements and the collating of the two sections is done by hand. The publishers of the *Morning Press* feel it would be too costly to purchase the necessary machinery when most of the time it would be used only during the summer months. Besides, they feel that hiring a number of vacationing students is a step toward better community relations. Each summer they hire approximately a dozen college students to work in the printing press building each night. The students usually put in between 7 and 14 hours. Because some editions have more advertising "stuffers" than others, the students do not know until they report for work whether that evening's work will be long or short. All time over 8 hours is considered overtime and is paid at time and a half. The normal hourly rate is $4.35.

The summer workers have a code among themselves that no matter what the work load, they will decide exactly how long to work each night. For example, if there seems to be an 8-hour load, the stuffing crew will purposely slow down in order to take 9 hours and thereby get paid overtime. On those occasions when the crew wants to finish early and get to the local disco before the 4 A.M. closing time, an estimated 7- or 8-hour job will be completed in about 6 hours. Newcomers to the crew are made to conform to the group's production norms through verbal abuse for noncompliance.

A member of the stuffing crew for the past two summers, Barbara Warren has supported this code. This summer, however, Warren was asked by the pressroom chief to supervise the work of the stuffing crew. She welcomed the extra 75¢ an hour she would be making and viewed with pride the thought of being able to apply her business school theories to her new "management-level" position.

After the first few nights, she noticed the code was working as it had for untold summers past. But this year she viewed its effects from the "other

Source: Peter L. Pfister, under the direction of James A. F. Stoner, in James A. F. Stoner and Charles Wankel, Management, *3d ed., copyright © 1986, p. 51. Reprinted by permission of Prentice-Hall, Englewood Cliffs, New Jersey.*

side." She realized that the slowdown lowered the profits of the paper by raising the labor costs. The drivers were delayed in making their deliveries. On occasion even the janitors had to sit about idle, waiting for the stuffing crew to finish their work.

Warren is puzzled as to what her proper course of action should be. Should she lower the boom and stop the wasteful practice, or should she let it continue? Neither alternative would be satisfactory to everyone concerned.

QUESTIONS

[Handwritten note in margin: Change OT to 40 hours a week]

1. Does Warren have more than the two choices she is considering? Discuss.
   - *[Handwritten:] Incentive: piecework*
   - *[Handwritten:] Educate ee to organize goals*
   - *[Handwritten:] selection criteria for next year*
   - *[Handwritten:] try to develop teamwork*
   - *[Handwritten:] ★ ask for their input to reset ground rules*

2. Why does the Morning Press management permit the "production" code to operate?
   - *[Handwritten:] Bottom line profit — minimal financial impact*
   - *[Handwritten:] good P.R.*

3. How would you handle this problem?
   - *[Handwritten:] Scholarship incentives*
   - *[Handwritten:] Bonus plan*

The Dashman Company

The Dashman Company was a large concern making many types of equipment for the armed forces of the United States. It had over 20 plants, located in the central part of the country, whose purchasing procedures had never been completely coordinated. In fact, the head office of the company had encouraged each of the plant managers to operate with their staffs as independent units in most matters. . . . When it began to appear that the company would face increasing difficulty in securing certain essential raw materials, Mr. Manson, the company's president, appointed an experienced purchasing executive, Mr. Post, as vice-president in charge of purchasing, a position especially created for him. Mr. Manson gave Mr. Post wide latitude in organizing his job, and he assigned Mr. Larson as Mr. Post's assistant. Mr. Larson had served the company in a variety of capacities for many years, and knew most of the plant executives personally. Mr. Post's appointment was announced through the formal channels usual in the company, including a notice in the house organ published by the company.

One of Mr. Post's first decisions was to begin immediately to centralize the company's purchasing procedures. As a first step, he decided that he would require each of the executives who handled purchasing in the individual plants to clear with the head office all purchase contracts that they made in excess of $10,000. He felt that if the head office was to do any coordinating in a way that would be helpful to each plant and to the company as a whole, he must be notified that the contracts were being prepared at least a week before they were to be signed. He talked his proposal over with Mr. Manson, who presented it to his board of directors. They approved the plan.

Although the company made purchases throughout the year, the beginning of its peak buying season was only three weeks away at the time this new plan was adopted. Mr. Post prepared the following letter to send to the 20 purchasing executives of the company:

Source: Copyright © 1947 by the President and Fellows of Harvard College. This case was prepared by George F. F. Lombard, Richard S. Meriam, Franklin E. Folts, and Edmund P. Learned as the basis for class discussion rather than to illustrate either effective or ineffective handling of an administrative situation. Reprinted by permission of the Harvard Business School.

Dear _____ :

The board of directors of our company has recently authorized a change in our purchasing procedures. Hereafter, each of the purchasing executives in the several plants of the company will notify the vice-president in charge of purchasing of all contracts in excess of $10,000 that they are negotiating at least a week in advance of the date on which they are to be signed.

I am sure that you will understand that this step is necessary to coordinate the purchasing requirements of the company in these times when we are facing increasing difficulty in securing essential supplies. This procedure should give us in the central office the information we need to see that each plant secures the optimum supply of materials. In this way the interests of each plant and of the company as a whole will be best served.

Yours very truly,

Mr. Post showed the letter to Mr. Larson and invited his comments. Mr. Larson thought the letter an excellent one, but suggested that, since Mr. Post had not met more than a few of the purchasing executives, he might like to visit all of them and take the matter up with each of them personally. Mr. Post dismissed the idea at once because, as he said, he had so many things to do at the head office that he could not get away for a trip. Consequently he had the letters sent out over his signature.

During the following two weeks replies came in from all except a few plants. Although a few executives wrote at greater length, the following reply was typical:

Dear Mr. Post:

Your recent communication in regard to notifying the head office a week in advance of our intention to sign contracts has been received. This suggestion seems a most practical one. We want to assure you that you can count on our cooperation.

Yours very truly,

During the next six weeks the head office received no notices from any plant that contracts were being negotiated. Executives in other departments who made frequent trips to the plants reported that the plants were busy, and the usual routines for that time of year were being followed.

QUESTIONS

1. How would you evaluate the control process that Mr. Post established?

   - New position should be communicated — responsibility
   - more time
   - poor control process

2. What would you have done if you were Mr. Post?

   met w̄ different ex̄ecs & explained changes — reasons & how; evaluate changes

3. What should Mr. Post do now?

   go back to find out what was wrong w̄ new process; use Larson
   restate goals
   meet w̄ ex̄ecs to establish goals & objectives
   admit he made a mistake

The Paragon Printing and Lithography Company

The Paragon Printing and Lithography Company is one of the largest printing and lithography firms in the southwestern United States, employing more than 180 persons and divided into two major divisions—Letterpress and Lithography. The company was formed in 1929 as an office supply firm, and gradually diversified its operations to include printing and lithography on a relatively small scale.

At the onset of World War II, the Paragon Company was called upon by the United States Government to print and publish military manuals. This increased activity resulted in the need for a tremendous expansion program. The office supply division was dissolved, and all subsequent activity was carried on in the printing and lithography trade.

In 1978, the major customer of the Paragon Printing and Lithography Company was still the United States Government, a situation that necessitated equipment capable of turning out tremendous quantities of printed matter, with the emphasis on *quantity* rather than quality.

The Camera and Platemaking Departments were, in effect, two separate departments under the supervision of Peter Vacher. In these departments were two people operating the two process cameras, six preparing the negatives, and four making plates for the lithographic presses. All of the personnel, including the supervisor, were members of the union.

Joe Matino, a journeyman lithographer in the Platemaking Department, had been with the company for seventeen years. Matino was classed as an "old-timer" by almost everyone in the plant, and he had seniority over all the personnel in his department. However, he was not classified as foreman of the Platemaking Department, which was regarded as a part of the Camera Department. The supervisor of both departments was Peter Vacher.

Peter Vacher was regarded by most of the men in his department as being "quite a capable man." However, the general belief among the people in the two departments was that Vacher never seemed very happy.

Source: Pp. 68–71 *from* The Human Side of Organizations, *2d ed. by Stan Kossen. Copyright © 1978 by Stanley Kossen. Reprinted by permission of Harper & Row, Publishers, Inc.*

On numerous occasions Vacher had complained vehemently about how poorly organized the management was. On one occasion he had said to Nat Stossen, an apprentice who worked the swing shift in the Platemaking Department and attended day classes at a nearby university, "As supervisor, I get it from both sides. I'm not supposed to get too friendly with the workers, but yet the management doesn't really accept me as part of management either. Those . . . won't even supply me with any cost information. The only way I can get it is to scrounge it out of Bill Johnson, the Purchasing Agent. How in . . . do they expect me to be cost-conscious if I don't even know anything about costs! Actually, Nat, management won't confide in any supervisor who is in the union!"

A month later, Betty Hanson, who was one of the two production managers, telephoned Vacher and asked him to come up to her office right away.

HANSON: Hi, Pete! Have a chair, will you?
VACHER: Thanks, Mrs. Hanson. What can I do for you?
HANSON: Well, at a recent meeting the Estimator revealed that he was having one . . . of a time trying to determine accurately just how much he should charge for labor to each job, since he doesn't have any labor time standards to go by. What I want you to do, Pete, is to go back to your departments and establish some time standards for the various operations in the Platemaking and Camera Departments. For example, I want you to determine how long it takes for a platemaker to make each of the various sizes of plates that are made in the department. Then submit a report back to me by tomorrow morning at 9:00 A.M.
VACHER: All right, Mrs. Hanson, I'll see what I can do.

Vacher went back to his departments to speak to Matino (the older platemaker).

VACHER: Joe, they're on our backs again. Now they want to know how long it takes for you guys to make plates. Will you please determine some sort of standard time for making each of the four different sizes and types of plates? I've got to have this info before 9:00 A.M. tomorrow so I can give it to the "efficiency expert."
MATINO: What in . . . is the matter with those crazy people upstairs? What do they think we are trying to do — put something over on 'em? Okay, I'll get it for you right away.

About half an hour later, Matino placed the report on Vacher's desk. When the swing shift reported to work the same afternoon, Matino complained to Hank Willows, the night shift journeyman platemaker, about his having established the new time standards.

MATINO: For some reason, Pete asked me to establish time standards for the platemaking in this department. I wrote down the new standard on this piece of paper for you, and be sure you don't go *under* it. Those

characters upstairs are trying to check up on us, and if we put out too much work, we'll work ourselves plumb out of work. So what I did was set a standard that we can do real easy. So don't work too . . . fast or you'll foul things up. Tell the 'professor,' your apprentice, about this.
WILLOWS: Sure will, Joe. I've seen this happen before in other shops. If you set the standard too high, they'll always expect you to make it, and then they'll give you . . . if you don't. Don't worry about a thing!

Later that evening, Willows told Nat Stossen, his apprentice, to slow down, that a standard had been set, and that he was not to attempt to "work us out of work." Stossen accepted the order reluctantly.

The regular hours of the swing shift were from 4:00 P.M. until 12:00 midnight. At about 10:00 P.M., the night after the standards had been established, production in the platemaking department halted.

WILLOWS: Well, professor, let's go home. We've done all we have to do, and if we do any more we'll go over the standard.
STOSSEN: Go home! It's only ten o'clock. We shouldn't go home yet.
WILLOWS: Don't worry, Nat, there aren't no supervisors on the swing shift, so who's gonna know?
STOSSEN: If you don't mind, I think I'll stick around a while longer. I don't want to jeopardize my job. I've got two more years of college to do, and I don't know of any other job where I could make this kind of money and work hours that will enable me to finish school.
WILLOWS: Heck, there are plenty of jobs where this one came from. Okay, suit yourself. But *don't* make any plates!

Every night thereafter Stossen took a textbook to work with him and studied from approximately 10:00 P.M. until 12 midnight.

QUESTIONS

1. Evaluate the leadership techniques of Peter Vacher. Should he have established the time standards himself?

2. What is your evaluation of Nat Stossen? Was it wrong for him to study on the job and be paid for those hours?

A Talk with Kirkeby's Son

"Did you want to see me?" Brad Kirkeby poked his head into the open doorway of his boss's office.

"Sure did, Brad. Come on in. I'll be finished with these overtime authorizations in a minute." Anthony Carboni continued initialing time cards while Kirkeby came in and sat down. Putting the cards to one side of his desk, Carboni looked up and smiled.

"Well, Brad, how's it going?"

"Boring as . . . !"

Carboni retained his composure. He cared little for the disrespectfulness of so many young people and their lack of tact. But Carboni had two reasons for restraint in this case. First, Brad Kirkeby was recently out of college and on an 18-month company rotational training program. He would be in Carboni's section for only another 45 days. Second, Brad was the son of Lawrence Kirkeby, one of Lockport Aircraft's most capable designers.

"I'm sorry to hear that," replied Carboni. "What seems to be the problem?"

"I'm going out of my mind with blueprint check." Kirkeby's response was emphatic but not hostile.

"Well," said Carboni, "someone has to check blueprints."

"But why me?" replied Kirkeby. "Can't a draftsman or a clerk do it?"

"Oh, I suppose he could," said Carboni, "but this is the way we've always developed potential structure designers . . . by having them learn all phases of the business from the bottom up."

"No disrespect intended, Mr. Carboni, but that argument escapes me. It's like saying that if you want to be an actor, you have to have experience as a stagehand. I joined Lockport Aircraft to design airplanes, not to check blueprints."

"And so you will, Brad . . . eventually."

Kirkeby laughed. "Eventually . . . in time, Brad . . . wait your turn, Brad. In the long run it will all work out. Mr. Carboni, do you know what Lord Keyes, the famous British economist, said about the long run?"

"No," replied Carboni, growing less patient each moment.

"Lord Keyes said, 'In the long run we'll all be dead!' "

Source: Robert D. Joyce, Encounters in Organizational Behavior, *copyright © 1972, Pergamon Press. Reprinted with permission.*

"Meaning?"

"Meaning that I don't want to die or retire before I'm given a meaningful job to do."

Carboni lit a cigar and puffed several times while looking directly at Kirkeby.

"I'm trying to understand you, Brad," he replied at last. "But you are simply going to have to adjust to the fact that you are out of college and in the real world now. It takes years of experience before you assume major structural design responsibility."

"That's because what they call experience in the Lockport Aircraft training program is merely a succession of routine tasks that could be done as well by a moron. Experience is learning and I'm not learning anything!"

"Look, Brad. I know you get all those aeronautical design theory courses in college and you expect to design planes your first week out of college. Face it, there's a certain amount of routine work in any job. Every day can't be a learning experience like it was in college."

"I don't see why not," replied Kirkeby. "If I was hired to eventually design planes, shouldn't I be working next to designers instead of piddling around with trivia?"

"The work in this section is hardly trivia!" Carboni was angry now but forced himself to keep from shouting. "But the work in this section is not the issue. You want to design airplanes like your father . . . right?"

"Right."

"Well," said Carboni, "your father has been with Lockport Aircraft for 25 years . . . eight years longer than I have. He started at the bottom and worked himself up step by step until, now, he's one of the most respected designers in the industry."

"My father is living proof of how ridiculous the system is. He had models at home when I was a boy . . . models he built in his spare time of wing and fuselage structures for as yet undreamed-of Mach 1 and Mach 1.5 power plants."

"Lawrence Kirkeby was always considered to be a very talented person," replied Carboni calmly.

Brad Kirkeby continued, "He was way ahead of his time. And what did this company have him doing most of those years? Did they use his creative talents to design planes, or on research to advance the state of the art? No. That would have been too obvious. They made him waste nearly 20 potentially creative years on trivial assignments before he became a designer with the authority to control technical considerations."

"How naive can you be, Brad Kirkeby? Do you really believe that your father alone came upon this advanced design information and was frustrated for years by a repressive and unresponsive management?" Carboni was angry now and let it show as he continued.

"Sure your father was talented. That's how he got to be chief designer at Lockport Aircraft. But he was and is still a mortal like the rest of us. Lawrence Kirkeby made his share of mistakes along the line. It was only after years of detailing and understudy with our top designers that his own ideas began to evolve and his real talents began to show. That's when he was moved to a responsible design position."

Brad Kirkeby started to reply, but Carboni cut him off.

"That's the trouble with you kids nowadays. You want everything in life without having to pay the price for it. You tell me you're bored with your job and ought to be designing planes instead. For your information, there are at least 30 bright young men currently in the company who have already passed this apprenticeship that you consider so useless and are now on detailing and limited design activity. Do you suggest I pass them up and promote you to the head of the class, simply because you're bored with your present assignment?"

"Of course not, but . . . " Brad Kirkeby made an attempt to intervene.

"You're . . . right I won't," shouted Carboni, answering his own question. "You've been in my section two months now and have turned in only mediocre work at best. You probably can justify that to yourself on the grounds that the work doesn't turn you on. Well, let me tell you something, Brad Kirkeby, talent is one hell of a lot more than just saying you have it. Talent is proving it in the work you do *now* . . . not the work you say you'll do next year or the year after! For all of your big talk about how great you are and how dull the work is, you have yet to prove to me you're anything but a phony!"

QUESTIONS

[Handwritten notes: BRAD — maybe he doesn't know why he's there — poor performance + attitude]

1. To what extent do you agree with the basic position(s) taken by Kirkeby?

   [Handwritten: Complained + griped — turn it into a proposal]

2. To what extent do you agree with the basic position(s) taken by Carboni?

   [Handwritten: Frustrated + upset at outset + became worse during conversation. Lost control — wrong. needed to develop Brad]

[Handwritten: — Explain value of job — ask for alternative proposal]

The Vice-President

Tom Brewster, one of the field sales managers of Major Tool Works, Inc., had been promoted to his first headquarters assignment as an assistant product manager for a group of products with which he was relatively unfamiliar. Shortly after he began this new assignment, one of the company's vice-presidents, Nick Smith, called a meeting of product managers and other staff to plan marketing strategies. Brewster's superior, the product manager, was unable to attend, so the director of marketing, Jeff Reynolds, invited Brewster to the meeting to help orient him to his new job.

Because of the large number of people attending, Reynolds was rather brief in introducing Brewster to Smith. After the meeting began, Smith—a crusty veteran with a reputation for bluntness—began asking a series of probing questions, which most of the product managers were able to answer in detail. Suddenly he turned to Brewster and began to question him quite closely about his group of products. Somewhat confused, Brewster confessed that he really did not know the answers.

It was immediately apparent to Reynolds that Smith had forgotten or had failed to understand that Brewster was new to his job, and was attending the meeting more for his own orientation than to contribute to it. He was about to offer a discreet explanation when Smith, visibly annoyed with what he took to be Brewster's lack of preparation, snapped, "Gentlemen, you have just seen an example of sloppy staff work, and there is no excuse for it!"

Reynolds had to make a quick decision. He could interrupt Smith and point out that he had judged Brewster unfairly; but that might embarrass both his superior and his subordinate. Alternatively, he could wait until after the meeting and offer an explanation in private. Inasmuch as Smith quickly became engrossed in another conversation, Reynolds followed the second approach. Glancing at Brewster, Reynolds noted that his expression was one of mixed anger and dismay. After catching his eye, Reynolds winked at Brewster as a discreet reassurance that he understood and that the damage could be repaired.

Source: From Cases and Problems for Decisions in Management, by Saul Gellerman. Copyright © 1984 by Random House, Inc. Reprinted by permission of Random House, Inc.

After an hour, Smith, evidently dissatisfied with what he termed the "inadequate planning" of the marketing department in general, abruptly declared the meeting over. As he did so, he turned to Reynolds and asked him to remain behind for a moment. To Reynold's surprise Smith immediately raised the question of Brewster himself. In fact, it turned out to have been his main reason for asking Reynolds to remain behind. "Look," he said, "I want you to tell me frankly, do you think I was too rough with that kid?" Relieved, Reynolds said, "Yes, you were. I was going to speak to you about it."

Smith explained that the fact that Brewster was new to his job had not registered adequately when they had been introduced, and that it was only some time after his own outburst that the nagging thought began to occur to him that what he had done was inappropriate and unfair. "How well do you know him?" he asked. "Do you think I hurt him?"

For a moment Reynolds took the measure of his superior. Then he replied evenly, "I don't know him very well yet. But, yes, I think you hurt him."

". . . That's unforgivable," said Smith. He then telephoned his secretary to call Brewster and ask him to report to his office immediately. A few moments later Brewster returned, looking perplexed and uneasy. As he entered, Smith came out from behind his desk and met him in the middle of the office. Standing face to face with Brewster, who was 20 years and four organization levels his junior, he said, "Look, I've done something stupid and I want to apologize. I had no right to treat you like that. I should have remembered that you were new to your job, but I didn't. I'm sorry."

Brewster was somewhat flustered. He muttered his thanks for the apology.

"As long as you are here, young man," Smith continued, "I want to make a few things clear to you in the presence of your boss's boss. Your job is to make sure that people like myself don't make stupid decisions. Obviously we think you are qualified for your job or we would not have brought you in here. But it takes time to learn any job. Three months from now I will expect you to know the answers to any questions about your products. Until then," he said, thrusting out his hand for the younger man to shake, "you have my complete confidence. And thank you for letting me correct a really dumb mistake."

QUESTIONS

1. Was Smith right to apologize to Brewster, or should he have left well enough alone?

2. What would it be like to have Nick Smith as a superior? As a subordinate?

The Reluctant Backhoe Operator

Clyde Jones had been a backhoe operator in the Kentucky Junction Utility Department for five years. Clyde was skilled at his job and continually won the praise of the city manager for the speed with which he installed water lines.

One year ago, a large federal grant was obtained to expand the city's water system to serve a large new subdivision. In order to accomplish the task and maintain the expanded system, twelve new employees were hired and divided into six-man crews. Clyde was promoted to crew chief with the responsibility of supervising one of the new six-man crews.

Billy Martin, a newly hired backhoe operator, reported to Clyde's team on a Monday morning and was immediately assigned to a backhoe by Clyde. That afternoon, while the crew was hard at work digging a trench for a new 8" water main, Billy accidentally backed over a section of pipe lying beside the trench. Clyde ran to inspect the damage and ordered Billy off the backhoe. ". . . you, kid, why the . . . can't you watch where you're going? I've been watching you and you're slow enough as it is, without making this mistake." As the rest of the crew watched, Billy apologized and began removing the broken pipe section. Clyde operated the backhoe the next two weeks himself.

One month later, Clyde was called into the city manager's office to explain why the progress of the project had slowed considerably for the past 30 days. Clyde's only explanation was that the men on his crew were just too lazy.

QUESTIONS

1. How should Clyde have handled this situation?

Source: Joseph Ohren, Northern Kentucky University, and Charles Atkins, Atkins-Elrod and Associates, 1978.

2. How do you think Billy felt?

3. How does the Peter Principle apply in this incident?

4. What should the city manager do?

The Sales Meeting

Progressive Packing Corporation (PPC) had traditionally held a meeting of its sales force each January at pleasant southern resorts. These meetings had three basic purposes: to reward the salespeople after a hard year's work, to inspire them with laudatory speeches, and to announce new products and strategies for the coming year.

But the last year had been particularly unfortunate. Due to an economic recession, sales were down, and the company had actually suffered a loss of market share, due to the aggressive introduction of new products by a competitor for which PPC had, as yet, no equivalent. Thus, many salespeople had failed to meet their yearly sales quotas. Their traditionally fat commissions had been comparatively slender.

Another blow to their morale was the resignation of their well-liked national sales manager, "Big Bob" Bailey, a forceful and colorful individual with an inspirational style of speaking who had tried unsuccessfully to champion the cause of sales with top management. A month after his departure, it was learned that he had joined a major competitor as vice-president of sales.

His replacement as national sales manager, Susan Evans, was a comparatively young woman who had risen rapidly through the ranks. Although she was respected for her capacity for hard work and ability to analyze sales problems, Evans lacked the charisma and showmanship of her predecessor, and additionally faced the problem that many of the sales staff were men who were older and more experienced than she was. She realized that she would be the subject of unfavorable comparison with Bailey unless she could quickly establish herself as an effective leader.

However, more than her personal prestige was involved. Evans was convinced that the confidence of the salespeople in their company was strongly influenced by their perceptions of their top sales executives. If their observations led them to believe that PPC was in retreat, they might try harder to protect "safe" business than to acquire new customers. If they felt PPC was on the verge of a rout, they might defect to more successful companies, especially the one that Bailey had joined. Her task,

Source: From Cases and Problems for Decisions in Management, *by Saul Gellerman. Copyright © 1984 by Random House, Inc. Reprinted by permission of Random House, Inc.*

therefore, was not merely to develop strategy for reversing the company's fortunes but also to convince the salespeople that they were capably led.

Evans's immediate problem was to cope with rumors that members of top management wanted to cancel the annual sales meeting. She announced that the meeting would be held on schedule and at a more glamorous resort than the ones usually used for this purpose. This was taken as a brave gesture, but, in itself, it did little to lighten the gloomy feelings among the salespeople.

At a party the night before the first general session, Elmer Detweiler, a veteran regional manager, expressed the opinion that Evans had erred in holding the meeting at all. Coming to a sales meeting under these circumstances, he said, was "like being invited to your own funeral." The remark seemed to catch the prevailing mood of futility, and by morning, everyone had heard it.

Evans briefly addressed the group that morning; her speech was delivered without flamboyance but with obvious sincerity. She began by explaining her reasons for holding the meeting: First, because they deserved it, having done what she considered a superb job against severe odds; second, as a clear demonstration that the company had not lost confidence in its salespeople; and third, and most important, to plan the strategies with which to restore a favorable sales trend. Instead of the customary lengthy review of the preceding year, she confined herself to saying, "It's over."

Next, she announced the immediate formation of "Management Advisory Boards." These ten-person panels, made up of field and headquarters managers and salespeople, would develop approaches to specific problems. She would define the problem for each board and indicate the financial and policy limits within which a solution would be acceptable. Evans promised to commit herself in advance to accept their recommendations, provided they were unanimous.

Then she announced the formation of three boards: one to devise strategies to counter the inroads of new competitive products, one to develop new applications for existing products, and another to maximize the effectiveness of the limited sales promotion budget. About half of the people attending the meeting were assigned to boards. She directed the boards to present their conclusions to the group the next morning. Then, to everyone's astonishment, she adjourned the general meeting until the next day. Those not assigned to boards were free to enjoy themselves, but with the understanding that they would be sitting on other boards in their turn.

The immediate reaction was very much in contrast to the cheering and elation that used to follow Bailey's speeches. After a moment of surprise, the salespeople became serious and thoughtful. Even those not chosen found themselves discussing the problems that had been presented to the boards. Many had half expected to be castigated for the year's poor performance, and they were relieved at Evans's positive approach.

But their primary reaction was not to her but to the problems she had posed. As they debated the intricacies of these problems, they began to see that tradeoffs were involved and that a long-range view had to be taken. Unanimous agreement was reached on only a few matters by the boards, but Evans was as good as her word: She put the recommendations into full effect.

The aftermath of the meeting was subtle. The salespeople were not particularly enthusiastic, as they had usually been after a meeting conducted by Bailey. But neither were they depressed and pessimistic, as they had been before the meeting. Their problems still seemed difficult, but no longer impossible.

During that year the sales force gradually reversed the losing trend, and as they did so, they began to regard Evans with increased admiration. Detweiler—a man known for his quotable remarks—summed up the eventual effects of the meeting by saying: "When we went down there we were writing our own obituaries. But she made us into live salespeople and managers again."

QUESTIONS

1. What adverse factors were affecting the performance of the sales force?

2. What was Evans trying to accomplish with her creation of Management Advisory Boards?

3. Why was a group problem-solving approach effective in this case?

The Puzzle Block Work Teams

The Atco Company is a large producer of children's plastic toys. Annual sales exceed $100,000,000, and they are growing at a yearly rate of 10 percent. One of the best selling products is a small plastic puzzle block. The Puzzle Block Department employs approximately 130 people. Organizationally, there is a department head, assistant department head, a general staff person, and three foreman — one per shift. Hourly employees work in teams which are headed up by a team leader. The main function of the department is to assemble the puzzle blocks, which have been one of Atco's most stable products over the last 10 years. Sales forecasts show that the puzzle block is expected to continue selling well and that sales volume should keep growing at a six to seven percent rate yearly for the next five years. Long range forecasts show a modest but continued growth of this product over the next 15-year period.

In the early stages of department growth, the puzzle blocks were assembled manually. Color coded plastic parts were fed into a small workplace and an operator would assemble the pieces in order to form the block. Indirect labor people were used to transport the plastic parts to the workplaces. They also transported the finished blocks into storage before they went on to the packaging department.

Within three years, as sales grew, the Atco Company could see that the product had to be produced by a more automatic process if sales forecasts were to be met. An automatic assembler was designed, built, and debugged by the company's Engineering Division. As the assembler was installed, maintenance personnel from the Solid Plastics Division (the Puzzle Block Department is part of this division) were trained to properly maintain it. These mechanics would do preventive maintenance and repair any breakdowns which might occur. At first, only one mechanic per shift was assigned to the department and he was on call for any breakdowns that might occur, as well as for performing routine maintenance work.

Within five years the department had grown from the initial three machines to a total of 20 machines. These were staffed with one operator

Source: Andrew J. DuBrin, Casebook of Organizational Behavior, copyright © 1977, Pergamon Press. Reprinted with permission. (I. R. Trojan researched and wrote this case.)

per machine and one support person per four machines. Each mechanic assigned to the department was responsible for the maintenance of four machines. This included trouble calls and routine maintenance functions required to keep the machines operating as efficiently as possible.

The support person was responsible for a variety of functions. He or she performed all the handling functions associated with the product, such as supplying parts and moving and storing the finished product. The inspection operation for four machines was also done by the support person, and he or she was responsible for the final quality of the product. If any of the machines was not producing a quality product the support person would shut down the machine and have the mechanic check the situation and make any necessary repairs.

At this time in the department's history, a new department head was appointed. Glen Aldridge, age 30 and with past experience as an industrial engineer, was appointed to the position of Head of the Puzzle Block Department. Having been the department's industrial engineer for the past five years, he was intimately familiar with its operation, equipment, and personnel.

During his years of work as an industrial engineer, Glen had developed a good working relationship with many of the operators in the department. Though production continued to improve at the rate of one to two percent annually, he thought this level could be improved. He also sensed that the operators were not satisfied with the type of work they were doing. As he saw the picture, Glen was faced with two problems which had to be solved in order to improve department efficiency and morale.

During his years in school, Glen had been exposed to behavioral science approaches to understanding management. As an industrial engineer he gained more knowledge of work groups or teams. He often felt that the team approach to the Puzzle Block Department's organization might help to improve efficiency and morale. After careful consideration he decided to try this approach to management.

Interviews held with the operators upheld Glen's hunches. The operators felt that they had no control over what they were producing due to the power held by the support person. They didn't know what level of quality they were producing because they didn't get to examine their final product. The support person also had control over their machine, and this gave the operators an uneasy feeling. Operators also alluded to feelings of boredom. Once parts were loaded into the assembler, the machine cycle gave them approximately 10 to 12 minutes before it had to be tended to again. They felt they could be given more responsibility than they presently held.

After the interviews, Glen and the rest of his department supervisors discussed how teams should be organized and what other types of responsibilities might be given to the operators. They decided to organize around a six-person team. According to their analysis, six people would be capable of operating five machines, performing all quality testing, handling all supplies, and following production schedules. It was reasoned that a team leader should be chosen for each group to organize the team and assist department supervision in evaluating departmental personnel.

Before the change was made, Industrial Engineering was asked to evaluate the plan's feasibility. A careful study of the operators and equipment was made. During this study the service provided by maintenance was also examined. The industrial engineers discovered that the mechanics, also, were not fully utilized. When the study was completed, the following recommendations were made:

1. The department should establish the work teams on an experimental basis.
2. The mechanics assigned to the department should be reassigned and given responsibility for five machines instead of four. It was also suggested that the given machines allotted to the mechanic would be those of a single work team.

These recommendations, along with Glen's, were taken to division supervision and approved. Shortly after division approval, work began to select an initial experimental team. Participants were carefully chosen to maximize the probability of success. The team was organized and prepared to operate three months after the initial idea.

The first month of operation showed little or no difference between the team operation and the normal operations. As time passed and the team became more of a unit, production began to show increases. The quality level also showed a modest increase. Within a five-month period, the work team was producing at a 10 percent increase over the rest of the department and the number of blocks rejected had dropped by 20 percent.

The next step was to establish two more teams, one per each of the other two shifts, and chart their results. The same pattern showed itself with the two new teams. It was at this point that supervision felt the change to work teams should take place in the entire department. In order to form the new work teams, one individual from each of the original teams was appointed team leader. He or she helped to organize the group and to start it into production. Within a two-year period, the entire departmental organization had been changed to a work team format. Production as well as the quality level of the product increased over the next two-year period. Employee satisfaction (measured through questionnaires administered after introduction of the work teams) was at a higher level than it had been previously.

In the later part of the second year and in the early part of the third year, two of the groups showed a productivity somewhat higher than the other groups. Performance was reviewed at mid-year, following the customary policy of the Atco Company. Shortly after this performance review, department supervision began to notice feeling of dissatisfaction coming from the two superior groups in the department. In the following two months, open dissatisfaction was visible in these two groups and productivity began to decline. Department supervision began to investigate the cause of this performance turnaround.

In the course of the investigation department supervision discovered that the main reason for the dissatisfaction was the performance evaluation system used and the way the department applied it to the teams and their members. When evaluating personnel, a 1–10 rating system was used, 1 being the highest rating and 10 being the lowest rating. Increases were based directly on the numerical value an individual received, with some discretion (1-2%) allowed the department head. Industrial Relations studied the work done by the operators and classified the job performed into a wage bracket, the only exception being team leaders, who were classified at a higher bracket. As one experienced worker explained her objections to the system:

"If we are all in the same wage bracket, we all get the same amount of money no matter how hard we work. It's fun to outperform other teams, but if putting out more puzzle blocks doesn't lead to more money, working hard gets old pretty fast."

As the work teams were started, Glen Aldridge and his assistants had to decide upon how teams would be evaluated. Consensus was reached on the following plan:

1. Teams would be rated as a team in comparison to each other. The discretionary part of the pay increase would be determined by this method.
2. Individuals would be evaluated on their effectiveness within the team rather than in the entire department.

When this plan was reviewed with the existing team members they had no objections and felt it was an equitable way to evaluate department personnel. However, the members of the two clearly superior teams felt that this program of evaluation did not treat them in an equitable manner. As a team individual in a superior team, the "poorest performer" might be rated a 3. As a member of one of the other teams, one of the employees may also be rated as a 3 in comparison to the other members of the group. Yet, when these individuals would be compared, not actually done by the department, the 3-rated individual in the superior team would be a higher caliber employee than the 3-rated individual in one of the other groups; but both of the employees would receive equal increases and their records would show equal capabilities.

Glen realized that in order to eliminate the dissatisfaction in his two top teams he would have to solve this problem. He was deeply committed to the team organization in the department and felt that evaluation had to continue in its present manner in order for teams to function as teams. He felt that if he began to rate each employee as an individual again rather than as part of a team, the organization which had been instituted would no longer function in the team manner.

QUESTIONS

1. What should Glen Aldridge do to enable the superior teams to regain their former levels of job satisfaction?

2. Would you recommend that Atco organize other toy departments into team operations? Why or why not?

Creativity Requires the Right Atmosphere

"Mr. Farnsworth, tell me about the size of your business," said Honey Levine, business reporter for a nationally circulated trade magazine. "Actually how big is the Maxwell restaurant chain?"

"My latest estimate is that our total annual sales volume is at the rate of $890 million. That's approaching $1 billion, and the figure improves every day. We are a worldwide operation, with outlets throughout the non-communist world. But we are concentrated in the United States, Canada, and Western Europe. As of this morning we had 2300 outlets. By this afternoon we will probably have added one or two more outlets. We are a moving, pulsating, dynamic, exploding operation. It is a true figure that over seven billion Maxwell Mini-Subs have been consumed by people."

"Mr. Farnsworth, we in the business writers' community cannot help but admire the success of your empire. We recognize that the failure rate is very high in the fast food franchise business. Could you speculate about the factors that underlie the success of your business?"

"Honey, I do not have to speculate. I *know* the reasons for our success. It's a simple case of creativity. Our small corporate staff is very creative. You have to be creative to prosper in this field. Applied creativity is undoubtedly the number one success factor in our business. I'll give you a few examples of the creative approaches we have used to promote our Mini-Subs, Maxade, and the total concept of our restaurants.

"One simple, but effective, example is our 'Q.S.T.' campaign. Every employee of our firm, from Maxwell Farnsworth down to the minimum wage floor mopper, wears a button whose initials signify our business motto: Quality, Service, Tidiness. And let me assure you, we are tidy around Maxwell's. Our team of field inspectors makes sure that every Maxwell location and every Maxwell employee is tidy looking. Anybody with an open sore is sent home for the day, usually with pay. Our refuse cans are shiny white enamel. Our dumpsters out back are also shiny and white. We will take a franchise away from an operator who violates our Q.S.T. code. It's written into the original contract.

Source: Andrew J. DuBrin, Casebook of Organizational Behavior, *copyright* © 1977, Pergamon Press. *Reprinted with permission.*

"Our Mini-Sub University is also a creative concept. We train potential franchise operators on every last detail of our operation. People take our course work quite seriously in their 10-day program at our university headquarters. Everybody leaving here knows the precise thickness of the slice of ham, and every other ingredient, that goes into a Maxwell Mini-Sub. They also know exactly how many shakes of oil are placed on top of the open sub. It's a precision operation. We want to insure that the Kansas City school teacher who visits Honolulu will be guaranteed a Maxwell sub there as tasty as the one she gets back in Kansas City.

"Perhaps our creativity reaches its greatest heights in our special promotions. In our business you need an ever changing number of promotions and special events. A Maxwell shop should be a happening, a place to go for excitement and adventure. One very successful promotion was 'Grandparent Day.' Every grandparent, accompanied by his or her grandchild or grandchildren on a given Wednesday from opening to closing, could order a sub for 10¢. Grandparent Day was a huge success. We wound up capturing a lot of the senior citizen business. Most chain restaurants make no special attempt to attract older people.

"The wildest promotion we ever had was in Columbus, Ohio. One of our executives selected Columbus as the site for trying out a 'Mini-Sub Submariner Look-Alike Contest.' Submariner, of course, gets right at the nostalgia kick. He was a superhero of the original Batman era. The three kids our judges decided looked the most like Submariner received a $50 gift certificate at Maxwell's. We received a good deal of T.V. and newspaper publicity on the basis of that promotion. A couple of local disc jockeys and Miss Ohio State judged the contestants."

"Maxwell, it's important for me to comment here that rumor has it you use very unconventional methods to bring about creativity in your staff. Is that true?"

"Honey, that is absolutely correct. Most people are not creative. That means that you have to set up the right atmosphere to induce creativity. Suppose I just issued a corporate directive that I wanted everybody to be creative in their jobs. Predictably, the response would be zilch. You need specialized techniques. All of our approaches to bringing about creativity are not unique, but some are.

"Our corporate Think Tank is certainly unique. When an executive has a creative assignment, he or she is urged to give our Tank a try. It consists mainly of a huge waterbed, some 12 feet in diameter at the bottom of a tank. The executive is supposed to lie on the bed alone until he or she comes up with a creative solution to the problem at hand. It seems to me that our Grandparent Day promotional stunt came out of the Think Tank. Even when an executive does not get the idea that he or she is seeking right away, it tends to clear one's head for later problems. Twenty minutes in the Think Tank and you are refreshed. Something like Transcendental Meditation.

"A very popular creativity inducing technique is our head massage. We have a young woman who gives an executive a gentle head massage in the privacy of his own office. So far no woman corporate staff executive has availed herself of this service. Melinda, the woman we call in for the massages, claims that the massaging stimulates the passage of blood through the brain cells, thus energizing one's thinking capacity. I find that the experience certainly does clear the mind. It seems to erase distracting thoughts.

"Another approach to bring about creativity similar to the Think Tank, is our No Distraction Room. Some call it solitary confinement. We have a room about 20 feet square, with pastel blue walls, and no furniture in it but a wire chair, something like what you might find in an old-fashioned candy parlor. According to the rules we have established, the executive entering this room is forced to concentrate on the problem at hand. No telephone messages, no distracting gazes at the outside world. It seems to work. Our special holiday promotion of subs in Christmas gift wrapping paper came out of the No Distraction Room."

Honey Levine, not content to base her story entirely on the perceptions of the company president, requested that she be allowed to interview a few executives to get their ideas on Maxwell Farnsworth's approach to fostering creativity. Howard Boyle, Vice President of Field Inspection, had praise for Maxwell's unconventional approach to eliciting creativity from his subordinates.

"It would fair to say that Maxwell is on to something important. Without his extra special emphasis on using your creativity, you could easily get trapped into solving every business problem in a mechanical way. When you're rushing from meeting to meeting, it's hard to be creative. Before Farnsworth came up with the Think Tank idea, I used to do all my thinking at home. I figured you didn't have time to think on the job. But thinking at home wasn't all that easy either. There are all kinds of distractions at home also. If you aren't shuffling papers other people in the family think you aren't working. People somehow don't equate thinking with working.

"Now thinking is a formalized activity at the office. You are given a separate place to think in an atmosphere that helps you become creative. I wouldn't be surprised if Maxwell Farnsworth goes down in history as the man who brought creativity to the fast food business."

An executive who asked Honey Levine for anonymity had another view of the creativity inducing programs of Maxwell's Mini-Subs: "Face it, this is a modern day reenactment of the fairy tale 'The Emperor's New Clothes.' In that story everybody knew that the Emperor was mistaken, that he was really naked and not dressed in fancy clothing, but nobody would face up to the fact. Maxwell Farnsworth is a great guy, but his ideas on making executives creative are far-fetched. People go along with his ideas to make him happy. I would venture to say that nobody would enter the Think Tank or the No Distraction Room if nobody was around to observe them enter. They would simply take their little problem back to their office and work out a solution.

"What really happens with Maxwell's gimmicks is that people go through the motion of entering the Think Tank or receiving head massage just to humor Farnsworth. If they do come up with a workable idea in one of those creativity sessions, it has to be refined further anyway. The person coming up with the idea usually then takes it to a few others to refine it in group discussions.

"It might even be that going off to a formal creativity exercise is counterproductive. Although I certainly do enjoy having an attractive woman stroke my head, I could think of a better way to finance the expansion of Mini-Sub shops without having her fingers run through my hair."

QUESTIONS

1. Should the dissenting executive confront Maxwell Farnsworth with his perception of the effectiveness of the company creativity training program? Why or why not?

2. One of Maxwell Farnsworth's former executives described him as "An old cornball who lucked out. His creativity bit is just hogwash." Based on the limited information provided in this case, what is your opinion of the preceding statement?

Emery Air Freight

The "power of positive reinforcement" is a topic that has been talked about by psychologists, organization behavior specialists, and managers for years. Much study has been done on the effects of positive reinforcement, but most of those studies have been with animals and humans in a laboratory setting. However, field studies, involving operating organizations, are now being reported in the literature, with some interesting results. The case of Emery Air Freight is one of those.

THE PROGRAM

Perhaps the most widely known example of the application of behavior modification in industry is that of Emery Air Freight. Under the direction of Edward J. Feeney, Emery selected behavior modification as a simple answer to the persistent problems of inefficiency and low productivity. In an air freight firm, rapid processing of parcels is important to corporate profitability.

Emery Air Freight began with a performance audit, which attempted to identify the kind of job behaviors which had the greatest impact on profit and the extent to which these behaviors were shown in the company. One area of special concern was the use of containers. Emery loses money if shipping containers are not fully loaded when shipped. Hence, one goal was to ensure that empty container space was minimized. Before the program was implemented, workers reported that they believed they were filling the containers about 90% of the time. However, the performance audit revealed that this was really so only about 45% of the time. In other words, over half of the containers were shipped unfilled.

THE RESULTS

Through the use of feedback (in the form of self-report checklists provided to each worker) and positive reinforcement (praise), the percentage

Source: Adapted, by permission of the publisher, from "Behavior Modification on the Bottom Line," by W. C. Hamner and E. P. Hamner, *Organizational Dynamics*, Spring 1976, pp. 8–21, copyright © 1976, American Management Association, New York. All rights reserved.

of full containers rose swiftly from 45% to 95%. Cost reductions for the first year alone exceeded $500,000, and rose to $2 million during the first three years. In other words, when workers were given consistent feedback and kept informed of their performance, subsequent output increased rapidly. As a result of this initial success, similar programs were initiated at Emery, including the setting of performance standards for handling customer problems on the telephone and for accurately estimating the container sizes needed for shipment of lightweight packages. Again, positive results were claimed.

QUESTIONS

1. What are the advantages and disadvantages of behavior modification to improve productivity? Consider each step: identifying key performance behaviors; providing feedback on performance; providing recognition and positive reinforcement for good performance.

2. How would you apply behavior modification principles to individual performance problems?

APPLICATIONS

Employee Performance Review — Rating Scale   285

Employee Performance Review — Paired Comparisons   293

Personality Traits and Job Demands Analysis   297

How Will You Spend Your Life?   303

Employee Performance Review — Rating Scale

Directions

Read the entire evaluation form carefully. Then, consider each item separately. Rate the employee as "failing," "below average," "above average," or "excellent" on each item by checking the appropriate box. The last item (15) is the overall evaluation of the employee. When rating this item, check the appropriate box and indicate whether the employee is at the high end (H) or the low end (L) of the scale.

Use the spaces provided in items 13, 14, and 15 to cite specific behaviors explaining your ratings and to identify steps to improve. These comments should be clear and complete so that the employee can understand your rating. Use the evaluation process to offer constructive help to your employees.

One useful variation is to ask employees to evaluate themselves. Compare your evaluations with theirs, and have a two-way discussion on what should be done to maintain or develop effective performance.

Use the following as a rating guide:

- *Failing.* This is the lowest possible rating. It tells the employee that job performance has been unsatisfactory. The employee has been either unable or unwilling to meet reasonable job requirements. If you check this box for any of the items on the evaluation, you should include comments and examples indicating where the employee's work is failing. This rating means that, unless there is improvement, the employee should be reassigned or transferred or disciplinary action should be taken.

- *Below average.* This is the second lowest rating. It informs the employee of serious shortcomings that interfere with work and may be a sign that the employee is exerting minimum effort. If you check this box for any item, it means that more training, a different assignment, or additional effort is required. Indicate by your comments what you see as the problem and the solution. Give examples and discuss them; make suggestions for improvement before it is too late.

Source: Joseph Ohren, Northern Kentucky University, 1976.

- *Average.* This is the middle rating. It indicates that the employee has done a satisfactory job throughout the rating period. Do not hesitate to explain on the form some possible avenues for further improvement.
- *Above average.* This is the second highest category and should be given only to those who perform consistently above average during the rating period. Reserve this rating for those employees who give more than you ask for. Show appreciation for positive contributions, and encourage all employees to strive for this rating.
- *Excellent.* This is the top performance rating. The employee who deserves this rating does everything right — there is almost no room for improvement. Job performance was consistent during the entire rating period. Comments that describe outstanding work should accompany this rating.

As you complete the evaluation, concentrate on the duties and requirements of the position held by the employee. What do you expect from the individual in the way of performance? Then, rate the employee's job behavior. Remember, you are evaluating work *behavior* — how the individual performs on the job. Include both strengths and weaknesses.

Avoid common rating problems such as being too lenient, being too strict, letting personal biases interfere, rating everyone alike, and allowing isolated events and recent performance to overinfluence you.

The purposes of employee performance reviews are to develop employee competence, to maintain morale, and to solve performance problems. Take a helpful, problem-solving approach in reviewing employee performance. Remember to listen to employees as they discuss job strengths and weaknesses and to suggest ways they may improve.

EMPLOYEE PERFORMANCE REVIEW

Employee _____   Title _____

Department _____   Date hired _____

Review period: from _____   to _____

---

1. *Job knowledge.* Evaluate the employee's familiarity with job requirements and standards and understanding of policies and procedures. Consider the following:
   - Is the employee familiar with the tools, equipment, and methods used?
   - Does the employee frequently need assistance in determining or understanding procedures?
   - Is work done correctly?

- Does the employee know what to do without having specific instructions?
- Is there a consistent pattern of mistakes reflecting misunderstanding or lack of job knowledge?

Failing	Below average	Average	Above average	Excellent

2. *Initiative.* Assess the employee's willingness to take on job assignments, and offer ideas and suggestions to improve performance. Consider the following:
    - Is the employee a self-starter?
    - Does the employee pitch in when something needs to be done, without waiting to be told to do so?
    - Does the employee make practical, workable suggestions for improvement?
    - Are suggestions and ideas shared freely with others?
    - Does the employee demonstrate a desire to improve?
    - Does the employee voluntarily participate in training or educational programs?

Failing	Below average	Average	Above average	Excellent

3. *Dependability.* Gauge the reliability of the employee. Consider the following:
    - Can you count on the employee to carry out assignments and meet obligations?
    - Are deadlines frequently missed?
    - Does the employee require close supervision?
    - Does the employee follow through on assignments?
    - Does the employee overcome obstacles to meet responsibilities?

Failing	Below average	Average	Above average	Excellent

4. *Work habits.* Analyze the employee's method of working. Consider the following:
    - Is the employee a safe worker?
    - Is the employee productive or merely busy?
    - Does the employee organize and coordinate actions for maximum effectiveness?

- Does the employee make effective use of time?
- Does the employee waste materials, lose tools, or otherwise waste resources?

Failing	Below average	Average	Above average	Excellent

5. *Judgment.* Appraise the employee's judgment and decision making on the job. Consider the following:
   - Does the employee demonstrate good judgment in handling routine problems?
   - Does the employee thoroughly analyze decisions before implementing them?
   - Does the employee weigh both positive and negative consequences of actions?
   - How effectively does the employee respond to difficult situations?
   - Does the employee have the ability to work under pressure?
   - Can the employee handle emergencies?
   - Does the employee recognize personal deficiencies and seek help when appropriate?

Failing	Below average	Average	Above average	Excellent

6. *Learning ability.* Evaluate the employee's ability to learn new tasks and methods. Consider the following:
   - Does the employee learn new methods quickly?
   - How does the employee adjust to changes and new conditions?
   - Does the employee profit from experience?
   - Is the employee open to personal and professional growth?

Failing	Below average	Average	Above average	Excellent

7. *Attitude.* Rate the employee's attitude and demeanor. Consider the following:
   - Does the employee want to do a good job?
   - Is assistance offered willingly?
   - Does the employee make a positive contribution to morale?
   - Does the employee show consideration and sensitivity to the feelings of others?

- Is constructive criticism accepted positively?
- Does the employee show pride in work?

Failing	Below average	Average	Above average	Excellent

8. *Relationships with people.* Assess the employee's interpersonal relationships. Consider the following:

    - How well does the employee get along with fellow employees?
    - Does the employee cause conflicts?
    - Does the employee disrupt the work of others?
    - Is the employee polite and courteous to others?
    - What kind of conduct and language is used with others?
    - Does the employee project a positive and professional image?
    - Can the employee communicate effectively?
    - Does the employee listen effectively?
    - Do customers complain about the employee?

Failing	Below average	Average	Above average	Excellent

9. *Attendance.* Review the employee's attendance and tardiness record. Consider the following:

    - Is the employee frequently absent from work?
    - Are absences justified? Documented?
    - Does the employee arrive for work on time?
    - Does the employee remain until the end of the work period?
    - If the job requires attending meetings or moving from one work location to another, is the employee punctual?
    - Does the employee give adequate notice for absence or tardiness?

Failing	Below average	Average	Above average	Excellent

10. *Appearance and fitness.* Assess the employee's personal appearance, cleanliness, grooming, and fitness. Consider the following:

    - Does the employee demonstrate cleanliness and good personal hygiene?
    - Are clothes neat and clean?
    - Does the employee have to be reminded of physical condition or appearance?

- Is the employee able to work consistently with only normal fatigue?
- Are clothes appropriate for the job?
- Do sleep, diet, and other health practices aid job performance?

Failing	Below average	Average	Above average	Excellent

11. *Use of equipment.* Appraise the employee's care in handling and maintaining property and equipment. Consider the following:
    - Does the employee take care of assigned equipment?
    - Does the employee demonstrate an understanding of how equipment is to be used?
    - Is equipment handled carefully, avoiding unnecessary damage?
    - Are routine maintenance procedures done properly?
    - Does the employee report defects when appropriate?
    - Does the employee follow procedures in the care and cleaning of equipment?

Failing	Below average	Average	Above average	Excellent

12. *Safety.* Examine the employee's attention to personal safety as well as to the safety of others. Consider the following:
    - Does the employee use assigned safety equipment?
    - Does the employee handle equipment safely, without injury?
    - Is care taken to avoid dangerous or unsafe conditions whenever possible?

Failing	Below average	Average	Above average	Excellent

13. *Productivity.* Weigh the amount of work completed in relation to the specific assignment. Consider the following:
    - How much work does the employee consistently produce?
    - Does the employee's output meet or exceed expectations?
    - Is the volume of work completed higher or lower than that of other individuals with similar assignments?

Failing	Below average	Average	Above average	Excellent

Remarks: _____

_____

Steps for improvement: _____

_____

14. *Quality.*   Analyze the quality of the employee's performance. Consider the following:
    - How innovative or creative is the employee?
    - How accurate is the employee's work?
    - How often does the employee's work need redoing?
    - How well do results meet standards?
    - Do customers or co-workers complain about the employee's work?

Failing	Below average	Average	Above average	Excellent

Remarks: _____

_____

Steps for improvement: _____

_____

15. *Overall rating.*   Evaluate the employee's overall job performance. This should be a composite rating.

Failing		Below average		Average		Above average		Excellent	
L	H	L	H	L	H	L	H	L	H

Remarks: _____

_____

Steps for improvement: _____
_____
_____

                              Employee's signature _____
                              Reviewer's signature _____
                              Date _____

Employee Performance Review — Paired Comparisons

The paired comparison is a systematic method for conducting performance reviews and making decisions. It forces comparisons between all workers being evaluated on common performance criteria. As the following quotation from Benjamin Franklin shows, the idea is not new:

Canceling Out Pros and Cons

When confronted with two courses of action, I jot down on a piece of paper all the arguments in favor of each one — then, on the opposite side, I write the arguments against each one. Then, by weighing the arguments pro and con and canceling them out one against the other, I take the course indicated by what remains.

Benjamin Franklin

EMPLOYEE PERFORMANCE REVIEW

Step I

State the performance criterion.* Use a single word, phrase, or sentence. For example, "Which employee is more valuable for the success of the organization?"

Performance criterion: _____

_____

---

*Common performance criteria include productivity, initiative, dependability, effort, and quality of work.

Source: Gene Archbold, Northern Kentucky Area Development District, 1976. Reprinted with permission.

Step II

Make a list of subordinates to be compared on the performance criterion. Assign a number to each name.*

1 _____   6 _____
2 _____   7 _____
3 _____   8 _____
4 _____   9 _____
5 _____   10 _____

Step III

Look at the first line of the grid below. You will see a 1 and a 2. Compare names 1 and 2 on your list, using the performance criterion. Who is more valuable? Circle your choice. Then go to the next pair (1 and 3). Continue in this manner until you have compared every employee with every other employee.

```
1 2
1 3     2 3
1 4     2 4     3 4
1 5     2 5     3 5     4 5
1 6     2 6     3 6     4 6     5 6
1 7     2 7     3 7     4 7     5 7     6 7
1 8     2 8     3 8     4 8     5 8     6 8     7 8
1 9     2 9     3 9     4 9     5 9     6 9     7 9     8 9
1 10    2 10    3 10    4 10    5 10    6 10    7 10    8 10    9 10
```

Step IV

Count the number of times each subordinate's number was circled on the grid. Enter the totals in the appropriate spaces below.

1___ 2___ 3___ 4___ 5___ 6___ 7___ 8___ 9___ 10___

---

*If you need to compare a list with more than ten names on it, add new rows to the bottom of the grid (1,11; 2,11; etc.) until you have all the numbers needed, arranged in pairs.

Step V

Recopy the list, beginning with the name of the subordinate whose number was circled most often. You have determined this individual to be the best employee at this time, based on the performance criterion. The name circled next most often is the second best employee, and so on. In case of a tie (if two names receive the same number of circles), look back on the grid to see which name you circled when you were comparing those two employees. This means you prefer one over the other; thus you break the tie. The rank order of employees is as follows:

1. _____
2. _____
3. _____
4. _____
5. _____
6. _____
7. _____
8. _____
9. _____
10. _____

Personality Traits and Job Demands Analysis

Use the following exercise to match personality traits with job demands. The manager should complete Part I, A View of the Job, and the employee should complete Part II, A View of the Person. The manager and employee should discuss Part III together.

Part I

A View of the Job

(To Be Completed by the Supervisor)

Directions

The following are job characteristics. Evaluate each characteristic for the job under consideration according to the following scale:

1. Never true
2. Rarely true
3. Sometimes true
4. Usually true
5. Always true

In order to succeed in this job:

a. _____ Unpopular decisions must be made.

b. _____ A routine work pattern is required.

c. _____ Close supervision is required.

d. _____ Steady persistence at simple tasks is required.

e. _____ The ability to initiate contact with strangers is required.

f. _____ Decisiveness must be exercised in uncertain situations.

g. _____ Policy must be executed with extreme caution.

h. _____ Various types of people must be coordinated.

Source: *Jerri Lynn Thomas and Naomi Miller, Northern Kentucky University, 1983.*

i. _____ Staying at one work station for long periods of time is required.

j. _____ The ability to overcome adversity, including the objections of others, is required.

k. _____ Systematic procedures and rules must be followed.

l. _____ The ability to solve human relation problems is required.

m. _____ The ability to compete with others to accomplish goals is required.

n. _____ An enthusiastic personality and the ability to motivate people are required.

o. _____ Deviation from prescribed procedures is prohibited.

p. _____ Risk taking is necessary.

q. _____ Repetitive work must be done quickly and accurately.

r. _____ Social poise and persuasive ability are required.

s. _____ Exact and detailed work is required.

t. _____ A dedication to duty is necessary.

u. _____ The ability to plan ahead on a large scale is necessary.

v. _____ Selling or counseling skills are required.

w. _____ The willingness to work as a member of a team is required.

x. _____ Personal patience and an even temper are required.

SCORING

Step One

Transfer your ratings for each item to the following key, and total each column.

	A	S	E	I
	a. _____	e. _____	b. _____	c. _____
	f. _____	h. _____	d. _____	g. _____
	j. _____	l. _____	i. _____	k. _____
	m. _____	n. _____	q. _____	o. _____
	p. _____	r. _____	s. _____	t. _____
	u. _____	v. _____	x. _____	w. _____
Totals	_____	_____	_____	_____
	Ascendancy	Sociability	Emotionality	Individuality

Step Two

Plot the total scores on the appropriate A, S, E, and I lines on the following job graph. Connect the points A and S, S and E, and E and I with straight lines (see the sample job graph).

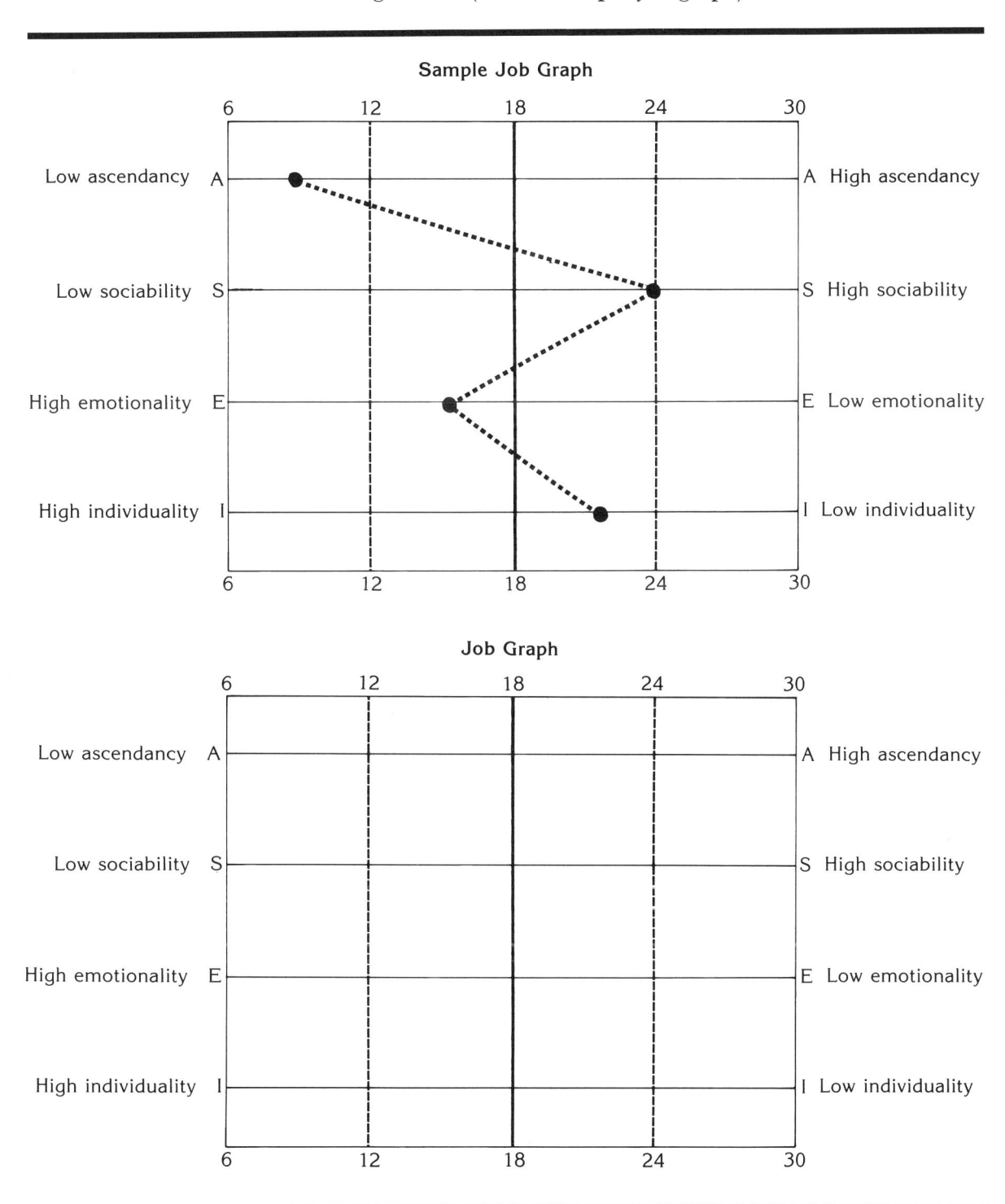

Sample Job Graph

	6	12	18	24	30	
Low ascendancy A	● (≈9)					A High ascendancy
Low sociability S				● (≈24)		S High sociability
High emotionality E			● (≈15)			E Low emotionality
High individuality I				● (≈22)		I Low individuality

Job Graph

	6	12	18	24	30	
Low ascendancy A						A High ascendancy
Low sociability S						S High sociability
High emotionality E						E Low emotionality
High individuality I						I Low individuality

Performance, Applications • Personality Traits and Job Demands Analysis   299

Part II
A View of the Person
(To Be Completed by the Employee)

Directions

For each of the following four traits—ascendancy, sociability, emotionality, and individuality—place an X at the position on the line that best reflects your personality.

A — Ascendancy

<----------------|---------------->

- Is peaceful, modest, and accommodating
- Likes a secure environment
- Dislikes making decisions
- Dislikes confrontations and arguments

- Is dominant in interpersonal relations
- Likes power and authority
- Meets problems head-on
- Likes to make decisions

S — Sociability

<----------------|---------------->

- Is reserved and reflective
- Likes to be alone
- Likes clear-cut decisions and black and white answers
- Wants privacy

- Likes to work with people
- Is outgoing and persuasive
- Has an open-door policy in dealing with others
- Enjoys counseling and teaching

E — Emotionality

<----------------|---------------->

- Likes adventure, variety, and change
- Is easily bored and restless

- Is calm and stable
- Is comfortable following established procedures

- Is impatient with slow speech, action, and progress
- Is quick to feel and express emotions

- Likes to concentrate on one project at a time
- Is deliberate and methodical in solving problems

I – Individuality

←——————————————|——————————————→

- Needs freedom and independence
- Dislikes routines and restrictions
- Avoids close supervision
- Likes individual assignments

- Wants structure and order
- Is comfortable with rules and policies
- Is a cooperative team player
- Is comfortable with formal supervision

Part III

Discussion

(Manager and Employee)

Directions

Compare the demands of the job (Part I) with the personality of the individual (Part II) by answering the following questions:

1. Ascendancy — is the individual *aggressive* enough, or *too* dominant, for this job?
2. Sociability — is the individual *outgoing* enough, or *too* people oriented, for this job?
3. Emotionality — is the individual *versatile* enough, or *too* variety loving, for this job?
4. Individuality — is the individual *independent* enough, or *too* individualistic, for this job?

Based on this analysis, is the personality of the individual compatible with the demands of the job?

If not, can the demands of the job be changed?

Discuss the importance of matching the personality traits of the individual with the demands of the job for optimum employee satisfaction and maximum job performance.

How Will You Spend Your Life?

Six areas of life concern most people: work and career; self-development (mental, physical, and spiritual); family and friends; civic and community involvement; leisure and recreation; and economic well-being. These six areas include most of the values that are important to us and most of the goals we want to accomplish. Living a fulfilled life requires an appropriate balance of activities within these areas. A box for each area follows.

What would you like to accomplish in each area? Think long range (at least three to five years), and write all of the goals you would like to achieve in each box. Write rapidly; don't evaluate; don't think about whether or not you can accomplish the goals. If you think of something you would like to do, write it down.

Work and Career

1. _____ 4. _____

2. _____ 5. _____

3. _____ 6. _____

Source: Naomi Miller, Northern Kentucky University, 1982. Based on David A. Kolb, Irwin M. Rubin, and James M. McIntyre, Organizational Psychology, 3d ed. (Englewood Cliffs, N.J.: Prentice-Hall, Inc., 1979), 423–67.

Self-Development
(Mental, Physical, and Spiritual)

1. _____   4. _____

2. _____   5. _____

3. _____   6. _____

Family and Friends

1. _____   4. _____

2. _____   5. _____

3. _____   6. _____

Civic and Community Involvement

1. _____   4. _____

2. _____   5. _____

3. _____   6. _____

Leisure and Recreation

1. _____   4. _____
   _____   _____
2. _____   5. _____
   _____   _____
3. _____   6. _____
   _____   _____

Economic Well-Being

1. _____   4. _____
   _____   _____
2. _____   5. _____
   _____   _____
3. _____   6. _____
   _____   _____

After you have filled in all of the boxes with your goals, review them. Change or modify your statements if necessary. Next, consider your priorities. Some of your goals may be more important to you than others. Rate each one with the 1, 2, 3 method: number 1's are most important, then number 2's, and then number 3's. Rank all of your 1's in order of importance, and assign a due date for accomplishing them using the following form.

Allocate time and resources to your most important goals first. Consider how you can best use your time and resources to accomplish as many of these goals as possible. At least once a year, repeat this exercise. Your birthday or New Year's Day are excellent times to think about who you are, where you are heading, what you are doing, and why you are doing it.

Goals	Priorities	Target Dates

APPENDIX A

Background Information, Teaching Suggestions, and Testing and Grading

The Human Side of Work is a series of desk books for managers, handbooks for practitioners, and workbooks for students. These are applied books that combine behavior theory with business practice. Each book teaches central concepts and skills in an important area of the world of work. The set of eight books includes stress management, communication skills, employee motivation, leadership principles, quality of work life, managing for excellence, employee participation, and the role of ethics.

Each book combines theory with practice, gives commonsense answers to real-life problems, and is easy to read and fun to use. The series may be used as a set or as stand-alone books. The subject areas are made more forceful and the impact greater by the self-evaluation questionnaires and practical exercises that are used for personal development.

AUDIENCE

The Human Side of Work is written for two audiences. One audience includes managers and professionals interested in personal and professional development on their own or within the context of a management development program. Another audience includes students in human relations, organization behavior, and other management-related courses.

The material is appropriate for use at the four-year college and university level as well as in community colleges, proprietary schools, extension programs, and management training seminars.

CONTENT AND STYLE

The difference between most organization behavior texts and *The Human Side of Work* can be compared to the difference between a lecture and a seminar. Although both are good educational vehicles, the lecture is better for conveying large amounts of information, while the seminar is better for developing skills. The good lecture is interesting and builds knowledge; the good seminar is stimulating and builds competency. *The Human Side of Work* emphasizes the interactive, seminar approach to learning.

The writing style is personal and conversational, with minimal professional jargon. True-life examples clarify points under consideration. Concepts are supported by stories and anecdotes, which are more meaningful and easy to remember than facts, figures, and lists. Each book includes learning activities to bridge the gap between classroom theory and on-the-job practice.

The Human Side of Work is more than a series of textbooks. These are "learning" books that actively involve the reader in the learning process. Our goal has been to include material that is interesting to read, relates to the reader's own concerns, and is practical to use. The following captures the spirit of our effort:

I Taught Them All

I have taught in high school for ten years. During that time, I have given assignments, among others, to a murderer, an evangelist, a pugilist, a thief, and an imbecile.

The murderer was a quiet little boy who sat on the front seat and regarded me with pale blue eyes; the evangelist, easily the most popular boy in school, had the lead in the junior class play; the pugilist lounged by the window and let loose at intervals with a raucous laugh that startled even the geraniums; the thief was a gay-hearted Lothario with a song on his lips; and the imbecile, a soft-eyed little animal seeking the shadows.

The murderer awaits death in the state penitentiary; the evangelist has lain a year in the village churchyard; the pugilist lost an eye in a brawl in Hong Kong; the thief, by standing on tiptoe, can see the windows of my room from the county jail; and the once gentle-eyed little moron beats his head against a padded wall in the state asylum.

All of these young men once sat in my room, sat and looked at me gravely across worn brown desks. I must have been a great help to those pupils—I taught them the rhyming scheme of the Elizabethan sonnet and how to diagram a complex sentence.

Naomi John White

The focus of *The Human Side of Work* is self-discovery and personal development as the reader "learns by doing." The material covered is authoritative and up to date, reflecting current theory and practices. The level of material is appropriate for all levels of expertise (new and experienced managers) and all levels of education (undergraduate and graduate).

TESTING AND REVIEW PROCESS

The Human Side of Work has been tested and refined in our classes at Northern Kentucky University. The information and activities have been used with hundreds of organizations and thousands of employees in business, industry, and government. Users include American Telephone and Telegraph Co., International Business Machines Corp., John Hancock, Marriott Corporation, Sun Oil, and Ford Motor Co. in the private sector and the Department of Transportation, the Environmental Protection Agency, the Internal Revenue Service, the National Institutes of

Health, and state governments in the public sector.

The following are sample evaluations:

> Good for student participation. My students like the exercises and learning instruments, and the fact each is a stand-alone book that is bite-size. Their reaction: "Everyone should read them!"
>
> *Joseph F. Ohren, Eastern Michigan University*

> A comprehensive series dealing with employee development and job performance. Information is presented in an interesting and easy-to-use style. Case studies and readings help teach the topics, and applications make the material more meaningful. It is an excellent guide for the practicing manager. Ideal as desk books.
>
> *David Duncan, IBM*

> I am a non-traditional student. As one who has worked for over twenty years, I thoroughly enjoyed the material. An understanding of the world of work is presented in a way that is usable at any level of an organization. The books present a common sense approach to management.
>
> *Naomi Miller, Northern Kentucky University*

> Best I've seen on the people side of work. Helps the person. Helps the company. Good for personal and management development. Popular with participants from all backgrounds.
>
> *Charles Apple, University of Michigan*

> This is an easy-to-read, comprehensive series in organization behavior. It puts theory into relevant, usable terminology. Methods for identifying and solving human relations problems are pinpointed. It sets the stage for understanding how people, environment and situations interact in an organization.
>
> *David Sprouse, AT&T*

TEACHING FORMATS

The Human Side of Work is versatile and can be used in many formats:

- for seminars and training programs
- as classroom texts
- as supplemental information and activities

The following is a discussion of each option.

Seminars and Training Programs

Books used for seminars and training programs should be selected to meet the objectives and needs of the participants—communication, stress, leadership, etc. Material can be mixed and matched for training programs in personal development, professional development, management development, and team building. Material in each book is appropriate for a variety of time periods: one-half day (3 to 4 hours), one full day (6 to 8 hours), and two full days (12 to 16 hours).

The books provide excellent learning activities and questionnaires to encourage participation and personalize the subject. Books then serve as "take-home" material for further reading and personal development. In this format, study quizzes are rarely used for grading, and homework assignments are seldom given. See the following table for appropriate audiences, program focus, and recommended books when using *The Human Side of Work* for seminars and training programs.

Classroom Texts

The series is appropriate for use as texts in college courses in human relations, organization behavior, and organizational psychology. The following is a sample lesson plan using the set for a one-semester course:

Week	Focus on the Person	
1	Stress	Part One, Part Two
2	Stress	Part Three, Part Four
3	Communication	Part One, Part Two
4	Communication	Part Three, Part Four
5	Human Behavior	Part One, Part Two
6	Human Behavior	Part Three
7	Ethics	Part One, Part Two
8	Ethics	Part Three, Part Four

	Focus on the Organization	
9	Morale	Part One, Part Two
10	Morale	Part Three
11	Leadership	Part One, Part Two
12	Leadership	Part Three, Part Four

USING THE HUMAN SIDE OF WORK FOR SEMINARS AND TRAINING PROGRAMS

Appropriate Audiences	Program Focus	Recommended Books
Personal and professional development	Focus on the individual	* Stress Without Distress: Rx for Burnout * Communication: The Miracle of Dialogue * Human Behavior: Why People Do What They Do * Ethics at Work: Fire in a Dark World * Morale: Quality of Work Life (optional) * Performance: Managing for Excellence (optional)
New and experienced managers	Focus on management	* Morale: Quality of Work Life * Leadership: Nine Keys to Success * Performance: Managing for Excellence * Groupstrength: Quality Circles at Work * Stress Without Distress: Rx for Burnout (optional) * Communication: The Miracle of Dialogue (optional) * Human Behavior: Why People Do What They Do (optional) * Ethics at Work: Fire in a Dark World (optional)
Employee development and team building	Focus on the organization	* Communication: The Miracle of Dialogue * Morale: Quality of Work Life * Groupstrength: Quality Circles at Work * Stress Without Distress: Rx for Burnout (optional) * Human Behavior: Why People Do What They Do (optional) * Performance: Managing for Excellence (optional)

Popular seminar and program titles with corresponding books are as follows:

Managing Change: Personal and Professional Coping Skills   * Stress Without Distress: Rx for Burnout
Communication: One to One; One to Many   * Communication: The Miracle of Dialogue
Human Relations and the Nature of Man   * Human Behavior: Why People Do What They Do
Business Ethics and Corporate Culture   * Ethics at Work: Fire in a Dark World
Quality of Work Life   * Morale: Quality of Work Life
The Human Side of Management   * Leadership: Nine Keys to Success
Managing for Productivity: People Building Skills   * Performance: Managing for Excellence
Employee Involvement: If Japan Can Do It, Why Can't We?   * Groupstrength: Quality Circles at Work

13	Performance	Part One, Part Two
14	Performance	Part Three
15	Groupstrength	Part One, Part Two
16	Groupstrength	Part Three

Related Activities and Homework Assignments

Week	Suggested Readings, Cases and Applications
1	*Anatomy of an Illness as Perceived by the Patient* (reading) *The Price of Success* (case)
2	*Death of a Salesman* (reading) *Scientific Relaxation* (application)
3	*Barriers and Gateways to Communications* (reading) *The Power of Vocabulary* (application)
4	*The Dyadic Encounter* (application) *Attitudes toward Women Working* (application)
5	*The Human Side of Enterprise* (reading) *Significant People and Critical Events* (application)
6	*Values Auction* (application) *Personal and Interpersonal Growth* (application)
7	*If Hitler Asked You to Electrocute a Stranger, Would You?* (reading) *How Could the Jonestown Holocaust Have Occurred?* (reading)
8	*Values Flag* (application) *The Kidney Machine* (application)
9	*Work* (reading) *The Joe Bailey Problem* (application)
10	*The Coffee Break* (case) *In Search of Excellence* (application)
11	*What Happened When I Gave Up the Good Life and Became President* (case) *Black, Blue, and White* (case)
12	*The Forklift Fiasco* (case) *Train the Trainers* (application)
13	*Games Mother Never Taught You* (reading) *How Will You Spend Your Life?* (application)

14   *How to Manage Your Time: Everybody's No. 1 Problem* (reading)
Chrysler's Turnaround Strategy (case)

15   *Groupthink* (reading)
The Dean Practices Participative Management (case)

16   *Decisions, Decisions, Decisions* (reading)
The Bottleneck (application)

This format for a one-semester course uses selected readings, cases, and applications from all eight books. For a two-semester course, additional readings, cases, and applications are provided.

Another popular format is to use fewer books in a one-semester course, and to use these more thoroughly. The books can be selected by the instructor or the class. For example, stress, communication, morale, and leadership may be best suited for a given group.

Testing and Grading

When using *The Human Side of Work* as classroom texts, study quizzes in each book can be used to evaluate content knowledge. Although quiz scores can be used to assign formal grades, students learn best when they are also asked to apply the concepts in some personal way. Examples include a term journal, a related research paper, a small-group project, a field assignment, and/or a self-improvement project.

Grades can be assigned on the basis of test scores and term project(s). Projects can be evaluated according to the three C's: clarity, comprehensiveness, and correctness. Half the course grade could be based on study quiz scores, and the other half on the term project(s).

Supplemental Information and Activities

The books in *The Human Side of Work* can provide supplemental information and activities for various college courses. State-of-the-art questionnaires and user-friendly exercises add variety and increase student involvement. Books matched with appropriate college courses are as follows:

Recommended Books	College Courses
Stress Without Distress: Rx for Burnout	Personal Development Personal Health Human Relations Organization Behavior Organizational Psychology Supervisory Development

Communication: The Miracle of Dialogue	Personal Development Communications Human Relations Organization Behavior Organizational Psychology Supervisory Development
Human Behavior: Why People Do What They Do	Personal Development Human Relations Organization Behavior Organizational Psychology Supervisory Development
Ethics at Work: Fire in a Dark World	Personal Development Business Ethics Human Relations Organization Behavior Organizational Psychology Supervisory Development
Morale: Quality of Work Life	Personnel/Human Resources Human Relations Organization Behavior Organizational Psychology Supervisory Development
Leadership: Nine Keys to Success	Management Principles Human Relations Organization Behavior Organizational Psychology Supervisory Development
Performance: Managing for Excellence	Management Principles Human Relations Organization Behavior Organizational Psychology Supervisory Development
Groupstrength: Quality Circles at Work	Personnel/Human Resources Human Relations Organization Behavior Organizational Psychology Supervisory Development

When used as supplemental material, books are rarely tested for grades. The emphasis is on using the questionnaires, exercises, cases, and applications to increase interest and participation and to personalize the subject.

APPENDIX B

Additional References

ADDITIONAL REFERENCES

The following books are recommended for further reading in the area of performance. Each is included because of its significance in the field, support to this text, and value for further personal development.

Bernardin, H. John. *Performance Appraisal*. Boston: Kent Publishing Co., 1984.

Blanchard, Kenneth H. *The One Minute Manager*. New York: William Morrow & Co., Inc., 1982.

Bolles, Richard. *What Color Is Your Parachute?* Berkeley, Calif.: Ten Speed Press, 1985.

Dale, Ernest. *Management Theory and Practice*. New York: McGraw-Hill, Inc., 1973.

Drucker, Peter. *Effective Executive*. New York: Harper & Row, Publishers, Inc., 1985.

Drucker, Peter. *Innovation and Entrepreneurship*. New York: Harper & Row, Publishers, Inc., 1985.

Drucker, Peter. *Management: Tasks, Practices, Responsibility*. New York: Harper & Row, Publishers, Inc., 1974.

Drucker, Peter. *Managing for Results*. New York: Harper & Row, Publishers, Inc., 1964.

Drucker, Peter. *Managing in Turbulent Times*. New York: Harper & Row, Publishers, Inc., 1982.

Drucker, Peter. *People and Performance: The Best of Peter Drucker on Management*. New York: Harper's College Press, 1977.

Fear, Richard A. *The Evaluation Interview*. New York: McGraw-Hill, Inc., 1972.

Henderson, Richard L. *Performance Appraisal*. Reston, Va.: Reston Publishing Co., 1984.

Kanter, Rosebeth. *The Change Masters*. New York: Touchstone Books, 1983.

Kuhn, Robert. *To Flourish Among Giants: Creative Management for Mid-Sized Firms*. New York: John Wiley & Sons, Inc., 1985.

Lakein, Alan. *How to Get Control of Your Time and Your Life.* New York: Peter H. Wyden, Inc., 1973.

Marvin, Philip. *The Right Man for the Right Job.* Homewood, Ill.: Dow Jones–Irwin, 1973.

Odiorne, George S. *The Change Resisters.* Englewood Cliffs, N.J.: Prentice-Hall, Inc., 1983.

Odiorne, George S. *Management by Objectives.* New York: Pitman Publishing Corp., 1965.

Odiorne, George S. *How Managers Make Things Happen.* Englewood Cliffs, N.J.: Prentice-Hall, Inc., 1961.

Peter, Laurence J., and Raymond Hull. *The Peter Principle: Why Things Always Go Wrong.* New York: William Morrow & Co., Inc., 1969.

Peters, Thomas J. *A Passion for Excellence.* New York: Random House, Inc., 1985.

Pinchot, Gifford. *Intrapreneuring.* New York: Harper & Row, Publishers, Inc., 1985.

Porter, Michael E. *Competitive Advantage: Creating and Sustaining Superior Performance.* New York: Free Press, 1985.

Sayles, Leonard. *Leadership: What Effective Managers Really Do . . . And How They Do It.* New York: McGraw-Hill, Inc., 1981.

Ullman, John E. *The Improvement of Productivity: Myths and Realities.* New York: Praeger Publishers, 1980.

Uris, Auren. *The Executive Deskbook.* Florence, Ky.: Van Nostrand Reinhold Co., Inc., 1979.

Uris, Auren. *Techniques of Leadership.* New York: McGraw-Hill, Inc., 1953.

APPENDIX C

Suggested Films

The following films are excellent learning aids. These are supplementary media that can enrich a class or training program. They are ideal for small-group discussion, panel debates, and question-and-answer periods. Topics are listed in the order in which they appear in the text.

LIFELINES: A CAREER PROFILE STUDY
(Document Associates, 26 min.)

In order to be fully satisfied and productive at work, a person must understand the forces that shape and nurture his or her career. Using illustrations from three case histories, this film explores Edgar Schein's concept of "career anchors," patterns by which individuals discover what they are good at and what they would like to do for the rest of their lives.

Document Associates, Inc.
211 East 43rd Street
New York, New York 10017

CAREER DEVELOPMENT: A PLAN FOR ALL SEASONS
(CRM, 24 min.)

Within organizations, career development programs offer one of the best means of analyzing an employee's desires and of coordinating them with organizational goals for positive results. This film shows how Collins Foods International, Inc., has promoted company goals through self-motivated employees.

A final segment of the film shows Skyline Career Development Center in Dallas. This center is one of many now committed to a program of early education for the career-oriented young person. It provides students with exposure to and training in a multitude of employment areas, from music to aeronautics.

CRM Educational Films
Del Mar, California 92014

JOB INTERVIEW: I GUESS I GOT THE JOB
(CRM, 13 min.)

This film presents vignettes illustrating different styles of approach to a job interview, focusing on the subtle cues that affect the interviewer's impression of the applicant.

CRM Educational Films
Del Mar, California 92014

PERFORMANCE APPRAISAL: THE HUMAN DYNAMICS
(CRM, 25 min.)

Results indicate that employees who have goals achieve their objectives. The more active the role of the employee in goal setting, the more chance there is of improving performance.

CRM Educational Films
Del Mar, California 92014

WHAT CAN I CONTRIBUTE?
(BNA, 25 min.)

Management consultant Peter Drucker stresses that promotions in the managerial ranks should go to those who have made their jobs different and bigger, not to those who have merely done their jobs well. Also dramatized are the information needs of one's colleagues and how to satisfy these needs to make team management a reality. As Drucker puts it, "Ask yourself, who in this company has to know what I am doing, and in what form do I have to present it so that he can understand and use it?"

BNA Communications, Inc.
5615 Fishers Lane
Rockville, Maryland 20852

NEED TO ACHIEVE
(Indiana University, 30 min.)

This film documents the research of David McClelland on various aspects of achievement motivation. McClelland's studies show that people with high needs for achievement usually are moderate risk-takers.

Indiana University
Audio-Visual Center
Bloomington, Indiana 47401

THE SELF-MOTIVATED ACHIEVER
(University of Illinois, 25 min.)

In addition to covering some of the research on achievement motivation, this film shows how to enhance self-motivation.

University of Illinois
Visual Aids Service
Division of University Extension
Champaign, Illinois 61820

WOMEN IN MANAGEMENT: THREAT OR OPPORTUNITY?
(CRM, 29 min.)

This film acquaints the viewer with the many responses that can be made to the challenge of the women's liberation movement. It shows how, once a supervisor can sort out substance from stereotype, the reality of women in managerial positions can offer opportunities for social and organizational improvement.

CRM Educational Films
Del Mar, California 92014

CREATIVE PROBLEM SOLVING
(CRM, 28 min.)

This film shows how creative problem solving can be learned, relates creativity to right and left brain function, and shows a creative problem-solving group in action.

CRM Educational Films
Del Mar, California 92014

A PSYCHOLOGY OF CREATIVITY
(Macmillan, 31 min.)

This film gives examples of creative behavior and achievements and explores techniques for encouraging creativity.

Macmillan Films
34 MacQuestion Parkway South
Mt. Vernon, New York 10550

PROBLEM-SOLVING STRATEGIES
(CRM, 27 min.)

This film provides a look at some recent innovations in creative problem solving.

CRM Educational Films
Del Mar, California 92014

MANAGING TIME
(BNA, 25 min.)

"Any executive," Peter Drucker says, "has to spend a great deal of time on things that do not contribute at all. Much time is inevitably wasted." In this film, Drucker introduces the use of the revealing and helpful time log to the harried, overextended president of Hudson-Lansing to help him determine how his valuable time disappears.

BNA Communications, Inc.
5615 Fishers Lane
Rockville, Maryland 20852

THE TIME OF YOUR LIFE
(Cally Curtis Films, 28 min.)

This award-winning film is excellent for teaching effective time management. Case examples are used to show common time wasters. James Whitmore stars; highest rating.

Cally Curtis Films
3384 Peachtree Rd. N.E.
Atlanta, Georgia 30326

MANAGING IN A CRISIS
(BNA, 30 min.)

Following a crisis, your first decision should be to keep it from happening again. Richard Beckhard shows you how to conduct a fact-finding session and keep it from turning into a name-calling, finger-pointing free-for-all.

You will learn how to determine the cause of the crisis, avoid recriminations, and channel antagonism into positive, constructive action. You will also find out how to conduct productive, fact-finding planning sessions involving large numbers of people.

BNA Communications, Inc.
5615 Fishers Lane
Rockville, Maryland 20852

BUSINESS, BEHAVIORISM, AND THE BOTTOM LINE
(CRM, 23 min.)

B. F. Skinner believes that we are capable of structuring an environmental framework in order to optimize behavioral results, but that we seldom succeed in doing so. In this highly recommended, award-winning film, Skinner describes the basic process of behavior modification as a system that includes both positive and negative reinforcement, and we see how such a system was applied in an industrial setting.

CRM Educational Films
Del Mar, California 92014

APPENDIX D

Management Performance Objectives

MANAGEMENT PERFORMANCE OBJECTIVES

Workshop I
Checklist for Management Values

	Management Values	Put a check next to each objective you accomplished last week.
Accuracy	I knew the facts; I paid attention to details; I passed along accurate information.	_____
Dependability	I was punctual; I worked until the job was completed; I was someone people could count on; I was someone who could be trusted.	_____
Honesty	I admitted mistakes I made, if any; I was honest in my dealings with others; I protected money and property.	_____
Pride	I was proud of the job I did; I was proud of the work of my employees.	_____
Respect	I showed respect for my co-workers; I took time to listen to my subordinates; I complimented those who consistently did a good job.	_____
Teamwork	I applied rules equally to all employees; I actively supported the policies of the company; I didn't isolate myself from my fellow employees.	_____
Understanding	I tried to understand the work of other supervisors and departments; I was tolerant of different types of people; I tried to understand the positions and ideas of my subordinates.	_____

Workshop II
Checklist for Leadership Principles

Leadership Behaviors	Put a check next to each objective you accomplished last week.
I gave recognition to subordinates for doing a good job.	_____
I made sure my subordinates knew what was expected of them and how they were doing.	_____
I encouraged and listened to suggestions from my subordinates.	_____
I avoided showing favoritism.	_____

Workshop III
Checklist for Stress Management

Stress Management Behaviors	Put a check next to each objective you accomplished last week.
Coping behaviors (go easy on criticism, talk it out, escape for a while, etc.) I: _____	_____
Positive thinking (appreciate family, health, job, etc.) I: _____	_____
Exercise and recreation (exercise three to five times each week) I: _____	_____
Relaxation and rest (obtain sufficient sleep every night) I: _____	_____

Diet and nutrition
(such as reduce caffeine, salt, and sugar consumption)

I: _____

_____

TLC
(such as spend an average of one hour every day helping someone else)

I: _____

_____

Workshop IV

Checklist for Delegation Skills

Effective Delegation Behaviors	Put a check next to each objective you accomplished last week.
I considered each subordinate's level of competence and work load before assigning tasks.	_____
I gave proper authority when I delegated tasks.	_____
I obtained commitments for completing assigned tasks.	_____
I listened to questions and suggestions from subordinates.	_____

Workshop V

Checklist for Effective Listening

Effective Listening Behaviors	Put a check next to each objective you accomplished last week.
I learned the names of at least three new employees or customers this week.	_____

One of my bad habits in listening is _____

_____ .

and I attempted to correct this by _____

_____ .   _____

One of my communication problems is _____

_____ ,

and I worked to eliminate this by _____

_____ .   _____

I was aware of the use of personal space and body language in interpersonal communications.   _____

I attempted to empathize with at least one person.   _____

Workshop VI

Checklist for Time Management Skills

Time Management Behaviors	Put a check next to each objective you accomplished last week.
I made a weekly time plan.	_____
I prepared a daily activity list that included priorities.	_____
I spent time reviewing work objectives and priorities with my subordinates.	_____
I eliminated at least one time waster within the past week.	_____
I kept my desk and office well organized and free of clutter.	_____
I met deadlines and finished tasks on time.	_____
I used travel and waiting time productively.	_____
I felt in control of my time and on top of my job.	_____

Workshop VII
Checklist for Public Speaking

Public Speaking Behaviors	Put a check next to each objective you accomplished last week.
I learned how stage fright affects me.	
Factors include _____.	_____
I spoke about a subject that was of interest to me.	
It was _____.	_____
I considered my audience in preparing my speech.	_____
I outlined my speech so it had a thesis and supporting material.	_____
I made notes from my outline.	_____
I practiced my speech at least twice.	_____

APPENDIX E
Study Quiz Answers

STUDY QUIZ ANSWERS

	Part One	Part Two	Part Three
1.	b	c	b
2.	c	a	e
3.	a	c	c
4.	d	a	a
5.	b	b	a
6.	c	a	a
7.	a	a	h
8.	d	b	c
9.	a	a	a
10.	c	a	a
11.	c	a	a
12.	c	b	
13.	c	b	
14.	b	a	
15.	a	a	
16.	a	b	
17.	b	a	
18.	b	a	
19.	a	a	
20.	d	f	
21.		b	
22.		a	
23.		a	
24.		b	
25.		a	
26.		a	
27.		a	
28.		a	

APPENDIX F

The Relationship of the Quiz Questions and the Discussion and Activities to the Part Objectives

The following chart shows the relationship of the quiz questions and the discussion and activities to the part objectives:

PART ONE

Objective Number	Quiz (Q), Discussion and Activities (D&A)
1	Q: 1 D&A: 9, 10
2	Q: 2 D&A: 6, 7, 8
3	Q: 3, 4, 5 D&A: 6
4	Q: 6, 7, 8 D&A: 7, 8
5	Q: 9, 10 D&A: 1
6	Q: 11, 12, 13, 14 D&A: 2, 3, 4
7	Q: 15, 16, 17, 18, 19, 20 D&A: 5
8	Q: 15, 16, 17, 18, 19, 20 D&A: 5

PART TWO

Objective Number	Quiz (Q), Discussion and Activities (D&A)
1	Q: 1, 2 D&A: 1, 4
2	Q: 4, 5 D&A: 2
3	Q: 1, 2, 3 D&A: 1

4	Q: 6, 7, 8, 9, 10, 11, 12, 13, 14, 15, 16, 17, 18, 19, 21, 22, 23, 24, 25, 26, 27, 28 D&A: 3, 5, 6
5	Q: 20 D&A: 8
6	Q: 6 D&A: 3

PART THREE

Objective Number	Quiz (Q), Discussion and Activities (D&A)
1	Q: 1, 2, 3, 4, 5, 6, 7 D&A: 1, 2, 3
2	Q: 8, 9, 10, 11 D&A: 4, 5